JavaScript Step by Step

Steve Suehring

PUBLISHED BY
Microsoft Press
A Division of Microsoft Corporation
One Microsoft Way
Redmond, Washington 98052-6399

Library of Congress Control Number: 2007942080

Printed and bound in the United States of America.

1 2 3 4 5 6 7 8 9   QWT   3 2 1 0 9 8

Distributed in Canada by H.B. Fenn and Company Ltd.

A CIP catalogue record for this book is available from the British Library.

Microsoft Press books are available through booksellers and distributors worldwide. For further information about international editions, contact your local Microsoft Corporation office or contact Microsoft Press International directly at fax (425) 936-7329. Visit our Web site at www.microsoft.com/mspress. Send comments to mspinput@microsoft.com.

Acquisitions Editor: Ben Ryan
Developmental Editor: Devon Musgrave
Project Editors: Kathleen Atkins and Lori Merrick
Editorial Production: ICC Macmillan Inc.
Technical Reviewer: Kurt Meyer; Technical Review services provided by Content Master, a member of CM Group, Ltd.
Cover: Tom Draper Design

Body Part No. X14-40140

To Rebecca and Jakob

Contents at a Glance

Table of Contents

What do you think of this book? We want to hear from you!

Microsoft is interested in hearing your feedback so we can continually improve our books and learning resources for you. To participate in a brief online survey, please visit:

www.microsoft.com/learning/booksurvey

What do you think of this book? We want to hear from you!

Microsoft is interested in hearing your feedback so we can continually improve our books and learning resources for you. To participate in a brief online survey, please visit:

www.microsoft.com/learning/booksurvey

Acknowledgments

And now the element that I most enjoy writing, the Acknowledgments. With a few books, and therefore a few acknowledgment pages under my belt, I no longer feel as though I need to thank everyone who I came in contact with while writing the book.

My wife Rebecca and I welcomed our first child, Jakob Edward, while this book was being written. If you'd like an exercise in futility, try writing a coherent chapter of a technology book with a newborn. As luck would have it, my wife was (and is) absolutely incredible and very understanding that deadlines are deadlines. She gave me the time, without any of the guilt, so that I could finish the book on time. Jakob arrived when I had about three chapters remaining and I believe his arrival resulted in three of the best chapters of the book.

I'd like to thank everyone at Microsoft Press. Writing for Microsoft Press was an excellent experience for me, and one I hope to repeat in the future. Ben Ryan and Devon Musgrave got the book kicked off and then Maureen Zimmerman, Michelle Goodman, Lori Merrick, and Kathleen Atkins all helped manage the project so thanks to all of them for dealing with an overtired writer. Thanks also to Kurt Meyer who did a great tech editing job. Kurt's meticulous work and persistence paid dividends on the final product.

Thanks to my agent Neil Salkind and everyone at Studio B for their hard work. Thank also to (in no particular order) the Tuescher family, John Hein, James Leu, Jeremy Guthrie, Jason Keup, Justin Hoerter, Chris Trawicki, Aaron Saray, Brian Pinter, Jenni Guggenheimer, Kelly Gardner, John O'Keefe, and the rest of the Triangle (I can't thank everyone, I can already see the end of the page coming). Tony Falduto and the server team, Eliot Irons, Andy Hale, and the rest of the data security team, Jeff Sanner, Aaron Deering and the architecture team, and Greg Pfluger, and everyone else I don't have room to thank from Sentry. See, I said I wasn't going to do this and here I am, thanking everyone again and this time I've put no forethought into it so someone is sure to be missed. Tim and Rob from Partners, Dave Marie, Johnny K, Pat Dunn, Sarah, Brian Page, Jay and Deb Schrank, Denise, Mark Little, Andy Berkvam, AJ Prowant, meek, Jim Oliva, John Eckendorf, Nightmare Squad, Kent Laabs, Kyle MacDonald, Dan Noah, Ron Mackay, where are you?, Chad Chasteen. And now I sit here and stare at the screen trying to remember who else needs to be remembered. Inevitably I'll forget someone. I like this part of the book because I can ramble with only a minimal amount of copy editing, thanks Susan! Apologies to anyone who wasn't included in these acknowledgments. I'm negotiating another book as I write this so hopefully I can include you next time!

Having sat at the screen for, well, for too long now, I'll wrap up these acknowledgments by thanking all of the readers of my other books who've written over the years. I enjoy receiving your e-mails even if I can't always answer each and every one. I'm consistently amazed when I receive e-mail from readers in many different countries. The books I've written seem to have a high readership in Brazil, Germany (and elsewhere in Europe), and Canada. I've been inspired to learn many different languages and I hope to visit Brazil and Germany soon (I've been to Canada a lot, I'll be back soon, and already speak the language, eh?)

Introducing JavaScript Step by Step

JavaScript is an integral language of Web application development. Whether adding interactivity to a Web page or creating an entire application, today's Web wouldn't be the same without JavaScript.

JavaScript is a standards-based language with a formal specification. However, as any Web developer will tell you, most every Web browser interprets that specification differently. This makes the job of a Web developer more difficult. Luckily, most Web browsers are converging in their support and interpretation of JavaScript's core functions.

This book provides an introductory look at JavaScript, including some of its core functions as well as newer features and paradigms, such as Asynchronous JavaScript and XML (AJAX). Today's Web users rely on many different platforms and many different browsers to view Web content. This fact was central to development of every aspect of the book, so you'll see screenshots in multiple browsers and an emphasis on standards-based, rather than proprietary, JavaScript development.

The first part of the book examines JavaScript and helps you get started developing JavaScript. No special tools are required for JavaScript development, so you'll see how to create JavaScript files in Microsoft Visual Studio, Eclipse, and Notepad (or any text editor). JavaScript's core language and functions are examined next, followed by the relationship of JavaScript and the Web browser. Finally, AJAX is demonstrated where you'll see how to build dynamic search forms.

Features and Conventions of This Book

This book takes you step by step through learning the JavaScript programming language. Starting at the beginning of the book and following each of the examples and exercises will help you to gain knowledge about the JavaScript programming language.

If you already have some familiarity with JavaScript, you might be tempted to skip the first chapter of this book. However, Chapter 1, "JavaScript Is More than You Might Think," details some of the background history of JavaScript as well as some of the underlying premise for this book, both of which might be helpful to frame the discussion for the remainder of the book. Chapter 2, "Developing in JavaScript," shows how to get started programming in JavaScript. If you're already familiar with Web development, you might already have a Web development program and therefore you might be tempted to skip Chapter 2 as well. Nevertheless, you should become familiar with the pattern used in Chapter 2 to create JavaScript programs.

The book contains a Table of Contents that will help you to locate a specific section quickly. Each chapter contains a detailed list of the material that it covers.

In addition, a companion CD accompanies the book. This CD contains the source code for many of the examples shown throughout the book.

Convention	Meaning
Lists	Step-by-step exercises are denoted by procedural lists with steps beginning with 1.
See Also	These paragraphs point you to other sources of information about a specific topic.
Tip/Note	Tips and notes feature additional bits of information that might be helpful for a given subject.
Inline Code	Inline code—that is, code that appears within a paragraph—is shown in *italic* font.
`Code Blocks`	Code blocks are shown in a different font to highlight the code.

Using the Book's CD

The CD included with this book contains much of the source code from examples shown throughout the book.

What's on the CD?

The source code on the CD is laid out on a per-chapter basis, with a directory for each chapter. Each chapter directory contains the step-by-step exercises used within that chapter. Some chapters contain additional source code shown in that chapter as well.

Minimum System Requirements

The CD will work on many platforms including Microsoft Windows, Linux, and Mac.

- Processor. A Pentium 133 megahertz (MHz) or greater (any computer capable of running a Web browser with JavaScript support, see below for more information).

- Memory. 64 megabytes (MB) of RAM or any amount that can run a computer capable of using a Web browser with JavaScript support, see below for more information).

- Hard disk. 2 MB free hard disk space.

- Operating System. Windows 98SE or later, most flavors of Linux and Mac OS X.

- Drive. CD or DVD drive.

- Display. Monitor with 640x480 or higher screen resolution and 16-bit or higher color depth.

- Software. Any Web browser capable of running JavaScript. Internet Explorer 6 or later, Mozilla Firefox 2.0 or later, Safari 2 or later, Opera 9, and Konqueror 3.5.2 or later are recommended.

Using the Sample Files

Because JavaScript is usually dependent on a surrounding Web page, the source code for the step-by-step exercises has been split within the directories. This enables you to copy and paste much of the repetitive HTML and concentrate on entering the JavaScript into the example.

Each chapter directory also contains a "CompletedCode" directory that contains the entire example. You can open the CompletedCode files as they are to see the example as laid out in the chapter.

Getting Help

Every effort has been made to ensure the accuracy of this book and the contents of its CD. If you run into problems, please contact the appropriate source, listed in the following sections, for help and assistance.

Getting Help with This Book and Its CD

If your question or issue concerns the content of this book or its companion CD, please first search the online Microsoft Press Knowledge Base, which provides support information for known errors in or corrections to this book, at the following Web site:

www.microsoft.com/mspress/support/search.asp

If you do not find your answer in the online Knowledge Base, send your comments or questions to Microsoft Learning Technical Support at:

mspinput@microsoft.com

Part I

JavaWhat? The Where, Why, and How of JavaScript

Chapter 1
JavaScript Is More Than You Might Think

Welcome to the introductory chapter. After reading this chapter, you'll be able to

- Understand the history of JavaScript.

- Recognize the parts of a JavaScript program.

- Use the *javascript* pseudoprotocol.

- Understand where JavaScript fits within a Web page.

- Understand what JavaScript can and cannot do.

A Brief History of JavaScript

JavaScript isn't Java. There, with that out of the way, we can move on to bigger, more important things, like how to make cool drop-down menus. In all seriousness, JavaScript is the colloquial name for a specification more formally known as ECMAScript. But the name ECMAScript doesn't exactly roll off the tongue. Go ahead, try saying it aloud: "ECMAScript." See? (More on ECMAScript a little later.)

Where did JavaScript come from? You might not know the rich and storied history of JavaScript—and arguably, you may not really care much about it, either. If that's the case, you might be tempted to jump ahead to the next chapter and go straight into coding JavaScript. This, of course, would be a mistake—you'd miss all of the wonderful text below about JavaScript. And besides, understanding a bit about the history of JavaScript is important to understanding how the language is implemented in various environments today.

JavaScript was originally developed by Brendan Eich at Netscape around 1995–1996. Back then, the language was called LiveScript. This would've been a great name for a new language and the story could've ended here. However, in an unfortunate decision, the folks in marketing had their way and the language was renamed to JavaScript. Confusion soon ensued. You see, the Java language was the hot new thing at the time, and someone decided to try to capitalize on Java's popularity. As a result, JavaScript soon found itself associated with the Java language. Unfortunately, Java, though popular in the sense that it was frequently used, had earned somewhat of a bad reputation because some Web sites used Java for presentation or to add useless enhancements to their Web sites (such as annoying scrolling text). The user experience suffered because Java required a plug-in to load into the Web browser, slowing down the browsing process and generally causing grief for those visitors, not to mention accessibility problems. JavaScript has been inexorably linked to Java and its problems ever since. Only recently has JavaScript begun to shake this association.

JavaScript is not a compiled language, which makes it have the look and feel of a language that lacks power. Power programmers of the Internet in the late 1990s initially dismissed JavaScript but soon came to realize its usefulness and strength to both simulate and create interactivity on the World Wide Web. Up until that point, many Web sites were made of simple Hypertext Markup Language (HTML), with graphics that lacked both visual appeal and the ability to interact with the site's content.

Early JavaScript concentrated on client-side form validation and working with images on Web pages to provide rudimentary, though helpful, interactivity and feedback to the visitor. When a visitor to a Web site would fill in a form, JavaScript could be used to instantly validate the contents of the Web form rather than making a round trip to the server. This was a great way to help applications be a little quicker and more responsive by saving the round-trip time, especially in the days before broadband was pervasive.

Enter Internet Explorer 3

With the release of Microsoft Internet Explorer version 3 in 1996, Microsoft included support for core JavaScript, known in Internet Explorer as JScript, along with support for another scripting language, VBScript. Unfortunately, although these languages were similar, they weren't exactly the same in their implementations. Therefore, methods were developed to detect which browser was being used by the Web site visitor and to respond with JavaScript that would work for that particular browser. This process is known as browser detection, which will be discussed in Chapter 14, "Browsers and JavaScript." Browser detection is still used, though it is now frowned upon for most applications.

And Then Came ECMAScript

In mid-1997 Microsoft and Netscape worked with the European Computer Manufacturers Association (ECMA) to release the first version of ECMAScript. Since this time, all browsers from Netscape and Microsoft have implemented versions of the ECMAScript standard. Other popular browsers, such as Firefox and Opera, have also implemented the ECMAScript standard.

The latest version of ECMAScript, formalized in the standard known as ECMA-262, was released in 1999. The good news is that browsers such as Internet Explorer 4 and Netscape 4.5 supported this standard and that every major browser since then has supported the version of JavaScript formalized in the ECMA-262 standard. The bad news is that each browser applies this standard in slightly different ways. This means that incompatibilities still plague developers who use JavaScript.

A fourth edition of ECMAScript is still a work in progress, soon to be released. See http://www. ecma-international.org/ *for more information on the standard.*

As a developer who will be incorporating JavaScript into your Web applications, you need to account for the differences between interpretations of JavaScript. Doing so might mean implementing a script in slightly different ways, and it also means that you need to test, test, and test again in various browsers and on various platforms. On today's Internet, there is little tolerance for poorly designed applications that work in only one browser.

> **Important**   It is imperative that you test your Web sites in multiple browsers, even Web appli-
> cations that you don't think will be used outside Internet Explorer. Even if you're sure that your
> application will be used only in Internet Explorer or that's all that you officially support, you still
> should test in other browsers. Not only is this important for security, but it also shows that you're
> being a thorough developer who understands today's Internet technologies.

So Many Standards...

If you're thinking that standards surrounding JavaScript programming are somewhat loosely defined, you'd be right. Each browser supports JavaScript with slight differences, making your job that much more difficult. Trying to write about all these differences is also more difficult than if the language were a single, specific entity, like a certain version of Microsoft Visual Basic or Perl. But it's not, and so your job (and mine) will be to keep track of these differences and account for them as necessary, trying to find common ground as much as possible.

The DOM

Another evolving standard relevant to the JavaScript programmer is the *document* object model (DOM) standard developed by the World Wide Web Consortium (W3C). The W3C defines the DOM as "a platform- and language-neutral interface that allows programs and scripts to dynamically access and update the content, structure, and style of documents." What this means for you is that there is a specification to which Web browsers adhere that you can use to work with a Web page in a dynamic manner. The DOM creates a tree struc- ture for HTML and Extensible Markup Language (XML) documents and enables scripting of those objects. JavaScript interacts heavily with the DOM for many important functions.

Like JavaScript, the DOM has been interpreted differently by different browsers, thus making life for a JavaScript programmer that much more interesting. Internet Explorer 4 and previ- ous versions of Netscape included support for an early DOM, known as Level 0. If you use the Level 0 DOM, you can be reasonably assured that you'll find support in those browsers and everything that came after.

Versions 5 and 5.5 of Internet Explorer included some support for Level 1 DOM, while Internet Explorer version 6 and later includes some support for Level 2 DOM. Other browsers, such as Firefox and Opera, support the W3C standards.

If there's one thing that you should take away while learning about JavaScript standards and the related DOM standards, it's that you need to pay particular attention to the code that you write (no surprise there) and the syntax used to implement that code. If you don't, JavaScript can fail miserably and make your page not render in a given browser. Chapter 10, "The Document Object Model," covers the DOM in much greater detail.

> **Tip** The W3C has an application that can test your Web browser for its support of the various DOM levels. This application can be found at *http://www.w3.org/2003/02/06-dom-support.html*.

What's in a JavaScript Program?

A JavaScript program consists of statements formed from tokens, operators, and identifiers placed together in an order that is meaningful to a JavaScript interpreter, which is contained in most Web browsers. This seems like a mouthful, but it's really not all that complicated to anyone who has programmed in just about any other language. A statement might be:

```
var smallNumber = 4;
```

In that statement, there is a token or reserved word, *var*, followed by other tokens, such as an identifier, an operator, and a literal. You'll learn more about each of these in Chapter 2, "Developing in JavaScript," and throughout the book. The purpose of this statement is to set a variable equal to the integer 4.

Like any programming language, statements get put together in an order that makes a program perform one or more functions. Speaking of functions, JavaScript has its own way to define functions, which you'll read much more about in Chapter 7, "Working with Functions." JavaScript defines several built-in functions that you can use within your programs.

Using the *javascript* pseudoprotocol and a function

1. Open a Web browser such as Internet Explorer or Firefox.

2. In the Address Bar, type the following code and press Enter:

   ```
   javascript:alert("Hello World");
   ```

3. When you press Enter, you'll see a dialog box similar to this one:

Congratulations! You've just programmed your first (albeit not very useful) bit of JavaScript code. With this little bit of code, however, you've now seen two important things that you'll likely use in your JavaScript programming endeavors: the *javascript* pseudoprotocol identifier in a browser, and, more importantly, the *alert* function. Each of these items will be examined in later chapters, but for now it's enough that you've already learned something that you'll use in the future!

JavaScript is also event-driven, meaning that it can respond to certain events or "things that happen," such as a mouse click or text change within a form field. Connecting JavaScript to an event is central to many forms or common uses of JavaScript. In Chapter 14, you'll see how to respond to events by using JavaScript.

Placing JavaScript on Your Web Page

If you're new to HTML, all you need to know about it for now is that it delineates elements in a Web page using a pair of matching tags in brackets. The closing tag begins with a slash character (/). Elements can be nested within each other. JavaScript fits within *<script>* tags inside of the *<head> </head>* and/or *<body> </body>* tags of a Web page, as in this example:

```
<html>
<head>
<title>A Web Page Title</title>
<script type = "text/javascript">
// JavaScript Goes Here
</script>
</head>
<body>
<script type = "text/javascript">
// JavaScript can go here too
</script>
</body>
</html>
```

JavaScript placed in the *<body>* tags executes as it is encountered. This is helpful when you need to write to the document by using a JavaScript function, as follows (the function calls are shown in bold type):

```
<head>
<title>A Web Page Title</title>
<script type = "text/javascript">
// JavaScript Goes Here
</script>
</head>
<body>
<script type = "text/javascript">
document.write("hello");
document.write(" world");
</script>
</body>
</html>
```

When you're using JavaScript on an Extensible Hypertext Markup Language (XHTML) page, the < and & characters are interpreted as XML, which can cause problems for JavaScript. To get around this use the following syntax in an XHTML page:

```
<script type="text/javascript">
<![CDATA[
// JavaScript Goes Here
]]>
</script>
```

Yes, it really is that ugly. However, there's an easy fix for this: use external JavaScript files. You'll see in Chapter 2 exactly how to accomplish this simple task.

Document Types

If you've been programming for the Web for any length of time, you're probably familiar with Document Type declarations, or DOCTYPE declarations as they're sometimes called. One of the most important things you can do with Web pages you design is ensure that an accurate and syntactically correct DOCTYPE declaration section exists at the top of the page. The DOCTYPE declaration, frequently abbreviated DTD, lets the browser (or other parsing program) know the rules that will be followed when parsing the elements of the document.

An example of a DOCTYPE declaration for HTML 4.01 looks like this:

```
<!DOCTYPE html PUBLIC "-//W3C//DTD HTML 4.01//EN"
    "http://www.w3.org/TR/html4/strict.dtd">
```

If you're using Microsoft Visual Studio 2005 or later to create a Web project, each page will automatically be given a DOCTYPE declaration for the XHTML 1.0 standard, like this:

```
<!DOCTYPE html PUBLIC "-//W3C//DTD XHTML 1.0 Transitional//EN" "http://www.w3.org/TR/
xhtml1/DTD/xhtml1-transitional.dtd">
```

If you fail to declare a DOCTYPE, the browser will interpret the page by using a mode known as Quirks Mode. Falling back to Quirks Mode means that the document might end up looking different than you had intended, especially when viewed through several browsers.

If you do declare a DOCTYPE, it's also important to then make sure that the resulting HTML, Cascading Style Sheet (CSS), and JavaScript also adhere to Web standards. You do this to ensure that the document can be viewed as intended by the widest possible audience, no matter what interface or browser they use to view the document. More on HTML and CSS validation will be discussed later in this book in Chapter 15, "JavaScript and CSS." The W3C makes available an online validator at *http://validator.w3.org/*, which you can use to validate any publicly available Web page.

Tip Use the Markup Validator regularly until you're comfortable with coding to standards, and always check for validity before releasing your Web project to the public.

What JavaScript Can Do

JavaScript is largely a complementary language, meaning that it's uncommon for an entire application to be written solely in JavaScript without the aid of other languages like HTML and without presentation in a Web browser. There is support for JavaScript in some Adobe products, but JavaScript is primarily used for Web-related programming.

As you'll see (or likely already know), JavaScript is also the J in the acronym AJAX (Asynchronous JavaScript and XML), the darling of the Web 2.0 phenomenon. Beyond that, though, JavaScript is an everyday language providing the interactivity expected, maybe even demanded, by today's Web visitors.

JavaScript can do many things on the client side of the application. It can add the needed interactivity to a Web site by such actions as creating drop-down menus, transforming the text on a page, adding dynamic elements to a page, and helping with form entry.

The rest of this book is about what JavaScript can do. But first let's look at some of the things JavaScript can't do, and please note that neither list is comprehensive.

What JavaScript Can't Do

Of the things that JavaScript can't do, many are the result of JavaScript's usage being somewhat limited to a Web browser environment. This section examines some of the tasks JavaScript can't do and some that JavaScript shouldn't do.

JavaScript Can't Be Forced on a Client

In practical terms, JavaScript relies on another interface or host program for its functionality. This host program is usually the client's Web browser, also known as a user agent. Because JavaScript is a client-side language, it can do only what the client allows it to do.

Some people are still using older browsers that don't support JavaScript at all. Still others won't be able to support many of JavaScript's fancy features due to accessibility, text readers, and other add-on software assisting the browsing experience. And some people might just choose to disable JavaScript because they can, because of security concerns (whether perceived or real), or because of the poor reputation JavaScript has among some people because of certain annoyances like pop-up ads.

No matter the reason, you need to perform some extra work to ensure that the Web site you're designing will be available to those individuals who don't have JavaScript. I can hear your protests already: "But this feature is really [insert your own superlative here: cool, sweet, essential, nice, splendiferous]." Regardless of how nice that feature may be, chances are you'd benefit from better interoperability and more site visitors. In the "Tips for Using JavaScript" section later in this chapter, I'll offer some pointers you can follow to ensure that JavaScript is used appropriately within your Web site.

It may be helpful to think of this another way. When you build a Web application that gets served from Internet Information Services (IIS) 6.0, you can be reasonably sure that the application should usually work when served from an IIS 6.0 server anywhere. Likewise, when you build an application for Apache 2, you can be sure that it will work on other Apache 2 installations. The same cannot be said for JavaScript, however. When you write an application that works fine on your desktop, it won't necessarily work on the next person's. You can't control how your application will work once it gets sent to the client.

JavaScript Can't Guarantee Data Security

Because JavaScript is run wholly on the client, the developer must learn to let go. As you might expect, letting go of control over your program has serious implications. Once the program is on the client's computer, the client can do many nasty things to the code itself before sending it back to the server. As with any other Web programming, you should never trust any data coming back from the client. Even if you've used JavaScript functions to validate the contents of forms, you still must validate this input again when it gets to the server. A client with JavaScript disabled might send back garbage data through a Web form. If you believe, innocently enough, that your client-side JavaScript function has already checked the data to ensure that it is valid, you may find that invalid data gets back to the server, causing unforeseen and possibly dangerous consequences.

> **Important** Remember that JavaScript can be disabled on your visitor's computer. Cute tricks like using JavaScript to disable right-clicks or to prevent visitors from viewing the page source simply cannot be relied upon to be successful and shouldn't be used as security measures.

JavaScript Can't Cross Domains

The JavaScript developer also must be aware of the *Same-Origin Policy*, which dictates that scripts run from within one domain do not have access to the properties from another Internet domain, nor can they affect the scripts and data from another domain. For example, JavaScript can be used to open a new browser window, but the contents of that window are somewhat restricted to the calling script. If a page from my Web site, braingia.org, contains JavaScript, it can't access any JavaScript executed from a different domain, such as microsoft.com.

This is the essence of the Same-Origin Policy: to be shared within sites, JavaScript has to be executed in the same location or originate from it.

The Same-Origin Policy frequently arises with frames and with AJAX's *XMLHttpRequest* object, where multiple JavaScript requests might be sent to different Web servers. I'll discuss some workarounds in Chapter 18, "A Touch of AJAX." For now, be aware that JavaScript is limited to doing things in your own browser window.

JavaScript Doesn't Do Servers

When developing server-side code such as Visual Basic .NET or PHP (PHP is a recursive acronym that stands for "PHP: Hypertext Preprocessor"), you can be reasonably certain that the server will implement certain functions, such as talking to a database or giving access to modules necessary for the Web application. JavaScript doesn't have access to server-side variables. For example, JavaScript cannot access databases that are located on the server. JavaScript code is limited to what can be done inside the platform on which the script is running, which is typically the browser.

Another shift in thinking if you're familiar with server-side programming is that you won't know what the client is capable of without testing on many different clients. When you're programming server-side, if the server doesn't implement a given function, you'll know it right away because the server-side script will fail when you test it. Naughty administrators aside, the back-end server code implementation shouldn't change on a whim, making it easier to know what you can and cannot code. The same cannot be said for JavaScript code that is intended to run on clients that are completely out of your control.

Tips for Using JavaScript

Several factors go into good Web design, and, really, who arbitrates what is and is not considered good, anyway? One visitor to a site might call it an ugly hodgepodge of colors and text created as if they were put in a sack and shaken until they simply fell out onto the page; the next might love the design and color scheme.

Since you're reading this book, I'll assume that you're looking for some help with using JavaScript to enhance your Web site. I will also assume that you want to use this programming language to help people use your site and to make your site look, feel, and work better.

Design of a Web site is not and will never be entirely objective. The goal of a Web site might be informational, which would dictate one approach, while the goal of another Web site might be connected to an application and therefore calls for specialized design and functionality. However, many popular and seemingly well designed sites have certain aspects in common. I'll try to break those down here, although I ask you to remember that I haven't created a comprehensive list and that these are simply one person's opinions.

A well-designed Web site emphasizes function over form.   When a user visits a Web site, he or she usually wants to obtain information. The more difficult your site is to navigate, the more likely the user will simply move to another site with better navigation.

Animations and blinking bits come and go, but what remain are sites that have basic information presented in a professional, easily accessible manner. Using the latest cool animation software or Web technology makes me think of the days of the HTML *<blink>* tag. The *<blink>* tag, for those who never saw it in action, caused the text within it to disappear and reappear on the screen. Nearly all Web developers seem to hate the *<blink>* tag and what it does to a Web page. Those same developers would be wise to keep in mind that today's cool bling or sweet effect on a Web page will be tomorrow's *<blink>*. Successful Web sites stick to the basics and use blinky bits only when the content requires them.

Use elements like a site map, alt tags, and simple navigation, and don't require special software or plug-ins for viewing the site's main content. Too often, I visit a Web site, only to be stopped because I need a plug-in or the latest version of this or that player (which I don't have) to navigate the site.

Although site maps, alt tags, and simple navigation may seem quaint, these are indispensible items for accessibility. Text readers and other such technologies that enable sites to be read aloud or navigated by those with disabilities use these objects and frequently have problems with complex JavaScript.

A well-designed Web site follows standards.   Web standards are there to be followed, so ignore them at your own peril. Using a correct DOCTYPE declaration and well-formed HTML helps to ensure that your site will display correctly to your visitors. Validation using the W3C's Markup Validator tool is highly recommended. If your site is broken, fix it!

A well-designed Web site renders correctly in multiple browsers.   Even when Internet Explorer had 90 percent market share, it was never a good idea for programmers to ignore other browsers. Doing so usually meant that accessibility was also ignored, so people with text readers or other add-ons couldn't use the site. People using operating systems other than Microsoft Windows might also be out of luck visiting those sites.

Though Internet Explorer is still the leader among Web visitors, there's a great chance that at least 2 or 3 of every 10 visitors might be using a different browser. Of course, this variance depends largely on the subject matter. The more technical the audience, the more you'll find you need to accommodate browsers other than Internet Explorer. Therefore, if your site appeals to a technical audience, you might need your site to work in Firefox, Safari, or even Lynx.

Regardless of the Web site's subject matter, you never want to turn away visitors because of their choice of browser. Imagine the shopkeeper who turned away 3 of every 10 potential customers just because of their shoes. That shop wouldn't be in business very long—or at the very least, it wouldn't be as successful.

If you strive to follow Web standards, chances are that you'll already be doing most of what you need to do to support multiple browsers. Avoiding proprietary plug-ins for your Web site helps to ensure that it renders correctly, too.

A well-designed Web site uses appropriate technologies at appropriate times.   Speaking of plug-ins, a well-designed Web site doesn't overuse or misuse technology. On a video site, it's appropriate to play videos. Likewise, on a music site, it's appropriate to play background music. This is not the case on other sites. If you feel as though your site needs to have background music playing, go back to the drawing board and examine why you want a Web site in the first place. I still shudder when I think of an attorney's Web site that I once visited. The site started playing the firm's jingle in the background, without my intervention. Friends don't let friends use background music on their site, unless your friend is from the band Rush and you are working on the band's Web site.

Where JavaScript Fits

Today's Web is still evolving. One of the more popular movements over the past year is known as unobtrusive scripting. The unobtrusive scripting paradigm is part of the larger movement called behavioral separation. Behavioral separation calls for structure to be separated from style, both of which are separated from behavior. In this model, HTML or XHTML provides the structure while CSS provides the style and JavaScript provides the behavior. The JavaScript is unobtrusive; it doesn't get in the way. If JavaScript isn't available in the browser, the Web site still works because there's still some other way for the visitor to use the Web site.

When applied properly, unobtrusive script means that any use of JavaScript will fail in a graceful manner. Not assuming that JavaScript will be available, the unobtrusive scripter either makes sure that the page will function without JavaScript or uses proper methods to ensure that JavaScript is available if it's actually required for the site. One such method will be covered in Chapter 14. Unobtrusive scripting is important because it helps to ensure accessibility for those with alternative browsers, text readers, or whatever the case may be.

I'm a proponent of unobtrusive scripting because it tends to mean that standards will be followed and the resulting site will follow the four recommendations I shared in the previous section. Granted, this isn't necessarily the case. One could separate the HTML, CSS, and JavaScript and still end up using proprietary tags, but the tendency when programming in an unobtrusive manner is to pay closer attention to detail and therefore care much more about the end result being standards-compliant.

Throughout this book, I'm going to strive to show you not only the basics of JavaScript but the best way to use JavaScript effectively and, as much as possible, unobtrusively.

A Note on JScript and JavaScript and This Book

This book will cover JavaScript as defined by the ECMA standard. In some areas, I'll highlight something related to Microsoft JScript and JScript .NET. For additional reference on JScript alone, I recommend the following sites:

JScript 7.1 — Visual Studio 2003 — .NET Framework 1.1: http://msdn2.microsoft. com/en-us/library/72bd815a(VS.71).aspx

JScript 8.0 — Visual Studio 2005 — .NET Framework 2.0: http://msdn2.microsoft. com/en-us/library/72bd815a(vs.80).aspx

---

Which Browsers Should the Site Support?

Backwards compatibility has been an issue for the Web developer for a long time. Choosing which browser versions to support becomes a tradeoff between the latest functionality available in the newest browsers and the compatible functionality required for older browsers to view the Web site. There is no hard and fast rule for which browsers you should support on your Web site, so the answer is: it depends.

Your decision depends on what you'd like to do with your site and whether you value visits by people using older hardware and software more than you value the added functionality available in later browser versions. Some browsers are just too old to support because they can't render CSS correctly, much less JavaScript. A key to supporting multiple browser versions is to test within them. Obtaining an MSDN account from Microsoft will give you access to legacy products, including older versions of Internet Explorer, so that you can see how your site reacts to a visit from Internet Explorer 4.

Many Web designs and JavaScript functions don't require newer versions of Web browsers. However, as I've already said, it's always a good idea to verify that your site renders correctly in various browsers. Even if extensive testing isn't possible, making the site fail in a graceful manner is also important so that it renders appropriately regardless of the browser being used.

Exercises

1. True or False: JavaScript is defined by a standards body and is supported on all Web browsers.

2. True or False: When a visitor whose machine has JavaScript disabled comes to your Web site, then you should block her or his access to the site since there's no valid reason to have JavaScript disabled.

3. Create a JavaScript definition block that would typically appear on an HTML page within the *<head>* block.

4. True or False: It's important to declare the version of JavaScript being used within the DOCTYPE definition block.

5. True or False: JavaScript can appear in both the *<head>* block and within the *<body>* text of an HTML page.

Chapter 2
Developing in JavaScript

After reading this chapter, you'll be able to

- Understand the options available for developing in JavaScript.
- Configure your computer for JavaScript development.
- Use Microsoft Visual Studio 2005 to create and deploy a JavaScript application.
- Use Eclipse to create and deploy a JavaScript application.
- Use Notepad (or another editor) to create a JavaScript application.
- Understand options for debugging JavaScript.

JavaScript Development Options

Because JavaScript isn't a compiled language, no special tools or development environments are required to write and deploy JavaScript applications. Likewise, no special server software is required to run the applications. Therefore, your options for creating JavaScript programs are virtually limitless.

JavaScript code can be written in any text editor, or in whatever program you use to write your Hypertext Markup Language (HTML) and Cascading Style Sheets (CSS) files, or in powerful Integrated Development Environments (IDEs) like Visual Studio—sometimes you might use all three approaches. You might initially develop the Web application with Visual Studio but then find that you have to use a text editor like Notepad to touch up a bit of JavaScript. Ultimately you should use whatever tool you're most comfortable with for developing JavaScript.

I will discuss in this book how to do development in JavaScript using Visual Studio, but at times I may just recommend (and show) the use of a text editor, such as Notepad or Vim (which can be obtained through the *http://www.vim.org* Web site). At other times, you'll be able to simply type the JavaScript code into the Location or Address bar of your Web browser using the *javascript:* pseudo protocol identifier, as you saw in Chapter 1, "JavaScript Is More Than You Might Think."

When you've been developing JavaScript for a while, you'll notice that you do some of the same things on every Web page. In such cases, the code can simply be copied and pasted into the Web page that you're developing. Better still, you'll likely be able to create an external file containing common functions that you'll use throughout the sites you develop. Chapter 10, "The Document Object Model," has more information about functions, though you'll see their use throughout the first 10 chapters.

Configuring Your Environment

This section looks at JavaScript development using a few different tools. I believe that you should be able to use whatever tool you feel most comfortable with for your JavaScript and Web site development, so don't consider this to be an exhaustive or prejudicial list of tools for JavaScript development.

One useful tool for JavaScript development is Visual Studio 2005. A Web server, Internet Information Services (IIS), comes with the installation of Visual Studio 2005, which makes deploying and testing the applications in this book a little easier. This does not mean, however, that you should go out and purchase Visual Studio 2005 just for JavaScript development. If you choose to use Eclipse, the second tool discussed in this chapter, you can still test the JavaScript code that you write. Likewise, you can test the JavaScript code even if you don't use an IDE at all.

You don't absolutely need a Web server for most JavaScript development. The notable exception to this is development with Asynchronous JavaScript and XML (AJAX). AJAX cannot use the *file://* protocol which, along with the same-origin policy covered in Chapter 1, prevents AJAX from working unless you use a Web server. The bottom line is if AJAX development is in your future you'll need a Web server.

AJAX notwithstanding, development does become a little easier if you have a Web server handy. Any Web server will do since all you're really looking to do is serve HTML and JavaScript and maybe a little CSS for fun. I have great luck with Apache, available from *http://httpd. apache.org*. Apache runs on many platforms, including Windows, and continues to be the most popular Web server on the Internet.

Configuring Apache or any Web server is beyond what this book can show, and again, having the Web server is not absolutely required. The Apache Web site has some good tutorials for installing Apache on Windows, and if you're using just about any version of Linux, Apache will likely be already installed or easily installable. Many of the examples used throughout the book will work whether you're using a Web server or just viewing the example locally. However, to take advantage of examples that use AJAX, a Web server will be necessary.

Writing in JavaScript with Visual Studio 2005

Visual Studio 2005 enables developers to quickly deploy Web applications with JavaScript enhancements. When you first start Visual Studio 2005, you are given options to select a certain style for your Visual Studio environment. Selection of the programming environment in Visual Studio 2005 gives differing views that are helpful to the programmer. An example of this dialog box is shown in Figure 2-1.

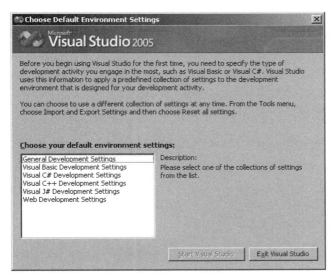

FIGURE 2-1 Choosing the development environment style

If you're using General Development Settings, your Visual Studio environment will be similar to that shown in Figure 2-2.

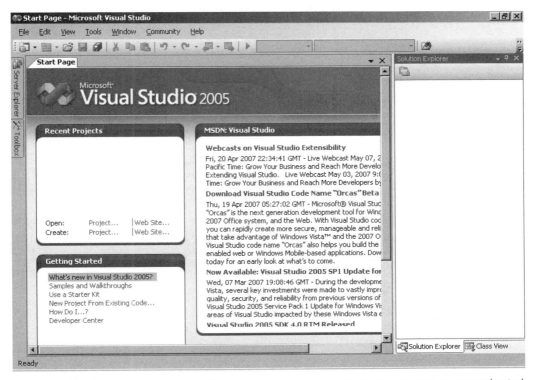

FIGURE 2-2 The General Development Settings provides an environment common to many programming tasks.

You can change to Web Development Settings by selecting Import And Export Settings from the Tools menu. This will open the Import And Export Settings Wizard. Select Reset All Settings, as shown in Figure 2-3, and then click Next.

 Note Changing the development environment settings isn't required.

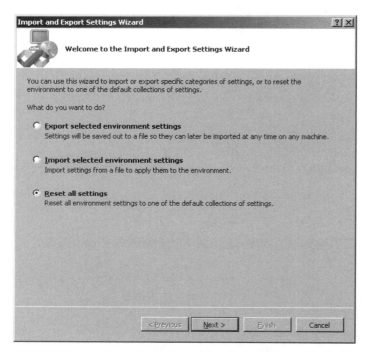

FIGURE 2-3 Preparing to change the settings in Visual Studio 2005 to Web Development Settings

The Save Current Settings page of the wizard now appears, as illustrated in Figure 2-4. If you have settings that you'd like saved, select Yes, Save My Current Settings. Otherwise, select No, Just Reset Settings, Overwriting My Current Settings. Click Next to continue.

The Choose A Default Collection Of Settings page of the wizard, shown in Figure 2-5, appears. Select Web Development Settings, and then click Finish.

After a short time, you'll receive a Reset Complete message. Click Close to reset your environment to the Web Development settings.

With the Web development settings, you'll have quick access to common tasks related to development of a Web site using not only ASP.NET, but also JavaScript, HTML, and CSS, the core languages of the Web. For more information about settings in Visual Studio 2005, see *http://msdn2.microsoft.com/en-us/library/zbhkx167(VS.80).aspx*.

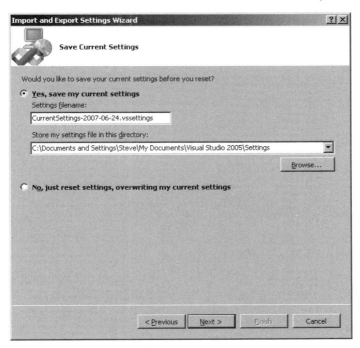

FIGURE 2-4 Saving the current settings enables you to keep any custom configuration that you may have specified for your environment.

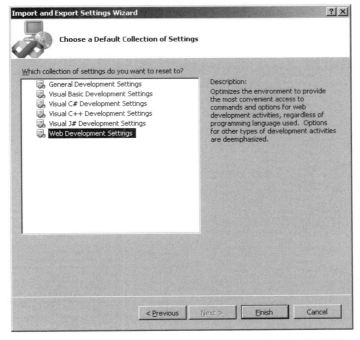

FIGURE 2-5 Selecting Web Development Settings in Visual Studio 2005

Your First Web (and JavaScript!) Project with Visual Studio 2005

Let's create a Web project and write a bit of JavaScript. If you're not using Visual Studio, skip ahead in this chapter to the section "Writing JavaScript with Eclipse" or the section "Writing JavaScript Without an IDE" for information on working within other development environments. I won't forget about you, I promise!

> **Note** The code found in these examples and throughout the book is included on the companion CD.

Creating a Web project with JavaScript in Visual Studio 2005

1. Within Visual Studio, using Web Development Settings, select New Web Site from the File menu. This opens the New Web Site dialog box.

2. Select Empty Web Site and set the name to Chapter2, with a path appropriate to your configuration. For example, I store my Visual Studio projects on a network drive, so the path information appears as shown here. When you have the information set, click OK. Visual Studio creates a new project.

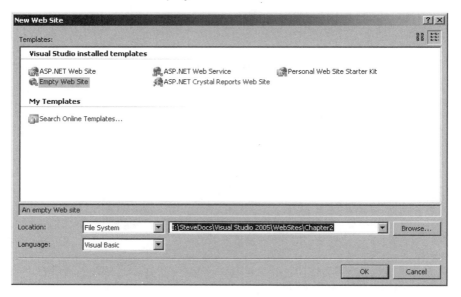

3. Next, create a new file by right-clicking the location within the Solution Explorer (usually found in the upper right-hand corner of the Visual Studio environment) and then selecting Add New Item. The Add New Item dialog box opens, as shown below. Select HTML Page, change the name to myfirstpage.htm, and then click Add. Visual Studio opens the new file and automatically enters the DOCTYPE and other starting pieces of an HTML page for you.

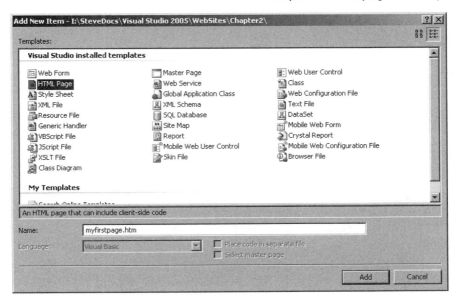

4. Within the myfirstpage.htm page, place your cursor between the *<title>* and *</title>* tags and change the title to **My First Page**. Your environment should look like the one shown here.

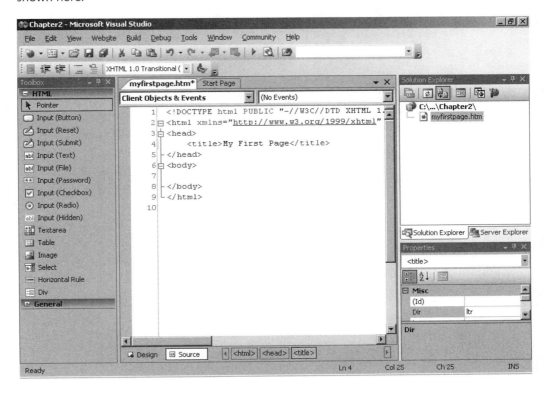

5. Within the *<head>* tags, after the closing *</title>* tag, add the following code:

```
<script type = "text/javascript">

function yetAnotherAlert(textToAlert) {
    alert(textToAlert);
}
yetAnotherAlert("This is Chapter 2");

</script>
```

6. Select Save All from the File menu. The finished script and page should resemble the screen here.

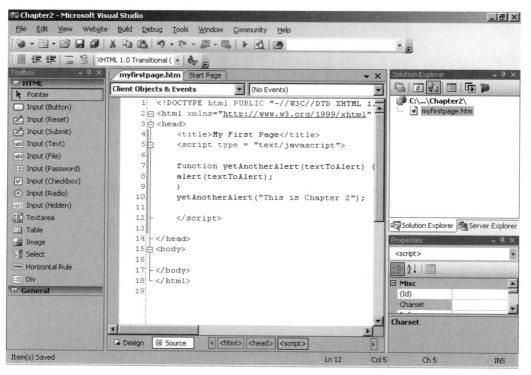

To view the page, select Start Without Debugging from the Debug menu. This will start the IIS server (if it's not already started) and take you to the page in your default browser. You should receive a page with an alert, similar to Figure 2-6. Click OK, then close the browser.

The script works like this:

First, the script tag is opened and declared to be JavaScript, as shown by this code:

```
<script type = "text/javascript">
```

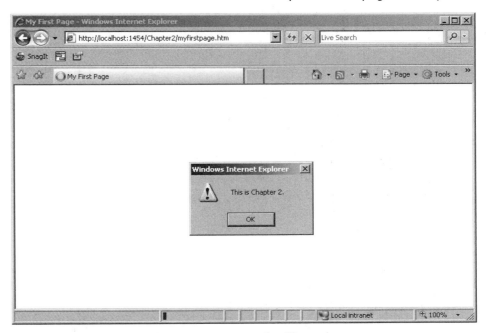

FIGURE 2-6 Running a JavaScript program courtesy of an IIS server

Note There are other ways to declare that your script is JavaScript, but the one that you see here is the most widely supported.

Next, the script declares a function, *yetAnotherAlert,* that accepts one argument, *textToAlert,* as follows:

```
function yetAnotherAlert(textToAlert) {
```

The function has one task: to pop an alert into the browser window with whatever text has been supplied as the function argument, which the next line accomplishes:

```
    alert(textToAlert);
```

The function is delineated by a closing brace (*}*). The script next calls the function you just declared with a quoted string argument, as follows:

```
yetAnotherAlert("This is Chapter 2");
```

With this script, you're now ready to develop JavaScript in Visual Studio 2005. But before you celebrate, consider sticking with me and learning about the use of external files to store your JavaScript code.

Using External JavaScript Files with Visual Studio 2005

JavaScript doesn't need to be contained wholly within the HTML files of your Web site. Therefore, you can take advantage of the *src* attribute to the *<script>* tag. Using the *src* attribute, you can define a source for your JavaScript file. The Web browser will then read the JavaScript contained within that file when it loads the Web page. Using external JavaScript files means that you have one place to maintain common JavaScript code, as opposed to maintaining it within each individual page—saving you a lot of work.

At this point, you should have a working Web page (built using Visual Studio) that displays an alert thanks to some nifty JavaScript. The Web page you developed in the previous section contains the JavaScript code within the *<head>* tag portion of the page. In this section I'll show you how to place JavaScript into an external file and then reference that code from within your HTML page.

Creating an external file for JavaScript using Visual Studio 2005

1. If the myfirstpage.htm code isn't open, open it by going into Visual Studio, and selecting Open Project from the File menu. Select the project in which you saved the myfirstpage.htm file and open the file itself. Your environment should look something like that from step 6 in the previous example.

2. Create a new file to hold the JavaScript code by selecting New File from the File menu. The Add New Item dialog box will appear. From the list of templates select JScript File and change the name to **myscript.js**, as shown here, then click Add. Note that your list may differ depending on your Visual Studio installation. This source file can be found within the Chapter 2 sample code, titled myscript.js.

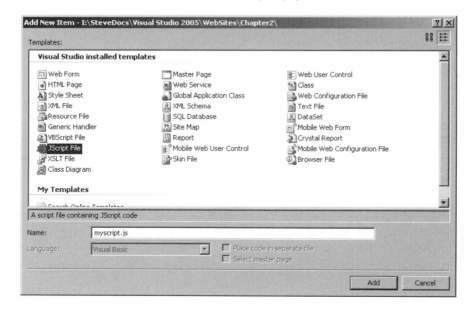

3. A new, nearly empty JavaScript (JScript) file opens and is added to your Web project. You should see a tab for the new myscript.js file and another for the myfirstpage.htm file, as shown here. If the myfirstpage.htm file isn't opened in a tab, open it by double-clicking it from the Solution Explorer.

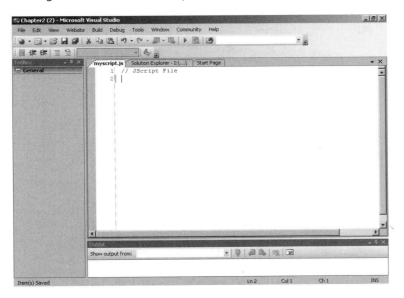

 Note Though not required, the colloquial extension for JavaScript and JScript is *.js*. I chose to use a JScript type of file in step 2 above simply because it automatically selects the correct file extension. You could just as easily have selected Text Document from the Add New Item dialog box, and then named the file with a *.js* extension.

4. Select myfirstpage.htm as the active tab and highlight the JavaScript code. Be sure to leave the actual JavaScript tags *<script>* and *</script>* intact and not highlighted. (We don't need these right now, but we'll be back.) This page can also be found within the Chapter 2 sample code, titled myfirstpage.htm.

5. Copy the code to the clipboard by highlighting the code and selecting Copy from the Edit menu.

6. Now select the myscript.js tab, move the cursor below the first line, and select Paste from the Edit menu. The code will be pasted. Change the text of the function call to be "This is the Second Example." as shown here:

```
function yetAnotherAlert(textToAlert) {
    alert(textToAlert);
}
yetAnotherAlert("This is the Second Example.");
```

7. Save the myscript.js file by selecting Save from the File menu. The file should look like this:

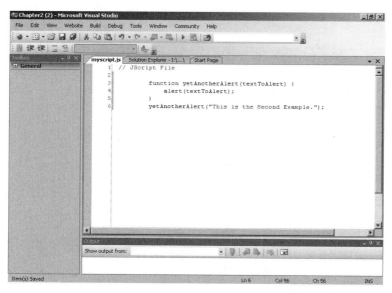

8. With the JavaScript code safely tucked away in its own file, myscript.js (you did save that file, right?), you can safely delete the code from the myfirstpage.htm file. Simply delete the code, leaving the script tags, as follows:

```
<script type = "text/javascript" >
</script>
```

9. Now add the *src* attribute to the opening *<script>* tag:

```
<script type = "text/javascript" src = "myscript.js">
```

10. If you wish, you can clean up the extra carriage return and make it look prettier by placing it on one line, like so:

```
<script type = "text/javascript" src = "myscript.js"></script>
```

The entire contents of myfirstpage.htm are now the following:

```
<!DOCTYPE html PUBLIC "-//W3C//DTD XHTML 1.0 Transitional//EN" "http://www.w3.org/TR/
xhtml1/DTD/xhtml11-transitional.dtd">
<html xmlns="http://www.w3.org/1999/xhtml" >
<head>
    <title>My First Page</title>
    <script type = "text/javascript" src = "myscript.js"></script>
</head>
<body>

</body>
</html>
```

11. Save myfirstpage.htm.

12. View the page in a Web browser by selecting Start Without Debugging from the Debug menu. The page will be served through the Web server and your browser window, if not already open, will open to the page. The result should be an alert with the text "This is the Second Example." An example of this is shown here:

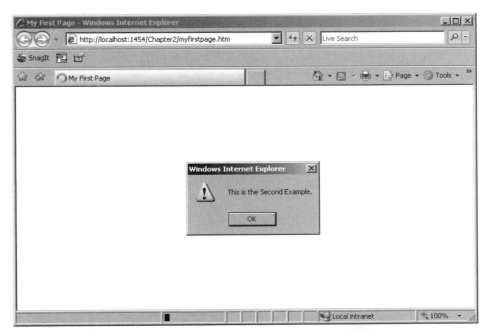

13. Click OK to clear the alert dialog box. Now view the source to see the difference. In your Web browser, select Source from the View menu. Note that the *<script>* tag now contains a reference to the external JavaScript file.

You've now developed JavaScript with Visual Studio 2005. From here, you can skip ahead to the section on debugging or keep reading to learn about JavaScript development using other tools.

Writing JavaScript with Eclipse

Another IDE that is popular among Web developers (and developers in many languages) is Eclipse. Eclipse is a development environment upon which the developer can install many different frameworks specific to the task at hand. For example, Web developers might use the Web Tools Platform or PHP Development Tools to make an environment that has many common tasks for those developers. Discussion of the many Eclipse projects is beyond the scope of this book, but I will discuss how to use the base Eclipse installation to develop JavaScript.

If you'd like to develop JavaScript with Eclipse, take a moment to download the software, and, if necessary, the Java Runtime Environment. Details and download locations are available from the Eclipse Web site (*http://www.eclipse.org*). In this section of the book, I assume that you've never used Eclipse before and that you'll be learning it for the first time. However, this section does not include a tutorial on installing Eclipse. I recommend reading the documentation included with Eclipse and on the Eclipse Web site for the most up-to-date information on installing Eclipse.

Your First Web (and JavaScript!) Project with Eclipse

It's now time to create a Web page with JavaScript using Eclipse. If you're not using Eclipse, then this section isn't for you. Later in the chapter, I'll show how to develop without an IDE, as well as some tips for debugging JavaScript.

> **Note**   Your Eclipse environment might look a little different than the screenshots included in this section.

Creating a Web project with JavaScript in Eclipse

1. Begin by opening Eclipse. When you run Eclipse, you'll be asked to select a workspace; choose the default. Also, the first time you run Eclipse, you'll be presented with a Welcome screen, like the one shown below. You can close that screen by clicking the *X* within its tab.

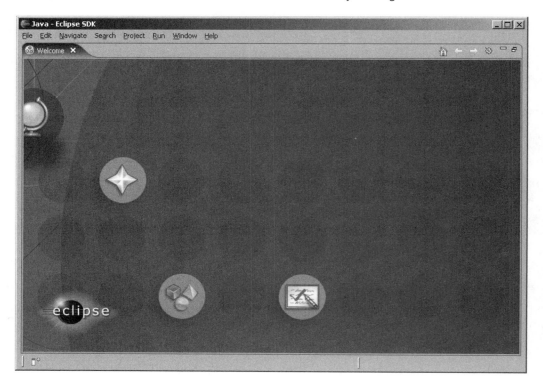

The default Eclipse configuration is for Java development. You can download one of the add-on projects for Eclipse and customize this workspace. The Java development configuration makes life a little difficult, so I'll show you how to switch out of that perspective shortly.

2. Create a new project by selecting New, then Project from the File menu. The New Project dialog box appears. Expand the General folder (if it's not already expanded) and select Project, as shown here. Click Next to continue.

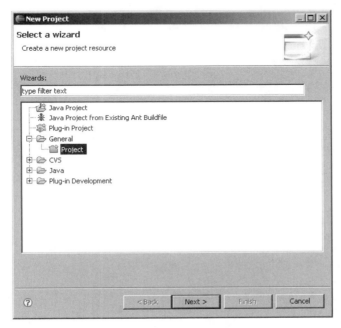

3. The next page of the New Project wizard, shown below, is for naming the project. Enter **Chapter2** in the Project name text box and click Finish.

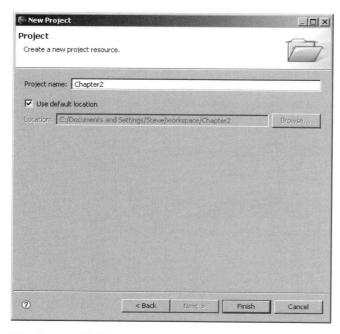

4. The Chapter2 folder opens in Package Explorer with no files underneath, as depicted here.

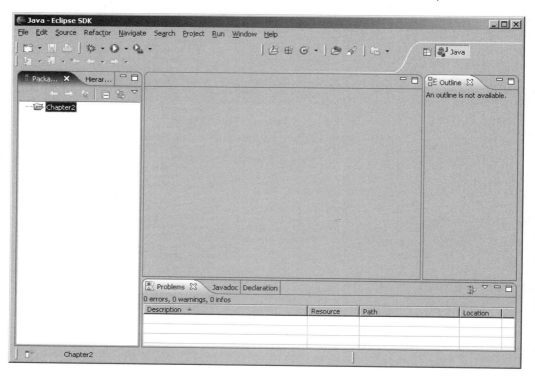

5. Right-click the Chapter2 folder, select New, and then File. The New File dialog box opens. Within the File Name text box, enter **myfirstpage.htm** and click Finish. An example is shown here. This file can be found within the Chapter 2 sample code, titled eclipse_myfirstpage.htm. If you'd like to use this file, rename it to myfirstpage.htm for the remainder of this exercise.

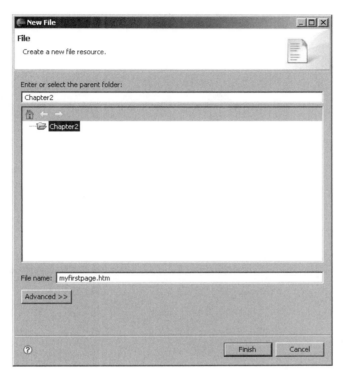

6. When you click Finish, Eclipse opens the page in its own Web browser. However, we want to edit the page, so right-click myfirstpage.htm within Package Explorer and select Open With and Text Editor. The page then opens in an editor right within Eclipse, as shown here.

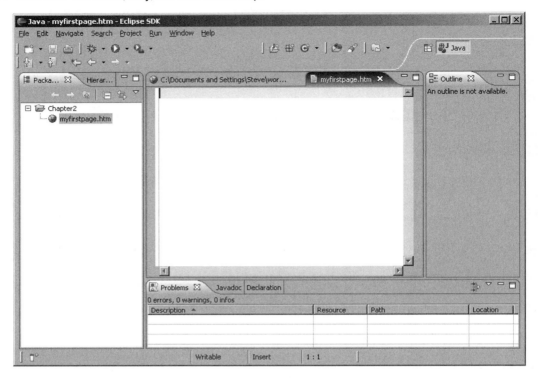

7. At last, it's time to write some code! Within the editor, place this code:

```
<!DOCTYPE html PUBLIC "-//W3C//DTD XHTML 1.0 Transitional//EN" "http://www.w3.org/TR/
xhtml1/DTD/xhtml1-transitional.dtd">
<html xmlns="http://www.w3.org/1999/xhtml" >
<head>
    <title>My First Page</title>
    <script type = "text/javascript">

function yetAnotherAlert(textToAlert) {
    alert(textToAlert);
}
yetAnotherAlert("This is Chapter 2");

</script>
</head>
<body>

</body>
</html>
```

Note For the purposes of this example, you can skip the DOCTYPE declaration if you don't want to type it, and just begin with an *<html>* tag on top. For real development, outside the context of this book, you would definitely want to have a DOCTYPE declared. See Chapter 1 for more information about why this is important.

8. Select Save from the File menu. The finished script and page should resemble the one shown below.

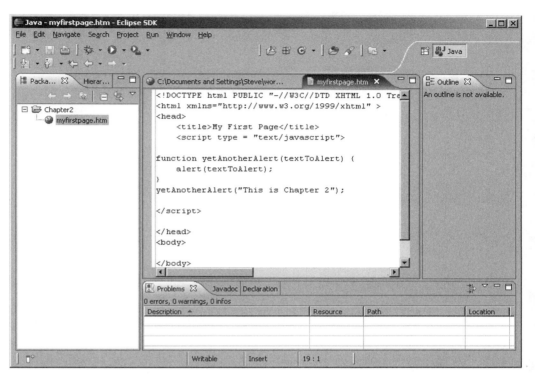

To view the page, select the Web browser tab located to the left of the editing tab of the screen shown above. Right-click that tab and select Refresh. You will see the file locally through the Eclipse browser, and you should receive a page with an alert, similar to that of Figure 2-7.

As an alternative, you could also view the file through a different Web browser on that same computer. Browse to the file (for example, my file is located in the C:\Documents and Settings\Steve\Workspace\Chapter2 folder), and double-click the file to view it through the default Web browser on your system.

> **Note** If you are using Microsoft Windows Internet Explorer you might receive an alert about viewing blocked content, depending on the security level set for your browser. The support article at *http://support.microsoft.com/kb/843017* has more information on this feature and how to disable it.

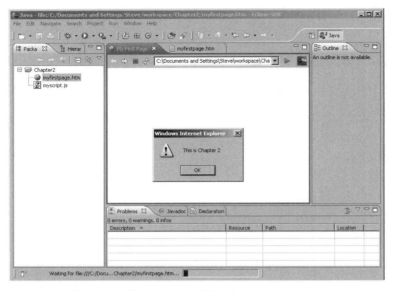

FIGURE 2-7 Viewing the file as developed in Eclipse

With this example, you've created a basic Web page with some JavaScript embedded within it. The JavaScript portion of the page contains just a few elements. First, the script tag is opened and declared to be JavaScript, as shown by this code:

```
<script type = "text/javascript">
```

> **Note** There are other ways to declare that your script is JavaScript, but the one that you see here is the most widely supported.

Next, the script declares a function, *yetAnotherAlert*, that accepts one argument, *textToAlert*:

```
function yetAnotherAlert(textToAlert) {
```

The function has one task: to pop an alert into the browser window with whatever text has been supplied as the function argument, which the next line accomplishes:

```
    alert(textToAlert);
```

The function is delineated by a closing brace:

```
}
```

The script then calls the function you just declared with a quoted string argument, as follows:

```
yetAnotherAlert("This is Chapter 2");
```

With this brief example, you've now seen how to code JavaScript using Eclipse. The next section shows how to place the JavaScript in an external file, a quite common approach to using JavaScript.

Using External JavaScript Files with Eclipse

By the time you read this, you should have a working Web page (created with Eclipse) that displays an alert. The Web page you developed in the previous section contains the JavaScript code within the *<head>* tag portion of the page. In this section I'll describe how to place JavaScript into an external file and then refer to that code from within your HTML page.

Creating an external file for JavaScript using Visual Studio 2005

1. If the myfirstpage.htm code isn't open, open it. Select the project in which you saved the myfirstpage.htm file and open the file itself through an editor by right-clicking the file and selecting Open With, and then Text Editor.

2. Create a new file to hold the JavaScript code by selecting New and then File from the File menu. The New File dialog box opens. Enter **myscript.js** in the File Name text box, as shown below, and click Finish.

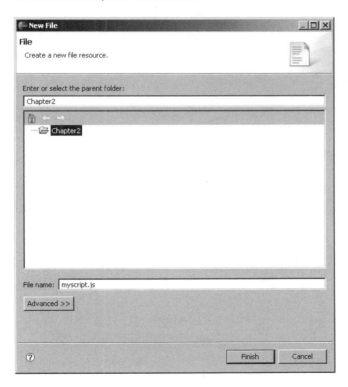

3. A new, nearly empty JavaScript (JScript) file is added to your project. Right-click the myscript.js file within Package Explorer and select Open With, and then Text Editor. You should see tabs for the new myscript.js file and the myfirstpage.htm file. You might also see the My First Page Web page.

> **Note** Though not required, the colloquial extension for JavaScript and JScript is *.js*. You don't have to use *.js* for JavaScript files, but doing so might make your life easier later.

4. Select myfirstpage.htm as the active tab and highlight the JavaScript code. Be sure to leave the actual JavaScript tags *<script>* and *</script>* intact and do not highlight them. (We don't need these right now, but we'll be back.)

5. Copy the code to the clipboard by highlighting it and selecting Copy from the Edit menu.

6. Now select the myscript.js tab and paste the code by selecting Paste from the Edit menu. Change the text of the function call to be "This is the Second Example." The code looks like this:

```
function yetAnotherAlert(textToAlert) {
    alert(textToAlert);
}
yetAnotherAlert("This is the Second Example.");
```

7. Save the myscript.js file by selecting Save from the File menu. The file should look similar to the screen shown below.

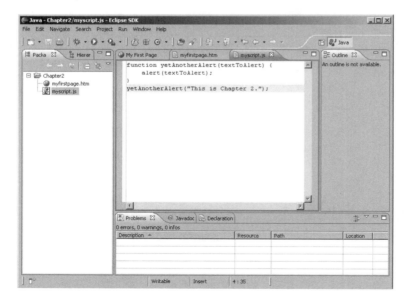

8. With the JavaScript code safely tucked away in its own file, myscript.js (you did save it, right?), you can safely delete the code from the myfirstpage.htm file. Simply delete the code, leaving the script tags, like so:

```
<script type = "text/javascript" >
</script>
```

9. Now add the *src* attribute to the opening *<script>* tag:

```
<script type = "text/javascript" src = "myscript.js">
```

10. You might also want to clean up the extra carriage return and make it look prettier by placing it on one line, like this:

```
<script type = "text/javascript" src = "myscript.js"></script>
```

The entire contents of myfirstpage.htm are now the following:

```
<!DOCTYPE html PUBLIC "-//W3C//DTD XHTML 1.0 Transitional//EN" "http://www.w3.org/TR/
xhtml1/DTD/xhtml1-transitional.dtd">
<html xmlns="http://www.w3.org/1999/xhtml" >
<head>
    <title>My First Page</title>
    <script type = "text/javascript" src = "myscript.js"></script>
</head>
<body>

</body>
</html>
```

11. Save myfirstpage.htm.

12. View the page in a Web browser by right-clicking myfirstpage.htm within Package Explorer and selecting Open With, and then Web Browser. The page is served locally and a browser window opens to the page. The result should be an alert with the text "This is the Second Example." It looks like this:

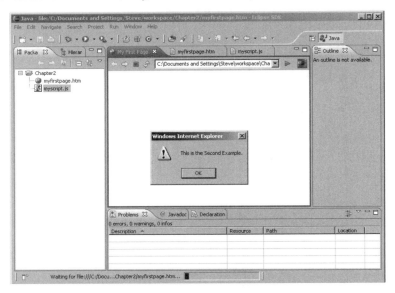

This wraps up the basic primer about JavaScript development with Eclipse. There's much more to it, though, and I recommend visiting the Eclipse Web site for more information about development with the Eclipse platform.

Writing JavaScript Without an IDE

You can just as easily forgo the IDEs in favor of a simpler approach to JavaScript development. Any text editor like Notepad or Vim will work fine for JavaScript development. I recommend against using word processors like Microsoft Office Word for JavaScript development because they can leave artifacts within the resulting file, which in turn can wreak havoc on the resulting Web site.

Your First Web (and JavaScript) Project with Notepad

This section shows an example of JavaScript development with Notepad.

Creating a Web page with JavaScript in Notepad

1. In Windows XP or Windows Vista, you can open Notepad by clicking Start and selecting All Programs, Accessories, and then Notepad. Within the document, place the
   following code:

   ```
   <!DOCTYPE HTML PUBLIC "-//W3C//DTD HTML 4.01//EN"
   "http://www.w3.org/TR/html4/strict.dtd">
   <html>
   ```

```
<head>
    <title>My First Page</title>
    <script type = "text/javascript">

function yetAnotherAlert(textToAlert) {
    alert(textToAlert);
}
yetAnotherAlert("This is Chapter 2");

</script>

</head>
<body>

</body>
</html>
```

 Note For the purposes of this example, you could skip the DOCTYPE declaration if you don't want to type it, and just begin with an *<html>* tag on top. For real-world development outside the context of this book, you would definitely want to have a DOCTYPE declared. See Chapter 1 for more information about why this is important.

2. Select Save from the File menu. You'll be presented with a Save As dialog box. By default, unfortunately, Notepad places a *.txt* extension on the document unless you use double quotes. Therefore, be sure to place double quotes around the filename myfirstpage.htm, or else Notepad will name it myfirstpage.htm.txt. An example of using double quotes around the filename is shown in the graphic. Be sure to note where you save this document.

[handwritten note in margin: save file in notepad w. " "]

3. To view the page, use the Web browser of your choice to browse to the location where you saved the file. If, as in the example shown in the previous step, Notepad by default saved the file within your My Documents folder, then that is the location to which you should browse. The view of the file from Firefox is shown here.

Note If you are using Windows Internet Explorer, you might receive an *alert()* dialog box about viewing blocked content, depending on the security level set for your browser. The support article at *http://support.microsoft.com/kb/843017* has more information about this feature and how to disable it.

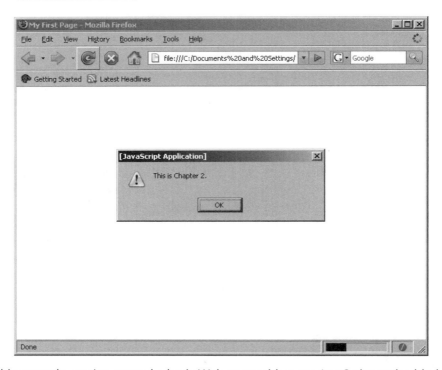

In this example, you've created a basic Web page with some JavaScript embedded within it. The JavaScript portion of the page contains just a few elements. First, the script tag is opened and declared to be JavaScript, as shown by this code:

```
<script type = "text/javascript">
```

Note There are other ways to declare that your script is JavaScript, but the one that you see here is the most widely supported.

Next, the script declares a function, *yetAnotherAlert*, that accepts one argument, *textToAlert*:

```
function yetAnotherAlert(textToAlert) {
```

The function has one task: to pop an alert into the browser window with whatever text has been supplied as the function argument, which the next line accomplishes:

```
    alert(textToAlert);
```

The function is delineated by a closing brace (*}*). The script then calls the function you just declared with a quoted string argument, like so:

```
yetAnotherAlert("This is Chapter 2");
```

In this brief example, you've now seen how to code JavaScript without an IDE. The next section shows how to place the JavaScript in an external file, a quite common approach to JavaScript usage.

Using External JavaScript Files Without an IDE

By the time you read this, you should have a working Web page (created in Notepad) that displays an *alert()* dialog box. The Web page you developed in the previous section contains the JavaScript code within the *<head>* tag portion of the page. This section shows how to place JavaScript into an external file and then refer to that code from within your HTML page.

Creating an external file for JavaScript using Notepad

1. If the myfirstpage.htm code isn't open, open it. If you're using Notepad, you might need to right-click the file and select Open With, and then Notepad.

2. Highlight the JavaScript code. Be sure to leave the actual JavaScript tags *<script>* and *</script>* intact and do not highlight them. Copy the code to the clipboard by highlighting it and selecting Copy from the Edit menu.

3. Create a new file to hold the JavaScript code by selecting New from the File menu. The new file opens. Paste the JavaScript code into the file by selecting Paste from the Edit menu. Change the text of the function call to be "This is the Second Example." The code reads as follows:

   ```
   function yetAnotherAlert(textToAlert) {
       alert(textToAlert);
   }
   yetAnotherAlert("This is the Second Example.");
   ```

4. Finally, save the file by selecting Save from the File menu. Enter **myscript.js** in the File Name text box, and be sure to include double quotes again because the extension needs to be *.js* and not *.txt*.

> **Note** Though not required, the colloquial extension for JavaScript and JScript is *.js*. You don't have to use *.js* for JavaScript files, but doing so might make your life easier later.

5. With the JavaScript code safely tucked away in its own file, myscript.js (you did save it, right?), you can safely delete the code from the myfirstpage.htm file. You'll need to open myfirstpage.htm again in Notepad. Within myfirstpage.htm, simply delete the JavaScript code that you pasted earlier, leaving the script tags:

> **Tip** Be sure you're viewing All Files and not just Text Documents when trying to open files that don't have a *.txt* extension, like the *.htm* or *.js* files that you just created. To do this, select All Files from the Files Of Type drop-down list in the Open dialog box.

```
<script type = "text/javascript" >
</script>
```

6. Now add the *src* attribute to the opening *<script>* tag, as follows:

```
<script type = "text/javascript" src = "myscript.js">
```

7. You might want to clean up the extra carriage return and make it look prettier by placing it on one line, like so:

```
<script type = "text/javascript" src = "myscript.js"></script>
```

The entire contents of myfirstpage.htm are now the following:

```
<!DOCTYPE HTML PUBLIC "-//W3C//DTD HTML 4.01//EN"
"http://www.w3.org/TR/html4/strict.dtd">
<html>
<head>
    <title>My First Page</title>
    <script type = "text/javascript" src = "myscript.js"></script>
</head>
<body>

</body>
</html>
```

8. Save myfirstpage.htm.

9. View the page in a Web browser. The result should be an alert with the text "This is the Second Example."

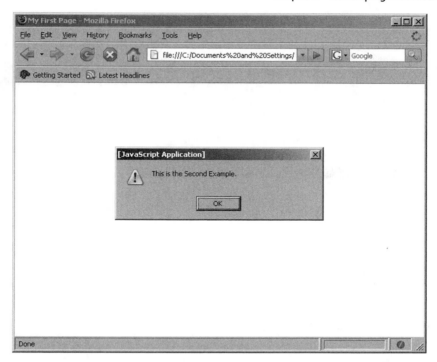

This wraps up the primer on JavaScript development without an IDE. Although this example used Notepad, several other editors might be more suited to basic development, including the aforementioned Vim and Textpad, from Helio Software Solutions, both of which are more powerful than Notepad.

Debugging JavaScript

Debugging JavaScript can be a hair-raising experience, especially in more complex applications. Some tools (such as Venkman) can assist in JavaScript debugging, but the primary tool for debugging JavaScript is the Web browser. Major Web browsers include some JavaScript debugging capabilities. Among the programs you should consider using is Firebug, a notable add-on to Firefox. It's small (only 258 kilobytes as of this writing), but it's quite powerful. Firebug is available at *http://www.getfirebug.com/*.

I find Firebug to be virtually indispensable for Web development, especially Web development with JavaScript and AJAX. This software allows you to inspect all the elements of a Web page, to see the results of AJAX calls, and to see CSS, all in real time, which makes debugging much easier. Figure 2-8 shows an example of Firebug in action on my Web site's home page.

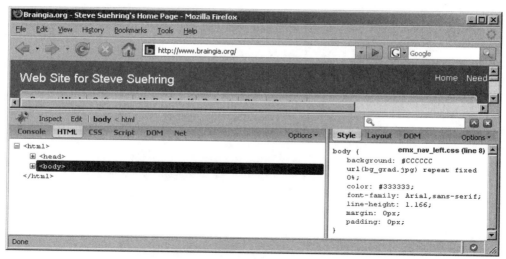

FIGURE 2-8 Firebug is an important tool in the Web developer's toolkit.

I recommend using Firebug for developing JavaScript and debugging it.

When debugging JavaScript, I find that the *alert()* function is quite useful. A few well-placed *alert()* functions can show you the values contained within variables and what your script is currently doing. Of course, because *alert()* causes a dialog box to open, if you place an *alert()* within a loop and then mistakenly cause that loop to repeat endlessly without exiting, you'll find that you need to exit the Web browser uncleanly, maybe using Task Manager.

Exercises

1. Create a new Web page and call it mysecondpage.htm. Create a script in JavaScript within the *<body>* portion of the page and have that script display an *alert()* dialog box with your name. Try this script in at least two different Web browsers.

2. Edit the Web page that you created in Exercise 1 and create a function within the *<head>* portion of the page and move the *alert()* dialog box that you currently have in the *<body>* script into your new function. Call the new function from the existing *<body>* script.

3. Move the function created in Exercise 2 to an external JavaScript file and link or call this file from within your Web page.

Chapter 3
JavaScript Syntax and Statements

After reading this chapter, you'll be able to

- Understand the basic rules of using the JavaScript programming language.

- Place JavaScript correctly within a Web page.

- Recognize a JavaScript statement.

- Recognize a reserved word in JavaScript.

A Bit of Housekeeping

The rest of the book looks more closely at specific aspects of JavaScript and how they relate to specific tasks. However, you must walk before you can run, so before examining JavaScript in more depth, you should learn some of its lexical structure—that is, the rules of the language, also known as *syntax rules*.

Case Sensitivity

JavaScript is case sensitive. The programmer must be aware of this fact when naming variables and using the language keywords. A variable called *remote* is not the same as a variable named *Remote* or one named *REMOTE*. Similarly, the loop control keyword *while* is perfectly valid, but naming it *WHILE* or *While* will result in an error.

Keywords are lowercase, but variables can be any mix of case that you'd like. So long as you are consistent with the case, you can create any combination you want. For example, all these examples are perfectly legal variable names in JavaScript:

```
buttonOne
txt1
a
C
```

> **Tip** You'll typically see JavaScript coded in lowercase except where necessary, like with function calls such as *isNaN()* which (as you'll learn in Chapter 4, "Working with Variables and Data") is a function to determine whether a value is Not a Number (the *NaN* in the function name).

There'll be much more on variables and their naming conventions in Chapter 4. For now, remember that you must pay attention to the case you use when you write a variable name in JavaScript.

White Space

For the most part, JavaScript ignores white space, or the space between statements in JavaScript. You can use spaces, indenting, or whatever coding standards to which you'd like to adhere that will make the JavaScript more readable. There are some exceptions to this rule. Some keywords, such as *return,* can be misinterpreted by the JavaScript interpreter if they're included on a line by themselves. You'll see an example of this problem a little later in this chapter.

Making programs more readable is a good enough reason to include white space as necessary. Consider the following code sample. It includes minimal white space and indenting:

```
function cubeme(incomingNum) {
if (incomingNum == 1) {
return "What are you doing?";
} else {
return Math.pow(incomingNum,3);
}
}
var theNum = 2;
var finalNum = cubeme(theNum);
if (isNaN(finalNum)) {
alert("You should know that 1 to any power is 1.");
} else {
alert("When cubed, " + theNum + " is " + finalNum);
}
```

Now consider the following code, with indenting. (This code can be found within the code on the companion CD called indentingexample.txt.)

```
function cubeme(incomingNum) {
    if (incomingNum == 1) {
        return "What are you doing?";
    } else {
        return Math.pow(incomingNum,3);
    }
}

var theNum = 2;
var finalNum = cubeme(theNum);

if (isNaN(finalNum)) {
    alert("You should know that 1 to any power is 1.");
} else {
    alert("When cubed, " + theNum + " is " + finalNum);
}
```

The second code sample performs just like the first, but it is generally easier to read and follow—at least it appears so to me! I find that it takes a short amount of time to actually write code, but then I spend the next several years working with that code. When I visit the code a year later, I'm much happier if I've made the code more readable and easier to follow.

Comments

Speaking of creating more readable code and maintaining that code over the long term, comments are your friends. Code that seems blatantly obvious now won't be nearly so obvious the next time you look at the code, especially if a lot of time has passed since you wrote it. Comments can be placed into JavaScript code in two ways: multiline and single line.

A multiline comment in JavaScript will look familiar to anyone who has coded in the C programming language. A multiline comment begins and ends with /* and */ respectively, as this code example shows:

```
/*  This is a multiline comment in JavaScript
It is just like a C-style comment insofar as it can
span multiple lines before being closed.  */
```

Single line comments begin with two front slashes (//) and have no end requirement because they only span a single line. An example is shown here:

```
// Here is a single line comment.
```

It's perfectly valid to use multiple single-line comments, and I find myself doing so for short comment blocks rather than using the multiline comment style previously shown. For example, look at this block of code:

```
// Here is another comment block.
// This one uses multiple lines.
// Each line must be preceded with two slashes.
```

> **Tip** You may find it quicker to use the two-slash method for small comments that span one line or a few lines. For larger comments, such as those at the beginning of a program or script, the multiline comment style is a better choice because it makes it easier to add or delete information if necessary.

Semicolons

Semicolons are used to delineate expressions in JavaScript. Technically, semicolons are not required for most statements and expressions. However, the subtle problems that you'll encounter if you don't use semicolons can add unnecessary errors and hence unnecessary debugging time. In some instances, the JavaScript interpreter will insert a semicolon when you may not have wanted one at all. For example, consider the statement:

```
return
(varName);
```

In all likelihood, you wanted to write:

```
return(varName);
```

But JavaScript, acting on its own, inserts a semicolon after the *return* statement, making the code appear like this to the JavaScript interpreter:

```
return;
(varName);
```

This code won't work; the interpreter will misunderstand your intentions. If you were to use this code in a function, it would return *undefined* to the caller, which is not likely what you want. This is an example where free use of white space is not allowed; you can't successfully use line breaks (explained below) to separate the *return* keyword from the value that it's supposed to return.

You'll find programming in JavaScript much easier if you use semicolons as a rule rather than trying to remember where you might not have to use them.

But you definitely shouldn't use semicolons in one instance: when using loops and conditionals. Consider this bit of code:

```
if (a == 4)
{
    // code goes here
}
```

In this case, you wouldn't use a semicolon at the end of the *if* statement. The reason is that the statement or block of statements in matching braces that follows a conditional is part of the *if* statement. A semicolon marks the end of the *if* statement and, if improperly placed, effectively dissociates the first part of the *if* statement from the rest of it. For example, this code is wrong (the code within the braces will execute regardless of whether *a* equals 4):

```
if (a == 4);
{
    // code goes here
}
```

> **Tip** When opening a loop or function, skip the semicolons.

Line Breaks

Related closely to white space and even to semicolons in JavaScript are line breaks, sometimes called *carriage returns*. Known in the official ECMA-262 standard as "Line Terminators," these characters separate one line of code from the next. Like semicolons, the placement of line breaks matters. As you saw from the example in the previous section, if you try to place a line break in the wrong place, it can result in unforeseen behavior or errors.

Not surprisingly, the most common use of line breaks is to separate individual lines of code for readability. To improve readability of particularly long lines of code, you can also separate some lines of code with line breaks as well. However, when doing so, you should be aware of issues like the one illustrated by the *return* statement cited earlier, where an extra line break can have unwanted effects on the meaning of the code.

Placing JavaScript Correctly

JavaScript can be placed in a couple of locations within a Hypertext Markup Language (HTML) page: in the *<head>* *</head>* section or between the *<body>* and *</body>* tags. The most common location for JavaScript has traditionally been between the *<head>* and *</head>* tags near the top of the page, though you may encounter some uses for it within the *<body>* section. In addition, you should declare what type of script you're using. Within the opening *<script>* tag, declare

```
<script type = "text/javascript">
```

Other script types could be declared here, but this is a JavaScript book, so that's the only one I'll be discussing.

One important distinction with JavaScript occurs with pages declared as Extensible Hypertext Markup Language (XHTML). In such pages, the *<script>* tag must be declared within a CDATA section because otherwise XHTML will try to parse the *<script>* tag as just another XML tag, and therefore code within the section might not work as you'd expect. Therefore, JavaScript used within strict XHTML should be declared as follows:

```
<script type="text/javascript">
<![CDATA[

//JavaScript goes here

]]>
</script>
```

If you place the actual JavaScript code in a separate file (as you've seen), then you don't need to use this ugly CDATA section at all. You'll likely find that for anything but the smallest of scripts, you'll want to define your JavaScript in separate files, usually with the file extension *.js*, and then link to those scripts within the page. The previous chapter showed this in full detail, but here's a reminder of how you link to a file using the *src* attribute of the *<script>* tag:

```
<script type="text/javascript" src="myscript.js">
```

JavaScript Statements

Like programs written in other languages, JavaScript programs consist of statements put together that cause the JavaScript interpreter to perform one or more actions. JavaScript statements can be simple or compound, which again is the same as with other programming languages. This section briefly examines the form of JavaScript statements, with the understanding that you've already seen several examples in the previous chapters and that you'll see others throughout the book.

What's in a Statement?

As covered in Chapter 1, "JavaScript Is More Than You Might Think," a JavaScript statement or expression is a collection of tokens, operators, and identifiers that are put together to create something that makes sense to the JavaScript interpreter. A statement usually ends with a semicolon, except in special cases like loop constructors such as *if*, *while*, and *for*, which are covered in Chapter 5, "Using Operators and Expressions."

Here are some examples of basic statements in JavaScript:

```
var x = 4;
y = x * 4;
alert("Hello");
```

The Two Types of JavaScript Statements

JavaScript statements come in two basic forms, simple and compound. I won't spend a lot of time discussing statements simply because you don't really need to know much about them. However, you should know the difference between simple and compound statements. A simple statement is just what you'd expect—it's simple, like so:

```
x = 4;
```

A compound statement combines multiple levels of logic. An if/then/else decisional such as the one given here provides a good example of this:

```
if (something == 1) {
    // some code here
} else {
    // some other code here
}
```

Reserved Words in JavaScript

Certain words in JavaScript are reserved, which means you can't use them as variables, identifiers, or constant names within your program because doing so will cause the code to have unexpected results, such as errors. For example, you've already seen the reserved word *var* in previous examples. Using the word *var* to do anything but declare a variable may cause an error or other weird behavior. Consider this statement:

```
var var = 4;
```

The code example won't result in a direct error to a browser, but it also won't work as you meant, possibly causing confusion when a variable's value isn't what you expect.

The following list includes the words that are currently reserved by the ECMA 262 specification.

break	delete	function	return	typeof
case	do	if	switch	var
catch	else	in	this	void
continue	finally	instanceof	throw	while
default	for	new	try	with

Several other words (shown in the following list) are reserved for future use and therefore shouldn't be used within your programs.

abstract	double	implements	private	throws
boolean	enum	import	protected	transient
byte	export	int	public	volatile
char	extends	interface	short	
class	final	long	static	
const	float	native	super	
debugger	goto	package	synchronized	

A Quick Look at Functions

You've already seen examples of functions in previous chapters. JavaScript has several built-in functions, or functions that are defined by the language itself. I have discussed the *alert()* function already, but there are several others. Built-in functions depend on the version of the language that you're using. Some functions are available only in later versions of JavaScript, which might not be supported by all browsers. Detecting functions (and objects) is a key method for determining if a visitor's browser is capable of using the JavaScript that you've created for your Web page. This topic is covered in Chapter 14, "Browsers and JavaScript."

> **Tip** You can find an excellent resource for compatibility on the Quirksmode Web site (*http://www.quirksmode.org/dom/compatibility.html*).

Similar to other programming languages, JavaScript also allows user-defined functions. An earlier example in this chapter defined a function called *cubeme()*, which raised a given number to the power of 3. That code provides a good opportunity to show the use of JavaScript in both the *<head>* and *<body>* portions of a Web page.

Placing JavaScript with a user-defined function

1. Using Microsoft Visual Studio, Eclipse, or another editor, edit the file example1.htm in the Chapter03 sample files folder.

2. Within the Web page, add the code shown below in bold type:

```
<!DOCTYPE HTML PUBLIC "-//W3C//DTD HTML 4.01//EN"
"http://www.w3.org/TR/html4/strict.dtd">
<html>
<head>
<script type = "text/javascript">
function cubeme(incomingNum) {
    if (incomingNum == 1) {
        return "What are you doing?";
    } else {
        return Math.pow(incomingNum,3);
    }
}
</script>
    <title>A Chapter 3 Example</title>
</head>

<body>
<script type = "text/javascript">
var theNum = 2;
var finalNum = cubeme(theNum);

if (isNaN(finalNum)) {
    alert("You should know that 1 to any power is 1.");
} else {
    alert("When cubed, " + theNum + " is " + finalNum);
}
</script>

</body>
</html>
```

3. Save the page, then run the code or view the Web page in a browser. You'll receive an alert like this:

The code in this example incorporates the code from the earlier example into a full HTML page, including a DOCTYPE declaration. The code declares a function, *cubeme()*, within the *<head>* of the document, like so:

```
function cubeme(incomingNum) {
    if (incomingNum == 1) {
        return "What are you doing?";
    } else {
        return Math.pow(incomingNum,3);
    }
}
```

This code accepts an argument called *incomingNum* within the function. An if/then decisional statement is the heart of the function. If the incoming number equals 1, the function returns the text string, "What are you doing?" If, on the other hand, the incoming number is less than or greater than 1, the *Math.pow* method is called and passes the *incomingNum* variable and the integer 3 as arguments. The call to *Math.pow* in effect raises the incoming number to the power of 3, and this value is then returned to the calling function.

All the previous code was placed within the *<head>* of the document so it can be called by other code, which is just what we're going to do. The browser then renders the *<body>* of the document, which includes another bit of JavaScript code. This next bit of code sets a variable, *theNum*, equal to the integer 2:

```
var theNum = 2;
```

The code then calls the previously defined *cubeme()* function using the *theNum* variable as an argument. You'll notice that the variable *finalNum* is set to receive the output from the call to the *cubeme()* function, as follows:

```
var finalNum = cubeme(theNum);
```

The final bit of JavaScript on the page is another if/then decisional set. This code checks to see if the returned value, now contained in the *finalNum* variable, is a number. To do so, the *isNaN()* function is used. If the value is not a number, then an alert is displayed reflecting the fact that 1 was used as the argument. (Of course, there could be other reasons why this isn't a number, but bear with me here and play along with my example.) If the return value is indeed a number, then the number is displayed, as you saw from the *alert()* dialog box shown in step 3 above.

Exercises

1. Which of the following are valid JavaScript statements? (Choose all that apply.)

   a. if (var == 4) {   // Do something }

   b. var testVar = 10;

   c. if (a == b) {   // Do something }

   d. testVar = 10;

   e. var case = "Yes";

2. True or False: Semicolons are required to terminate every JavaScript statement.

3. Examine this bit of JavaScript. What will be the likely result? (Assume that the JavaScript declaration has already taken place and that this code resides properly within the *<head>* section of the page.)

```
var orderTotal = 0;
function collectOrder(numOrdered) {
    if (numOrdered > 0) {
        alert("You ordered " + orderTotal);
        orderTotal = numOrdered * 5;
    }
    return orderTotal;
}
```

Chapter 4
Working with Variables and Data

This chapter discusses data types and variables in JavaScript. After reading this chapter, you'll be able to

- Understand the six different data types used in JavaScript.
- Use functions associated with the six data types.
- Create variables.
- Define objects and arrays.
- Understand the scope of variables.
- Debug JavaScript with Firebug.

Data Types in JavaScript

The data types of a language describe the basic elements that can be used within that language. You're likely already familiar with data types from other languages, such as strings or integers. Depending upon whom you ask, JavaScript defines anywhere from three to six data types. You'll work with all these data types regularly, some more than others.

The six data types in JavaScript are

- Numbers
- Strings
- Booleans
- Null
- Undefined
- Objects

The first three data types—numbers, strings, and Booleans—should be fairly familiar to programmers in any language. The latter three—null, undefined, and objects—beg for some additional explanation. I'll examine each of the data types in turn, and explain objects further in Chapter 8, "Objects in JavaScript."

Numbers

Numbers in JavaScript are just what you might expect them to be: they're numbers. What might be a surprise, however, for those familiar with data types in other languages like C is that there are no special or separate types for integers versus floating point numbers. All these are perfectly valid numbers in JavaScript:

```
4
51.50
-14
0xd
```

The last example, 0xd, is a hexadecimal number. Both hexadecimal and octal are valid in JavaScript, and as you might expect, JavaScript allows math to be performed using those number formats. Try this exercise:

Performing hexadecimal math with JavaScript

1. Using Microsoft Visual Studio, Eclipse, or another editor, edit the file example1.htm in the Chapter04 sample files folder.

2. Within the Web page, add the code shown below in bold type:

```
<!DOCTYPE HTML PUBLIC "-//W3C//DTD HTML 4.01//EN"
"http://www.w3.org/TR/html4/strict.dtd">
<html>
<head>
<title>Hexadecimal Numbers</title>
<script type = "text/javascript">
var h = 0xe;
var i = 0x2;
var j = h * i;
alert(j);
</script>
</head>
<body>
</body>
</html>
```

3. View the Web page in a browser. You should see a dialog box similar to this one:

This script defines two variables (you'll learn about defining variables later in this chapter) and sets them equal to two hexadecimal numbers, 0xe (14 in base 10 notation) and 0x2 respectively:

```
var h = 0xe;
var i = 0x2;
```

Then a new variable is created and set to the product of the previous two variables as follows:

```
var j = h * i;
```

The resulting variable is then passed to the *alert()* function, which displays the dialog box shown above. It's interesting to note that even though you multiplied two hexadecimal numbers, the output in the alert dialog box is in base 10 format.

Numeric Functions

JavaScript has some built-in functions (and objects too, as you'll see) to work with numeric values. In fact, the European Computer Manufacturers Association (ECMA) standard defines several of them. One of the more common numeric functions is the *isNaN()* function. By common, I mean that *isNaN()* is a function that I use frequently in JavaScript programming. Your usage may vary, but here's an explanation nonetheless.

NaN is an abbreviation for "Not a Number," and it is used to represent an illegal number. The *isNan()* function is used to determine whether a number is legal. For example, a number divided by zero would be an illegal number in JavaScript. The string value "This is not a number" is obviously also not a number. Though humans may interpret it otherwise, the string "four" is also not a number to the *isNaN()* function, but the string "4" is a number. The *isNaN()* function requires some mental yoga at times since it attempts to prove a negative, that the value in a variable *is not* a number. Here are a couple examples that you can try.

Testing the *isNaN()* function

1. Open your Web browser, such as Microsoft Windows Internet Explorer or Firefox.

2. In the address bar, type the following (also available in the code on the companion CD in a file called isnan.txt):

   ```
   javascript:alert(isNaN("4"));
   ```

You'll receive an alert with the word "false", as shown here:

The function *isNan()* returns false from this expression because the integer value 4 *is* a number. Remember the meaning of this function is, "Is 4 Not a Number?" Well, 4 *is* a number, so the result is false.

Now consider this example:

1. Open your Web browser, such as Windows Internet Explorer or Firefox.

2. In the address bar, type:

```
javascript:alert(isNaN("four"));
```

You'll receive an alert with the word "true", like this:

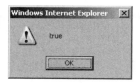

In this case, because 4 is represented as a string, "four," with nonnumeric characters, the function returns true: the string "four" is not a number. I purposefully used double quotes in each example, "4" and "four," to show that the quotes don't matter for this function. Because JavaScript is smart enough to realize that "4" is a number, it does the type conversion for you. However, this can sometimes be a bad thing, like when you're really counting on a variable or value to be a certain type.

The *isNaN()* function is used frequently when validating input to determine if something, maybe a form variable, was entered as a number or as text.

Numeric Constants

Other numeric constants are available in JavaScript, as described in Table 4-1. These constants might or might not be useful to you in your JavaScript programming, but you can rest assured that they are there if you need them.

TABLE 4-1 Selected Numeric Constants

Constant	Description
Infinity	Represents positive infinity
Number.MAX_VALUE	The largest number representable in JavaScript
Number.MIN_VALUE	The smallest number representable in JavaScript
Number.NEGATIVE_INFINITY	A value representing negative infinity
Number.POSITIVE_INFINITY	A value representing positive infinity

The *Math* Object

The *Math* object is a special built-in object used for working with numbers in JavaScript. The *Math* object has several properties that are helpful to the JavaScript programmer. Included are properties that return the value of pi, the square root of a number, a pseudo-random number, an absolute value, and many others. Most of the properties act like functions, but some, like the *PI* property, are static and don't accept arguments. Consider this example:

```
javascript:alert(Math.PI);
```

The result is shown in Figure 4-1.

FIGURE 4-1 Using the Math.PI method

Dot Notation

Dot notation is so named because a single period, or dot, is used to access the members of an object. The single dot (.) creates an easy visual delineator between elements. For example, to access a property that you might call the "length of a variable *room*," you would write *room.length*. The *dot* operator is similarly used in many programming languages.

Several other properties of the *Math* object may be helpful to your program. Some of them act as functions, several of which are listed in Table 4-2. You can obtain a complete list of properties for the *Math* object within the ECMA-262 specification at *http://www.ecma-international.org/publications/files/ECMA-ST/Ecma-262.pdf*.

TABLE 4-2 Select Properties of the *Math* Object

Property	Definition
Math.random()	Returns a pseudo-random number
Math.abs(x)	Returns the absolute value of *x*
Math.pow(x,y)	Returns x to the power of *y*
Math.round(x)	Rounds x to the nearest integral value

Strings

Strings are another basic data type available in JavaScript. They consist of one or more characters surrounded by quotes. The following are examples of strings:

- "Hello world"
- "B"
- "This is 'another string'"

The last example bears some explanation. Strings are surrounded by either single or double quotes. Strings quoted with single quotes can contain double quotes. Likewise, a string enclosed in double quotes, like the one you see in this example, can contain single quotes. So basically, if the string is surrounded by one type of quote, you can use the other type within it. Here are some more examples:

- 'The cow says "moo".'
- 'The talking clock says the time is "Twelve Noon".'
- "'Everyone had a good time' was the official slogan."

Escaping Quotes

If you choose or need to use the same style of quote both to enclose the string and within the string, then the quotes must be escaped. A single backslash character escapes the quote, as in these examples:

- 'I\'m using single quotes both outside and within this example. They\'re neat.'
- "This is a \"great\" example of using \"double quotes\" within a string that's enclosed with \"double quotes\" too."

Other Escape Characters

JavaScript enables other characters to be represented with specific escape sequences that can appear within a string. Table 4-3 shows those escape sequences.

TABLE 4-3 Escape Sequences in JavaScript

Escape Character	Sequence Value
\b	Backspace
\t	Tab
\n	Newline
\v	Vertical tab
\f	Form feed
\r	Carriage return
\\	Literal backslash

Here's an example of some escape sequences in action. (Let me be the first to apologize for the continued use of the *alert()* function. I promise to get into more complex ways to display output in due course.)

Using escape sequences

1. Open your Web browser, such as Windows Internet Explorer or Firefox.

2. In the address bar, type the following (also found in the code in on the companion CD in the escapesequences.txt file):

```
javascript:alert("hello\t\thello\ngoodbye");
```

The following box appears. (If it does not appear, close and reopen your browser.)

This rather contrived example shows escape sequences in action. The alert outputs the words "hello" surrounding two tabs, represented by their escape sequence of /t, followed by a newline character represented by its escaped sequence of \n, finally followed by the word "goodbye."

String Methods and Properties

JavaScript defines several properties and methods to work with strings. These properties and methods are accessed using dot notation ("."), which will be familiar to many programmers.

Like other elements of JavaScript, the ECMA-262 specification contains several properties and methods of which only a subset will be shown in this text. Refer to the ECMA specification for more information.

The *length* property or a string object gives the length of a string, not including the enclosing quotes. The *length* property can be called directly on a string literal, as in this example that can also be found in the source code on the companion CD in a file called stringlength.txt:

```
alert("This is a string.".length);
```

However, it's much more common to call the *length* property on a variable, like this:

```
var x = "This is a string.";
alert(x.length);
```

Both give the same result, which you can see by following this example.

Obtaining the length of a string

1. Open your Web browser, such as Windows Internet Explorer or Firefox.

2. In the address bar, type:

```
javascript:alert("This is a string.".length);
```

The result should be a box showing "17", as seen here:

3. Now try the same thing with this code:

```
javascript:var x = "This is a string."; alert(x.length);
```

The result should be a box showing "17", the same as in the previous example.

The substring method returns the characters from the first argument up to but not including the second argument, such as in the following example:

```
alert(x.substring(0,3));
```

This code would return the first through third characters of the string *x*. For example:

```
var x = "Steve Suehring";
alert(x.substring(0,5));
```

The result is a message box displaying the string "Steve".

Odd Indexing

The indexes used for the substring method are a bit odd—or at least I think they are. The first character is represented by the integer 0. This is all well and good because 0 is used numerous other places within programming to represent the first index. However, the last index of the substring method represents not the last character that you'll see, but one greater than the last character.

For example, you might think that with index values of 0 and 5 (as in the example above), the output would be the first six characters, 0 through 5 inclusive, resulting in a string of "Steve" with the additional space on the end. However, this is not the case. The output is really "Steve"—just the first five characters. So the key is to remember that the second index value of the substring is really one greater than what you want; it's not inclusive.

As I stated previously, there are numerous string properties and methods. I could devote an entire chapter to strings and the nuances of their properties and methods, but I'm not going to in this book. Throughout the remainder of the book, however, I'll feature other string properties and methods, and you can always find a complete list within the ECMA specification at *http://www.ecma-international.org/publications/files/ECMA-ST/Ecma-262.pdf*.

Booleans

Booleans are a bit of a hidden data type in JavaScript. By "hidden," I mean that you don't work with Booleans in the same way that you work with strings and numbers; you can define and use a Boolean variable, but typically you simply use an expression that evaluates to a Boolean value. Booleans have only two values, true and false, and in practice you rarely set variables as such. Rather, you use Boolean expressions within tests such as an if/then/else statement.

Consider this statement:

```
If (myNumber > 18) {
    //do something
}
```

A Boolean expression is used within the *if* statement's condition as the arbiter of whether the code within the braces will be executed. If the contents of the variable *myNumber* is greater than the integer 18, then the Boolean expression will evaluate to true; otherwise, the Boolean will evaluate to false.

Null

Null is another special data type in JavaScript (as it is in most languages). Null is simply nothing. It represents and evaluates to false. When a value is null, it is nothing and contains nothing. Don't confuse this nothingness with being empty, however. An empty value or variable is still full of emptiness. This situation is different from null, which is just plain nothing. For example, defining a variable and setting its value to an empty string looks like this:

```
var myVariable = '';
```

The variable *myVariable* is empty, but it is not null.

Undefined

Undefined is a state, sometimes used like a value, to represent a variable that hasn't yet contained a value. This state is different from null, though both null and undefined can evaluate the same way. You'll learn how to distinguish between a null value and an undefined value in Chapter 5, "Using Operators and Expressions."

Objects

Like functions, objects are special enough to get their own chapter (Chapter 8, to be exact). But I'll still discuss objects here briefly. JavaScript is an object-based language, as opposed to a full-blown object-oriented language. JavaScript implements some object-oriented-like functionality, and for most basic usages of JavaScript, you wouldn't notice the difference.

Objects in JavaScript are a collection of properties, each of which contains a primitive value. These properties—think of them as keys—enable access to values. Each value stored in the properties can be a value, another object, or even a function. You can define your own objects with JavaScript, and there are several built-in objects as well.

Objects are created with curly braces, so the following code creates an empty object called *myObject*:

```
var myObject = {};
```

Here's an object with several properties:

```
var dvdCatalog = {
    "identifier": "1",
    "name": "Coho Vineyard "
};
```

The code example creates an object called *dvdCatalog,* which holds two properties, one called *identifier* and the other called *name*. The values contained in each property are 1 and "Coho Vineyard", respectively. You could access the name property of the *dvdCatalog* object like this:

```
alert(dvdCatalog.name);
```

Here's a more complete example of an object, which can also be found in the source code for on the companion CD:

```
// Create a new object with curly braces
var star = {};
// Create named objects for each of four stars.
star["Polaris"] = new Object;
star["Deneb"] = new Object;
star["Vega"] = new Object;
star["Altair"] = new Object;
```

Examples later will show how to add properties to these objects as well as how to access properties. There's much more to objects and Chapter 8 gives that additional detail.

Arrays

You've seen in the previous example how to create an object with a name. However, you can also use unnamed objects that are accessed by a numbered index value. These are the traditional arrays familiar to programmers in many languages. The previous example showed several objects, each named for a star. The following code creates an array of the same objects. This code can also be found on the companion CD in a file called stararray.txt.

```
var star = new Array( );
star[0] = "Polaris";
star[1] = "Deneb";
star[2] = "Vega";
star[3] = "Altair";
```

The same code could also be written like this, using the implicit array constructor of square brackets:

```
var star = ["Polaris", "Deneb", "Vega", "Altair"];
```

Arrays can also contain nested values, as in this example that combines the star name with the constellation in which it appears:

```
var star = [["Polaris", "Ursa Minor"],["Deneb","Cygnus"],["Vega","Lyra"],
["Altair","Aquila"]];
```

Finally, although less common, you could also call the *Array()* constructor with arguments:

```
var star = new Array("Polaris", "Deneb", "Vega", "Altair");
```

> **Note** Calling the *Array()* constructor with a single numeric argument will set the length of the array rather than the value of the first element as you might expect.

Defining and Using Variables

Variables should be familiar to programmers in just about any language. Variables store data that might change during its lifetime. You've seen several examples of declaring variables throughout the previous chapters of this book. This section formalizes the use of variables in JavaScript.

Declaring Variables

Variables are declared in JavaScript with the *var* keyword. Examples can be found in the source code on the companion CD in the variablenaming.txt file. The following are all valid variable declarations:

```
var x;
var myVar;
var counter1;
```

Variable names can contain uppercase and lowercase letters as well as numbers, but they cannot start with a number. Variables cannot contain spaces or other punctuation, with the exception of the underscore character ("_"). (In practice, though, I haven't seen very many underscore characters in JavaScript variables.) The following variable names are invalid:

```
var 1stCounter;
var new variable;
var new.variable;
var var;
```

Take a look at the last example. Where the other three variable names are invalid because of the use of characters that aren't valid at all (or aren't valid in that position, as is the case with the first example), the last variable name, *var,* is invalid because it uses a keyword. For more information on keywords or reserved words in JavaScript, refer to Chapter 2, "Developing in JavaScript."

It's also possible to declare multiple variables on the same line of code, as follows:

```
var x, y, zeta;
```

These can be initialized on the same line, too:

```
var x = 1, y = "hello", zeta = 14;
```

Variable Types

Variables in JavaScript are not strongly typed. It's not necessary to predeclare whether a given variable will hold an integer, a floating point number, or a string. You can also change the type of data being held within a variable through simple reassignment. Consider this example, where the variable *x* first holds an integer, but then through another assignment, it changes to hold a string:

```
var x = 4;
var x = "Now it's a string.";
```

Variable Scope

A variable's *scope* refers to the locations from which its value can be accessed. Variables are globally scoped when they are used outside a function. A globally scoped variable can be accessed throughout your JavaScript program. In the context of a Web page, or a document as you might think of it, a global variable can be accessed and used throughout that document.

Variables defined within a function are scoped solely within that function. This effectively means that the values of those variables cannot be accessed outside the function. Function parameters are scoped locally to the function as well.

Here are some practical examples of scoping, which you can also find in the code on the companion CD in the scope1.txt file:

```
<script type = "text/javascript" >
var aNewVariable = "I'm Global.";
function doSomething(incomingBits) {
    alert(aNewVariable);
    alert(incomingBits);
}
doSomething("An argument");
</script>
```

The code defines two variables: a global variable called *aNewVariable,* and a variable called *incomingBits,* which is local to the *doSomething()* function. Both variables are passed to re-spective *alert()* functions within the *doSomething()* function. When the *doSomething()* func-tion is called, the contents of both variables are sent successfully and displayed to the screen, as depicted in Figures 4-2 and 4-3.

FIGURE 4-2 The variable *aNewVariable* is globally scoped.

FIGURE 4-3 The variable *incomingBits* is locally scoped to the function.

Here's a more complex example for you to do:

Examining variable scope

1. Using Microsoft Visual Studio, Eclipse, or another editor, edit the file scoping.htm in the Chapter04 sample files folder.

2. Within the page, add the code shown below in bold type:

```
<!DOCTYPE HTML PUBLIC "-//W3C//DTD HTML 4.01//EN"
"http://www.w3.org/TR/html4/strict.dtd">
<html>
```

```
<head>
    <title>Scoping Example</title>
    <script type = "text/javascript" >
    var aNewVariable = "is global.";
    function doSomething(incomingBits) {
        alert("Global variable within the function: " + aNewVariable);
        alert("Local variable within the function: " + incomingBits);
    }

    </script>

</head>
<body>
<script type = "text/javascript" >

    doSomething("is a local variable");
    alert("Global var outside the function: " + aNewVariable);
    alert("Local var outside the function: " + incomingBits);

</script>
</body>
</html>
```

The result will be three alerts on the screen.

The first alert:

The second alert:

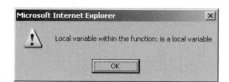

The third alert:

But wait a minute. Examine the code. How many calls to the *alert()* function do you see? Hint: There are two in the *<head>* portion and another two within the *<body>*, for a total of four calls to the *alert()* function. So why were there only three alerts on the screen when there are four calls to the *alert()* function within the script?

Since this is a section on variable scoping (and I've already explained the answer), you may already have figured it out. But this provides a good chance to demonstrate how to trouble-shoot JavaScript problems when things don't work as you expect.

Installing Firebug

The next procedure requires the use of the Firebug add-on to the Mozilla Firefox Web browser. As a Web developer I'm going to assume that you have Firefox installed (see Chapter 1, "JavaScript Is More Than You Might Think," for reasons why you should). If you don't yet have Firefox, download it from *http://www.mozilla.com/firefox/.* This first procedure will walk you through installing Firebug into Firefox. While Windows Internet Explorer has a script debugger and you could also use the Microsoft Script Debugger, Firebug is much more powerful and flexible.

1. With Firefox installed, it's time to get the Firebug add-on. Accomplish this task by going to *http://www.getfirebug.com/.* Once at the site, click the install link.

2. If you're installing Firebug for the first time, you may receive a warning that Firefox has prevented the site from installing software.

3. Click Edit Options to allow the Getfirebug.com site to install the software. Doing so will display the Allowed Sites dialog box:

4. Within the Allowed Sites dialog box, the *www.getfirebug.com* address will already be shown. Click Allow and then click Close.

5. With the Getfirebug.com site allowed, again click the install link on the Web page.

6. A Software Installation dialog box opens, as shown below. Click Install Now.

7. The Add-Ons dialog box opens, as shown below, and the Firebug add-on downloads. The installation completes when you restart Firefox, so click Restart Firefox after the add-on finishes downloading.

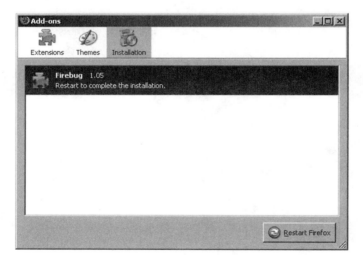

8. Firefox closes and opens again. Congratulations—Firebug is installed. You'll now notice a small icon in the lower right-hand corner of the Firefox browser window. Click this icon to open the Firebug console:

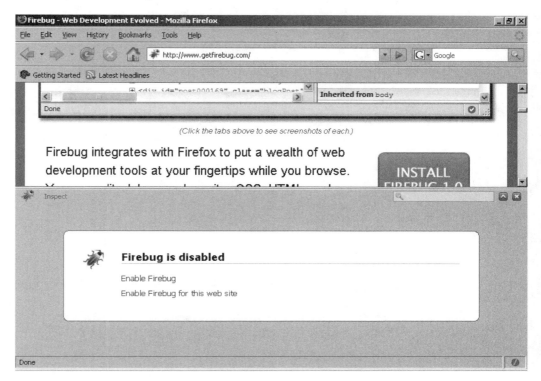

9. Firebug is disabled, but don't worry—the next procedure will walk you through enabling and using it. But feel free to experiment with Firebug by enabling it for this site only or for all Web sites.

Installing Firebug allows you to troubleshoot the problem where only three of the four expected alerts were displayed when running the scoping example given previously.

Troubleshooting with Firebug

1. Open Firefox and select the Scoping.htm example that was created earlier in this chapter. The JavaScript code again executes as before, showing the three alerts. After you clear the alerts, you'll end up with a blank page loaded in Firefox.

2. Click the Firebug icon in the lower right-hand corner of the Firefox browser window and select Enable Firebug For This Web Site. Firebug opens:

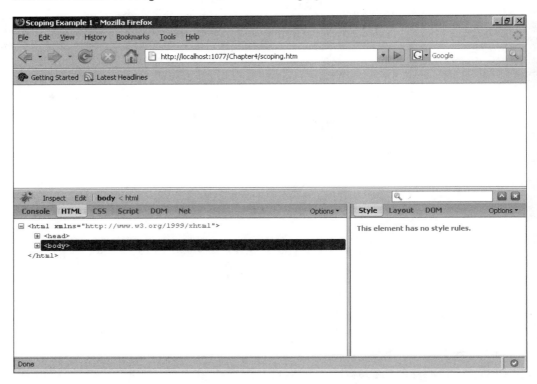

3. Click the Reload button on the toolbar or select Reload from the View menu. The page reloads, and the JavaScript executes again. All three alerts are displayed again, but notice now that Firebug has discovered an error, denoted by the red X and "1 Error" indication on the lower right-hand corner of the status bar, as shown here.

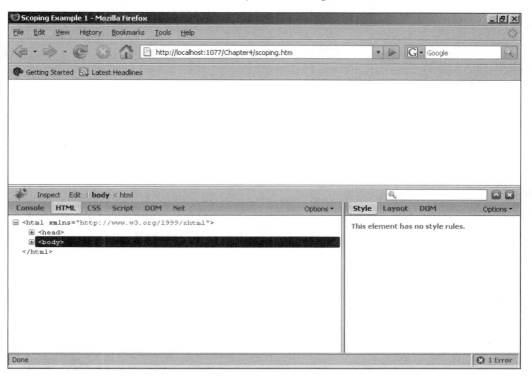

4. Click the Console tab within the Firebug portion of the window. This action reveals the error, which is that the variable *incomingBits* isn't defined. It also shows the line number where the problem occurred. Note, however, that the line number might not always be accurate in your original source code because of the way in which the document is parsed. Regardless, you can now see that *incomingBits* is not defined within the *<body>* of the Web page because its scope was limited to the *doSomething()* function.

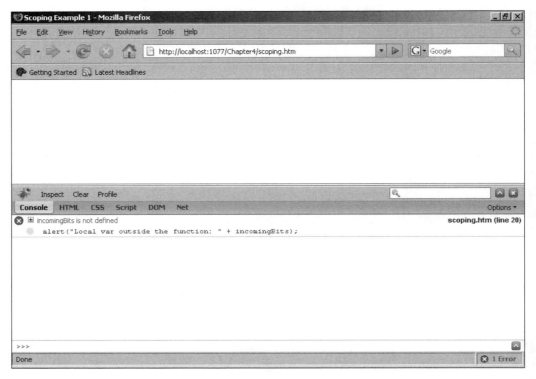

This procedure demonstrated not only the use of Firebug but also the effect of local versus global scoping of variables. Firebug is an integral part of JavaScript (and Web page) debugging. I invite you to spend some time with Firebug on just about any site to see how JavaScript, Cascading Style Sheets (CSS), and HTML all interact.

References and Garbage Collection

Some types of variables or the values they contain are primitive, while others are reference types. The implications of this might not mean much to you at first glance; you might not even think you'll ever care about this. But you'll change your mind the first time you encounter odd behavior with a variable that you just copied.

First, a bit of explanation: objects, arrays, and functions operate as reference types, while numbers, Booleans, null, and undefined are known as primitive types. Strings don't operate as either reference or primitive, so they aren't relevant to this discussion.

When a number is copied, the behavior is what you might expect of a copied value: the original and the copy both get the same value, but if you change the original, the copy is not affected. Here's an example (also available in the source code on the companion CD called garbagecollection1.txt and garbagecollection2.txt):

```
// Set the value of myNum to 20.
var myNum = 20;
// Create a new variable, anotherNum, and copy the contents of myNum to it.
// Both anotherNum and myNum are now 20.
var anotherNum = myNum;
// Change the value of myNum to 1000.
myNum = 1000;
// Display the contents of both variables.
// Note that the contents of anotherNum haven't changed.
alert(myNum);
alert(anotherNum);
```

The alerts display 1000 and 20, respectively. Once the variable *anotherNum* gets a copy of *myNum*'s contents, it holds on to them no matter what happens to the variable *myNum* after that. This is because numbers are primitive types in JavaScript.

Contrast that example with a variable type that's a reference type, as in this example.

```
// Create an array of three numbers in a variable named myNumbers.
var myNumbers = [20, 21, 22];
// Make a copy of myNumbers in a newly created variable named copyNumbers.
var copyNumbers = myNumbers;
// Change the first index value of myNumbers to the integer 1000.
myNumbers[0] = 1000;
// Alert both.
alert(myNumbers);
alert(copyNumbers);
```

In this case, because arrays are reference types, both alerts display 1000,21,22, even though only *myNumbers* was directly changed in the code.

The moral of this story is to be aware that object, array, and function variable types are reference types, so any change to the original will change any copies as well.

Loosely related to the difference between primitive types and reference types is the subject of garbage collection. *Garbage collection* refers to the destruction of unused variables by the JavaScript interpreter to save memory. When a variable will no longer be used within a program, the interpreter will free up the memory for reuse.

This behavior is different from other languages, where the programmer must perform the garbage collection task manually. As a JavaScript programmer, you don't need to do this—the JavaScript interpreter does it for you, and that's all you really need to know about garbage collection.

Type Conversions

Before we wrap up the discussion on data types and variables, you should know a bit about type conversions, or converting between data types. JavaScript usually performs implicit type conversion for you. However, in many cases you can also explicitly cast or convert a variable from one type to another.

Number Conversions

You've already seen a conversion between two number formats, hexadecimal to base 10, with the example given earlier in the "Data Types" section of this chapter. However, you can convert numbers to strings as well. JavaScript will implicitly convert a number to a string when the number is used in a string context.

To explicitly convert a number to a string, call the *String()* function or use the *toString()* method, as in these two examples, which can also be found in the file on the companion CD called numberconversion.txt:

```
// Convert myNumString as a string with value of 100
var myNumString = String(100);
// Set myNum and then convert it to a string.
var myNum = 100;
myNum.toString(100);
```

String Conversions

Just as numbers can be converted to strings, so can strings be converted to numbers. This is accomplished with the help of the *Number()* function, like this. (You can also find this example in the source code on the companion CD in the stringconversion.txt file.)

```
var myNumString = "100";
var myNum = Number(myNumString);
```

> **Tip** JavaScript also converts strings to numbers automatically when those strings are used in a numeric context. However, I've had hit-or-miss luck with this implicit conversion in practice, so I usually just convert to a number whenever I want to use a number. The downside of doing this is that you have to execute a bit of extra code, but it's better than the uncertainty inherent in leaving it up to a JavaScript interpreter.

Boolean Conversions

Booleans are converted to numbers automatically when used in a numeric context. The value of true becomes 1, and the value of false becomes 0. When used in a string context, true becomes "true" and false becomes "false". The *Boolean()* function also exists if you need to explicitly convert a number or string to a Boolean value.

Exercises

1. Declare three variables—one number and two strings. The number should be 120, and the strings should be "5150" and "Two Hundred Thirty".

2. Create a new array with three numbers and two strings or words.

3. Use the *alert() function* to display the following string, properly escaped: Steve's response was "Cool!".

4. Convert the string types created in Exercise 1 to numbers. Did they both convert? If not, why not?

5. Use Firebug to examine three of your favorite Web sites. Look closely for any JavaScript errors that Firebug reports. Bonus: Use Windows Internet Explorer to view those same three Web sites and debug the errors using Windows Internet Explorer tools and other related tools.

Chapter 5
Using Operators and Expressions

After reading this chapter, you'll be able to

- Understand the operators available in JavaScript.
- Use JavaScript operators to perform math, assignments, relational tests, and equality tests.
- Use the void operator to open a new window through a link.

Meet the Operators

The ECMA-262 standard defines assorted operators of various forms. These include:

- Additive operators
- Multiplicative operators
- Bitwise operators
- Equality operators
- Relational operators
- Unary operators
- Assignment operators

Operators can be used both on literal values, like the number 10, and on variables and other objects in JavaScript.

Additive Operators

The term *additive operators* includes both addition and subtraction operators. It seems a bit of a misnomer, really. But as my fifth-grade math teacher would remind me, subtraction is just addition with a negative number. As you might guess, the operators for addition and subtraction are + and −, respectively. Here are some examples of how they are used:

```
4 + 5;  // This would be 9.
x + y;  // Adds x and y together.
5 - 1;  // Results in 4.
```

The addition operator operates in different ways depending on the type of value being added. When a string is used, the addition operator concatenates the left and right arguments.

You can get odd results when JavaScript unexpectedly converts a type before performing a math operation. For example, you won't get the expected results when you think you have a number variable but the JavaScript interpreter treats it as a string. Here are some specific examples:

```
var aNum = 947;
var aStr= "Rush";
var anotherNum = 53;
var aStrNum = "43";
var result1 = aNum + aStr;    // result1 will be the string "947Rush";
var result2 = aNum + anotherNum;  // result2 will be the number 1000;
var result3 = aNum + aStrNum;  // result3 will be 94743;
```

As discussed in Chapter 4, "Working with Variables and Data," in many cases JavaScript allows you to explicitly change or convert one type to another. Take a look at the *result3* variable in the previous example. In all likelihood, you would want *result3* to hold the result of the mathematical expression 947 + 43. But because the second value, represented by *aStrNum*, is a string, the expression concatenates the two values rather than adding them mathematically as numbers. Using the *Number()* function converts *aStrNum* to a number, thus enabling it to be used in a mathematical expression, such as addition. Here's the relevant code, corrected to do what you might think it would:

```
var aNum = 947;
var aStrNum = Number("43");
var result3 = aNum + aStrNum;   // result3 will be 990;
```

Multiplicative Operators

Like additive operators, multiplicative operators behave in the way you might expect: they perform multiplication and division. In addition, multiplicative operators include the modulo operator, %. The multiplication operator, *, multiplies two numbers, while the division operator, /, divides numbers. The modulo operator, %, gives the remainder of the division of two numbers. For example, the modulo of 4 divided by 3 is 1, as in this example:

```
javascript:alert(4 % 3);
```

The result is shown here:

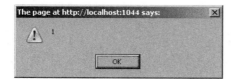

Bitwise Operators

Bitwise operators include *AND*, *OR*, *XOR*, *NOT*, Shift Left, Shift Right With Sign, and Shift Right With Zero Fill, as depicted in Table 5-1.

TABLE 5-1 Bitwise Operators

Operator	Function
&	AND
|	OR
^	XOR
~	NOT
<<	Shift Left
>>	Shift Right With Sign
>>>	Shift Right With Zero Fill

More information on bitwise operators is available within the ECMA-262 specifications. They won't be discussed further in this book.

Equality Operators

Equality operators are used to test whether two expressions are the same. They always return boolean types: either true or false. The equality operators in JavaScript are listed in Table 5-2.

TABLE 5-2 Equality Operators

Operator	Function
==	Tests whether two expressions are equal
!=	Tests whether two expressions are not equal
===	Tests whether two expressions are equal using stricter methods
!==	Tests whether two expressions are not equal using stricter methods

As you can see from Table 5-2, there are different ways to test for equality or inequality. These methods differ in their strictness—in other words, what degree of equality they require to determine if equal is really equal. The stricter of the two, ===, requires not only that the values of a given expression are equal, but the types as well. When using the strict test, a string with the value "42" is not equal to a number with the value of 42, whereas the less strict equality test would find that they were equal. An example is helpful.

Testing the equality operators

1. Using Microsoft Visual Studio, Eclipse, or another editor, edit the file equality.htm in the Chapter05 sample files folder.

2. Within the Web page, add the code, shown below in bold type.

```
<!DOCTYPE HTML PUBLIC "-//W3C//DTD HTML 4.01//EN"
"http://www.w3.org/TR/html4/strict.dtd">

<html>
<head>
    <title>Equality</title>
    <script type = "text/javascript">
    var x = 42;
    var y = "42";
    if (x == y) {
        alert("x is equal to y with a simple test.");
    } else {
        alert("x is not equal to y");
    }
    </script>
</head>
<body>

</body>
</html>
```

3. Point your Web browser to the newly created page. The code is fairly simple in its operation. Two variables are set, *x* and y. The variable *x* is set to the number value 42, while *y* is set to the string value of "42" (notice the double quotes). The test for equality is next, using the simple test, ==. This type of equality test measures only the values and ignores whether the variable types are the same. The appropriate *alert()* function is called based on the result. You should receive an alert like this:

4. Change the equality test so that it uses the strict test. First change the equality test to use the stricter of the two equality tests (that is, ===) and then change the alert to read *strict* instead of *simple*. The full code should look like this (the changed lines are shown in bold type):

```
<!DOCTYPE HTML PUBLIC "-//W3C//DTD HTML 4.01//EN"
"http://www.w3.org/TR/html4/strict.dtd">

<html>
<head>
    <title>Equality</title>
    <script type = "text/javascript">
```

```
var x = 42;
var y = "42";
if (x === y) {
    alert("x is equal to y with a strict test.");
} else {
    alert("x is not equal to y");
}
</script>
</head>
<body>

</body>
</html>
```

5. Again point your Web browser to the page. The test for equality now uses the stricter test, ===. Like the less strict equality test, this test examines the values, but unlike the simpler test, the stricter test also tests variable types. Since variable *x* is a number and variable *y* is a string, this equality test fails. The appropriate *alert()* function is called based on the result. This time the alert looks as follows:

Relational Operators

Relational operators test expressions to find out if they are greater or less than each other or whether a given value is in a list or is an instance of a certain type. Table 5-3 lists the relational operators in JavaScript.

TABLE 5-3 Relational Operators

Operator	Function
>	Greater than
<	Less than
>=	Greater than or equal to
<=	Less than or equal to
in	Tests whether a value is found in an expression
instanceof	Tests whether an expression is an instance of an object

You are probably quite familiar with the first four relational operators in Table 5-3, but here are some quick examples nonetheless:

```
if (3 > 4) {
    // do something
}
```

Obviously, the integer 3 is never greater than the integer 4, so this will never evaluate to true; therefore the code inside the *if* statement will never be executed. Likewise, the following code tests whether the variable *x* is less than *y*:

```
if (x < y) {
    // do something
}
```

The *in* Operator

The *in* operator is most commonly used to evaluate whether a given index is contained within an object. Be aware that the *in* operator searches for an index and not a value. Therefore, because there is an index called "star" within the *mjObj* object, the following code will work:

```
var myObj = { star: "Algol", constellation: "Perseus" };
if ("star" in myObj) {
        // do something fancy
}
```

The *in* operator expects to work with string types, so it won't work for numbers. A common use of the *in* operator is to iterate through an object. You'll see an example of this usage in Chapter 8, "Objects in JavaScript."

The *instanceof* Operator

The *instanceof* operator tests whether a given expression, usually a variable, is an instance of the object included as part of the statement. Yes, that's awkward. Rather than fumble around some more, I'll just skip ahead to an example, and then it'll all make sense:

```
var myDate = new Date();
if (myDate instanceof Date) {
        //do something
}
```

Because the variable *myDate* is an instance of the built-in *Date* object, the *instanceof* evaluation returns *true*. The *instanceof* operator works on user-defined objects as well as on built-in objects as in the previous example.

Unary Operators

Unary operators have a single operand or work with a single expression in JavaScript. The unary operators include those in Table 5-4.

TABLE 5-4 Unary Operators

Operator	Function
delete	Removes a property
void	Returns undefined
typeof	Returns a string representing the data type
++	Increments a number
--	Decrements a number
+	Converts the operand to a number
-	Negates the operand
~	Bitwise NOT
!	Logical NOT

Because the use of unary operators isn't necessarily self-evident in the same way that an addition or subtraction operator is, I'll explain it a bit more.

Incrementing and Decrementing

The ++ and -- operators are used to increment and decrement a number, respectively. They are used as follows:

```
var aNum = 4;
aNum++;
++aNum;
```

The placement of the operator in relation to the operand to which it is applied determines the value that the code returns. When appended to the variable (referred to as *postfixed*), as in the second line of code in the previous example, the operator returns the value *before* it is incremented (or decremented, as the case may be). When prefixed, as in the last line of code from the previous example, the operator returns the value *after* it is incremented (or decremented).

Here are a couple of examples of the difference between prefixing and postfixing in code. The first example is postfixing:

```
var aNum = 4;
var y = aNum++;  // y now has the value 4
```

The second example is prefixing:

```
var aNum = 4;
var y = ++aNum;  // y now has the value 5.
```

In practice, you'll use the postfix increment operator more often than the prefix increment operator or the decrement operator because of its common usage within a loop structure. You'll learn about looping in JavaScript in Chapter 6, "Controlling Flow with Conditionals and Loops."

Converting to a Number with the Plus Sign

The plus sign (+) attempts to convert a value to a number. In practice, however, I find it to be somewhat unreliable, or at least not reliable enough to use in production code. When I need to convert something to a number, I use the *Number()* function explicitly. You can, however, use the plus sign as a unary operator to attempt conversion, as follows:

```
var x = +"43";
```

This code will result in the string "43" being converted to a number by JavaScript and the numeric value 43 being stored in the variable *x*.

Creating a Negative Number with the Minus Sign

It may come as no surprise that when you use a minus sign (-) in front of a number, the number is converted to its negative counterpart, as in this code:

```
var y = "754";
var negat = -y;
alert(negat);
```

Bitwise Not and Logical Not

The tilde (~) character is a bitwise not, and the exclamation point (!) is a logical not. These operators negate their counterparts. In the case of bitwise not, its bit complement is given, so a 0 changes to a -1 and a -1 to a 0. A logical not, which is the negation you'll use most frequently in JavaScript programming, negates the expression. If the expression was *true*, the logical not operator will make it *false*.

The *delete* Operator

The *delete* operator takes the property of an object or the index of an array and removes it or causes it to become undefined. Here's a simple example using an array:

```
var myArray = ("The RCMP", "The Police", "State Patrol");
delete myArray[0];   // myArray now has "The Police" and "State Patrol"
```

This code creates an array called *myArray* and then promptly deletes the value at the first index. The *delete* operator works with objects too, as you can see in this next example.

Using the *delete* operator with objects

1. Using Visual Studio, Eclipse, or another editor, edit the file deleteop1.htm in the Chapter05 sample files folder.

2. The first task is to create the contents for a base page from which you'll use the *delete* operator in a later step. Within the page, add the following code shown in bold:

```
<!DOCTYPE HTML PUBLIC "-//W3C//DTD HTML 4.01//EN"
"http://www.w3.org/TR/html4/strict.dtd">

<html>
<head>
    <title>The Delete Operator</title>
    <script type = "text/javascript" >

    var star = {};

    star["Polaris"] = new Object;
    star["Mizar"] = new Object;
    star["Aldebaran"] = new Object;
    star["Rigel"] = new Object;

    star["Polaris"].constellation = "Ursa Minor";
    star["Mizar"].constellation = "Ursa Major";
    star["Aldebaran"].constellation = "Taurus";
    star["Rigel"].constellation = "Orion";

    </script>
</head>
<body id = "mainbody">
<script type = "text/javascript">

    for (starName in star) {
        var para = document.createElement('p');
        para.id = starName;
        para.appendChild(document.createTextNode(starName +
            ": " + star[starName].constellation));
        document.getElementsByTagName("body")[0].appendChild(para);
    }

</script>

</body>
</html>
```

3. Within the *<head>* portion of the code, you have created an empty *star* object and several additional *star* objects, each named *star["starname"]*. Then you have given the objects a *constellation* property with a value of the constellation within which each star appears in the sky. Within the *<body>* portion of the code, a *for* loop executes to iterate through each of the stars in the star object. This code uses the Document Object Model (DOM), which is covered in Chapter 10, "The Document Object Model (DOM)."

For now, don't concern yourself too much with what the code inside the *for* loop is doing. Save the file and view it in your Web browser. The output is shown here:

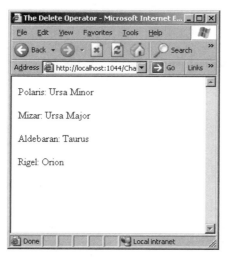

4. Now add the *delete* operator above the *for* loop in the code to remove the constellation from Polaris. The code will look like this:

```
<!DOCTYPE HTML PUBLIC "-//W3C//DTD HTML 4.01//EN"
"http://www.w3.org/TR/html4/strict.dtd">

<html>
<head>
    <title>The Delete Operator</title>
    <script type = "text/javascript" >

    var star = {};

    star["Polaris"] = new Object;
    star["Mizar"] = new Object;
    star["Aldebaran"] = new Object;
    star["Rigel"] = new Object;

    star["Polaris"].constellation = "Ursa Minor";
    star["Mizar"].constellation = "Ursa Major";
    star["Aldebaran"].constellation = "Taurus";
    star["Rigel"].constellation = "Orion";

    </script>
</head>
<body id = "mainbody">
<script type = "text/javascript">

    delete(star["Polaris"].constellation);

    for (starName in star) {
        var para = document.createElement('p');
```

```
            para.id = starName;
            para.appendChild(document.createTextNode(starName +
                ": " + star[starName].constellation));
            document.getElementsByTagName("body")[0].appendChild(para);
        }

    </script>

    </body>
    </html>
```

Notice the addition of the *delete* operator in the *<script>* tag in the document's body (shown in bold type).

5. Save the file and view it in a Web browser. The output will look like this:

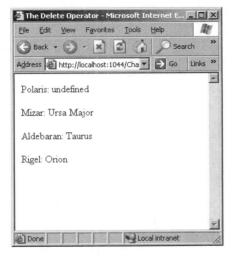

6. The use of the *delete* operator caused the constellation for Polaris to become undefined. You could also delete the entire Polaris object like this:

```
        delete(star["Polaris"]);
```

The *typeof* Operator

Unsurprisingly, the *typeof* operator returns the variable type of the given operand. Using this operator, you can determine whether a given variable has been created and is being used as a string, a number, or a Boolean; whether that variable is a certain type of object or function; and other related tasks. For example, consider this code:

```
var star= {};
if (typeof(star) == "object") {
        alert("star is an object");
}
```

The *typeof* operator will return "number" if a number is evaluated, "string" if a string type is evaluated, and (as you saw from the example), "object" if an object is evaluated. When used with properties, JavaScript is smart enough to know that you want to know the type of variable that the property actually is, rather than the object. As a result, the type of the value is returned. Here's an example that steals a little code from earlier in the chapter:

Using the *typeof* operator

1. Using Visual Studio, Eclipse, or another editor, edit the file typeof.htm in the Chapter05 sample files folder.

2. Within the Web page, add the following code shown in bold:

```
<!DOCTYPE HTML PUBLIC "-//W3C//DTD HTML 4.01//EN"
"http://www.w3.org/TR/html4/strict.dtd">
<html>
<head>
    <title>The Typeof Example</title>

    <script type = "text/javascript" >
        var star = {};

        star["Polaris"] = new Object;
        star["Polaris"].constellation = "Ursa Minor";

        alert(typeof star["Polaris"].constellation);
    </script>

</head>
<body>

</body>
</html>
```

3. The code within the *<script>* tags creates a new object for the star Polaris and sets its *constellation* property to the string "Ursa Minor". An alert dialog box is then called with the *typeof* operator to show that the type of the *star["Polaris"].constellation* property is a string. Save the file and view it in a Web browser. You'll get an alert like this:

Using the *typeof* operator, you can see the difference between null and undefined.

The *void* Operator

If you've done any behind-the-scenes examination of source code in JavaScript, you've likely seen the *void* operator. The *void* operator returns *undefined* after evaluating its argument. This means that the *void* operator enables the Web developer to call a function without the results being shown in the browser.

A common use of the *void* operator is to submit a form or to open a new window. The following example shows the *void* operator in use:

```
void(window.open());
```

More commonly, the *javascript:void* code would be placed inside a link on a Web page to open a new window, as follows:

```
<a href="javascript:void(window.open())">Open a new window by clicking here.</a>
```

Let's incorporate that into a Web page.

Using the *void* operator

1. Using Visual Studio, Eclipse, or another editor, edit the file void.htm in the Chapter05 sample files folder.

2. Within the Web page, add the following code shown in bold:

```
<!DOCTYPE HTML PUBLIC "-//W3C//DTD HTML 4.01//EN"
"http://www.w3.org/TR/html4/strict.dtd">

<html>
<head>
    <title>Void</title>

</head>
<body>
<p><a href="javascript:void(window.open('http://www.braingia.org/books/
javascriptsbs/'))">
Click here to open a new window.</a></p>
</body>
</html>
```

3. Save this code and view it in your Web browser. The page should look like this:

4. The code operates within the *<body>* tags and creates a standard Web link, this time calling the *window.open()* method to open a new window pointing to my *JavaScript Step By Step* Web site, as follows:

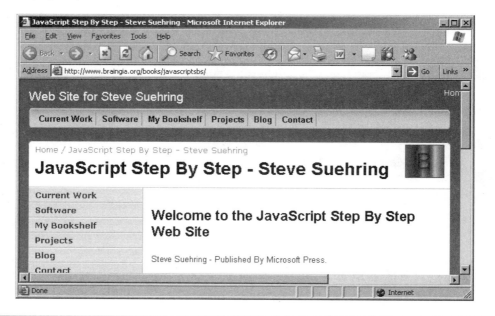

 Note The *void* operator, or more specifically, the use of the *javascript:* pseudoprotocol within an *href*, has fallen into disfavor in some Web design circles.

Assignment Operators

We've already reviewed assignments in this chapter, and you've seen them throughout the book. The primary (or most frequently used) assignment operator is the equals sign (=). This type of operator is known as a *simple assignment*. However, JavaScript has many more assignment operators, including:

*=	/=	%=
+=	-=	<<=
>>=	>>>=	&=
^=	|=	

These other operators are called *compound assignment operators*. The compound assignment operators provide shortcuts that save a few keystrokes and bytes. However, I won't go into detail about any of these operators because some of them are fairly specialized and rarely used.

The Importance of Byte Conservation

Though there'll never be any telethons, fundraisers, or benefit concerts, conserving bytes is an important topic for every JavaScript programmer. Byte conservation refers to programming with shortcuts so that the resulting program in JavaScript (or any other language, for that matter) consumes less memory and bandwidth. Each time that the programmer can take advantage of features like compound assignment statements to save bytes, the better off the program will be.

Saving bytes wherever possible means that the user will have a smaller script to download. It's difficult to quantify how many bytes you can save, or how much saving bytes will assist you. Some might argue that the effect is negligible, and for smaller scripts that's probably true, especially since more and more users are adopting broadband or faster connections. But the effect of smart shortcuts is very real for larger scripts, especially when they have to be downloaded using a dial-up or other slow type of connection.

Be wary of too much byte saving, though. I've seen scripts where virtually all the carriage returns and as much white space as possible are removed. The result is a script that saves bytes but is impossible to read or debug. The militant byte savers argue that this is the logical conclusion of running an optimized JavaScript program. I argue against this interpretation and recommend against sacrificing readability (and maintainability) for the sake of those bytes. As I stated in Chapter 1, "JavaScript Is More than You Might Think," you'll spend minutes, hours, or maybe even days writing the code—a relatively short time—but then you'll spend years maintaining it.

Exercises

1. Use the additive operator (+) to send three *alert()* dialog boxes to the screen (you can use three separate programs). The first alert should add two numbers. The second should add a number and a string. The third should add two strings. All should be represented by variables.

2. Use the postfix increment operator (++) to increment a number stored in a variable. Display the value of the variable before, while, and after incrementing. Use the prefix increment operator to increment the number and display its results before, while, and after incrementing using an alert.

3. Use the *typeof* operator to check the type of variables you created in Exercise 1.

4. True or False: Unary operators don't appear in JavaScript very often.

5. True or False: It's always best to save bytes (using JavaScript shortcuts whenever possible), rather than using returns and indenting that can slow down the loading of the page.

Part II
Applying JavaScript

Chapter 6
Controlling Flow with Conditionals and Loops

After reading this chapter, you'll be able to

- Understand the different types of conditional statements in JavaScript.

- Use the *if else* conditional statement to control code execution.

- Use the *switch* statement.

- Understand the different types of loop control structures in JavaScript.

- Use a *while* loop and a *do...while* loop to execute code repeatedly.

- Use different types of *for* loops to iterate through ranges of values.

If (and how)

The *if* statement is used to determine which way to go within a program or which code to execute based on one or more conditions. If you've ever booked a flight on the Internet, you know about making decisions. You might want to go on a quick weekend getaway, for example, so when pricing the ticket, you would say, "If the ticket costs less than $350, I'll book the flight, otherwise I'll find a different getaway spot."

Another real-world example is taking out the trash. Should I take the garbage to the curb tonight or wait until the morning? If the weather forecast is windy overnight, the trash might get blown all over the neighbor's lawn, but if I wait until morning, I might miss the garbage truck. (A third option would be to tell my wife that it's her turn to take out the garbage, but that's never worked in the past.)

JavaScript won't help you make these decisions. However, if you want to decide how to act depending on whether a variable contains a certain value or whether a form field has been filled in correctly, JavaScript can be a great help. This section looks at the syntax of the *if* statement in JavaScript.

Syntax for *if* Statements

The *if* statement has a specific syntax that might be familiar to you if you've programmed in other languages, including Perl or PHP. The basic structure of an *if* statement is

```
if (some condition) {
    // do something here
}
```

> **Note** The *if* statement is sometimes called the *if* conditional. I'll use these terms interchangeably within this and other chapters to get you comfortable with hearing the statement referred to in different ways. But don't confuse the *if* conditional (the entire *if* statement) with the *if* condition, which is the Boolean expression that the *if* statement evaluates.

The validity or truthfulness of the condition is examined to determine whether the code within the conditional (inside the braces) will be executed. A boolean expression is tested, and if the condition evaluates to *true*, the code will be executed. (You can negate an expression in the condition to cause the code to run if the expression evaluates to *false*.) Recall the use of boolean and unary operators from Chapter 5, "Using Operators and Expressions." Here's an example:

```
if (! some condition) {
    // do something here
}
```

In this case, the condition would need to evaluate to *false* for the code inside the conditional to execute.

Looking back at those real-world examples from earlier in the chapter, they might look like this in pseudocode:

```
if (flightCost < 350) {
    bookFlight();
}
```

The garbage example might look like this:

```
if (forecast != "windy") {
    takeGarbageOut();
}
```

If the flight costs less than $350, then the code within the conditional will execute. Later in this chapter, I'll show how to use the *else* statement to cause other code to execute when the condition is true.

The *if* statement is where you'll use many of the operators that you learned about in Chapter 5, especially relational operators that test whether one value is greater or less than another and equality operators that test whether two values are equal to each other (). Take a look at these examples:

```
var x = 4;
var y = 3;
// Equality test
if (x == y) {
    // do something
}
```

Because the value in variable *x* (4), does not equal the value in variable *y* (3), the code within the *if* conditional (inside the braces) doesn't execute. Here's an example with a relational operator:

```
var x = 4;
var y = 3;
// Relational test
if (x > y) {
    // do something
}
```

In this case, because the value in variable *x* (4) is greater than the value in variable *y* (3), the code within the braces is executed.

The next section shows an example that you can perform yourself. This example takes advantage of the *prompt()* function to get input from the visitor through a simple interface.

The *prompt()* Function in Windows Internet Explorer 7

With the introduction of Microsoft Windows Internet Explorer 7, the *prompt()* function is no longer enabled by default. If you attempt to use the *prompt()* function with Internet Explorer 7, you'll receive either a security warning like the one shown in Figure 6-1 or possibly a page with the word *null*, like the one in Figure 6-2.

FIGURE 6-1 A security warning caused by the *prompt()* function in Windows Internet Explorer 7.

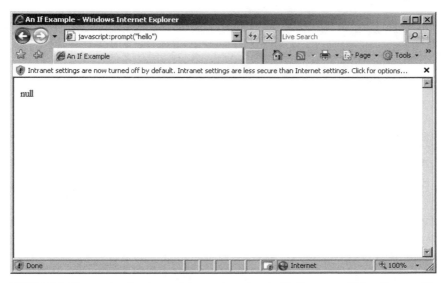

FIGURE 6-2 When using the *javascript:* pseudoprotocol with the *prompt()* function, you'll receive a page with the word *null*.

You can reliably get around this feature by clicking the Information Bar (shown in Figure 6-1) and selecting an option to allow scripts or by changing the security settings. You can change security settings in Windows Internet Explorer 7, for example, by selecting Internet Options on the Tools menu, clicking the Security tab, clicking Custom Level, and enabling the Allow Web Sites To Prompt For Information Using Scripted Windows option. However, you can't rely on your visitors doing the same with their Windows Internet Explorer settings.

Therefore, the *prompt()* function is no longer as useful as it was before Windows Internet Explorer was introduced. Granted, some might argue that the *prompt()* function was annoying (and I agree that it creates problems sometimes). However, the *prompt()* function did have its uses, and disabling it does very little to enhance security.

See http://msdn2.microsoft.com/en-us/ie/Aa740486.aspx for more information on Windows Internet Explorer 7 and the prompt() *function.*

Using *if* to make decisions about program flow

1. Using Microsoft Visual Studio, Eclipse, or another editor, edit the file ifexample.htm in the Chapter06 sample files folder.

2. Within the page, add the following code shown in bold:

```
<!DOCTYPE HTML PUBLIC "-//W3C//DTD HTML 4.01//EN"
"http://www.w3.org/TR/html4/strict.dtd">
<html>
<head>
    <title>An If Example</title>
</head>
<body>

<script type = "text/javascript" >
var inputNum = prompt("Please enter a number below 100:");

if (inputNum > 99) {
    alert("That number, " + inputNum + ", is not below 100.");
}

</script>

<p>This is an example from Chapter 6.</p>

</body>
</html>
```

3. Save the page and view it in a Web browser. If you're attempting to view the page in Windows Internet Explorer 7 and receive a security warning, you'll need to change your security settings as described previously. You could also use Firefox or another browser instead.

4. When you view the page, you'll see a prompt asking for a number below 100. Internet Explorer will likely fill in the text "undefined" in the dialog. Enter a number and click OK. I entered 51, as you can see here.

5. When you click OK, you'll see a page like the one here:

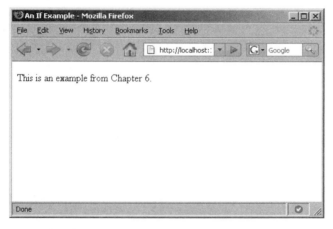

6. Now reload the page in the browser, and this time, enter a number larger than 100 when prompted. You'll receive an alert like this one:

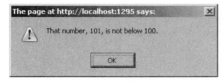

Aside from the Hypertext Markup Language (HTML) and opening script tags, which you've seen in previous examples, the code works as follows:

The first line within the body's *<script>* tag establishes a variable, *inputNum*, and then sets it equal to the result from the *prompt()* function:

```
var inputNum = prompt("Please enter a number below 100:");
```

The next lines of code use an *if* statement to examine the value in the *inputNum* variable. If the value is greater than 99, then an alert is shown:

```
if (inputNum > 99) {
    alert("That number, " + inputNum + ", is not below 100.");
}
```

This example begs for improvements in many areas, and later examples will show those improvements, taking advantage of what you've already learned and a little of what's to come.

Compound Conditions

Many times you'll find that you need to test for more than one condition within the same *if* statement. Going back to the previous example, if you wanted to have the visitor enter a number between 99 and 51 inclusive, you could combine those tests within one *if* statement like this:

```
if ((inputNum > 99 ) || (inputNum < 51)) {
    alert("That number, " + inputNum + ", is not between 50 and 100.");
}
```

> **Note** You could also write that *if* statement without the extra parentheses on the first line; however, I find it helpful to add them since it improves readability.

For those of you playing along at home, the full code from the earlier example is shown in Listing 6-1 (which can also be found in the book's source code as listing6-1.htm) with the new addition for a compound *if* statement shown in bold.

LISTING 6-1 A Compound *if* Statement

```
<!DOCTYPE HTML PUBLIC "-//W3C//DTD HTML 4.01//EN"
"http://www.w3.org/TR/html4/strict.dtd">
<html>
<head>
    <title>An If Example</title>

</head>
<body>

<script type = "text/javascript" >
var inputNum = prompt("Please enter a number between 50 and 100:");
```

```
if ((inputNum > 99) || (inputNum < 51)) {
    alert("That number, " + inputNum + ", is not between 50 and 100.");
}

</script>

<p>This is an example from Chapter 6.</p>

</body>
</html>
```

The statement uses the logical *OR* operator and reads, "If *inputNum* is greater than 99 or *inputNum* is less than 51, do this."

Nested Conditions

Compounding and nesting is also possible within a conditional with the appropriate placement of parentheses. Consider again the example we've been using for much of this chapter. If you enter a number greater than 99 or less than 51, you'll receive an alert. But what if the input is not a number at all? What if you entered the word *boo*? You wouldn't receive the alert because the condition being used checks only whether the variable is above or below specified numbers.

The code should check whether the value contained in the variable is a number. Accomplish this task with the help of the *isNaN()* function and nesting of the decision, like this:

```
if (isNaN(inputNum) || ((inputNum > 99) || (inputNum < 51))) {
    alert("That number, " + inputNum + ", is not between 50 and 100.");
}
```

The conditional is now evaluated to check whether the value in the *inputNum* variable is a number. If this initial check fails, no further processing is done, thus saving the rest of the statement from being evaluated. After that, the checks for the range of numbers are nested together into its own conditional set. The result when run with the value of "boo" is shown in Figure 6-3.

FIGURE 6-3 Running the example with the *isNaN()* function in a nested conditional

The full code is shown in Listing 6-2. The nested condition is shown in bold.

LISTING 6-2 A Nested *if* Statement

```
<!DOCTYPE HTML PUBLIC "-//W3C//DTD HTML 4.01//EN"
"http://www.w3.org/TR/html4/strict.dtd">
<html>
<head>
    <title>An If Example</title>

</head>
<body>

<script type = "text/javascript" >
var inputNum = prompt("Please enter a number between 50 and 100:");

if (isNaN(inputNum) || ((inputNum > 99) || (inputNum < 51))) {
    alert("That number, " + inputNum + ", is not between 50 and 100.");
}

</script>

<p>This is an example.</p>

</body>
</html>
```

Else if and *else* Statements

The next problem with the code example used so far is that the alert dialog box seen in Figure 6-3 indicates that a number has been entered. This obviously isn't the case—I entered the word *boo*. What we really need is a way to perform multiple separate condition checks. How can we do this? Enter *else if* and *else*.

> ## *Else if*
>
> Most modern programming languages have the *if/else if/else* conditional constructs, but they differ in the actual use of those constructs within a program, especially in the area of the spelling or construction of the *else if* statement.
>
> Some languages, like JavaScript, define the *else if* statement as two words. Other languages define it as *elsif*, all one word (and misspelled at that). Still others define it as *elseif*, all one word but spelled correctly. Keeping these constructs straight is a challenge, and this doesn't even consider the use of braces to define the code to be executed.
>
> For JavaScript programming, you'll use *else if*—two words, both spelled correctly.

Using *else if* and *else,* you can create multiple levels of conditions, each of which is tested in turn. The code within the first matching condition is executed. If nothing matches, then the code inside the *else* condition, if present, is executed. Listing 6-3 shows code that first checks to see if the *inputNum* variable contains a number. If the value is indeed a number, it is checked to make sure it's within the appropriate range. The correct *alert()* function is called based on the matching condition.

LISTING 6-3 Using an *else if* Condition

```html
<!DOCTYPE HTML PUBLIC "-//W3C//DTD HTML 4.01//EN"
"http://www.w3.org/TR/html4/strict.dtd">
<html>
<head>
    <title>An If Example</title>

</head>
<body>

<script type = "text/javascript" >
var inputNum = prompt("Please enter a number between 50 and 100:");

if (isNaN(inputNum)) {
    alert(inputNum + " doesn't appear to be a number.");
}
else if ((inputNum > 99) || (inputNum < 51)) {
    alert("That number, " + inputNum + ", is not between 50 and 100.");
}

</script>

<p>This is an example from Chapter 6.</p>

</body>
</html>
```

Multiple Levels of Conditionals

Just as *else if* and *else* are used to test several conditions, it is also possible (sometimes even necessary) to use multiple levels of conditions. For example, you can test for a certain condition, and when successful, execute further conditions. Here's an example that takes advantage of the *match()* function and a regular expression.

Don't Be Afraid of Regular Expressions

Just hearing the phrase *regular expressions* causes many a programmer to cringe. For those that haven't heard of regular expressions before, Wikipedia defines them as "a string that is used to describe or match a set of strings, according to certain syntax rules." Regular expressions can look rather intimidating, but they're really not all that scary when you dissect them. Here's a not-so-intimidating regular expression:

```
s/([0-9]+)\.([0-9]+)(\/[0-9]+)/$1\.$2\.0$3/;
```

This regular expression would look for digits and then perform a substitution to reformat an Internet Protocol (IP) address block using grouping. What this example does is not really relevant to our discussion beyond showing a regular expression (it was part of a script that parsed an Asia Pacific Network Information Centre (APNIC) network list on a firewall, if you must know).

Regular expressions provide an excellent way to match lines of text or input strings where you don't really know or care what the string is—just that it fits a certain pattern. E-mail addresses are one place where regular expressions are used. E-mail addresses, by the way, are one of the most difficult (and argued about) regular expressions to use correctly.

There will be much more about regular expressions in Chapter 11, "Using JavaScript with Web Forms." You're going to see an example of a regular expression in the next step-by-step procedure. Don't be scared by it!

Using multiple levels of conditionals and a regular expression

1. Open an editor and, if you followed the earlier procedure, open the file you updated, ifexample.htm.

2. The file should have the following code. (If you didn't follow the earlier example, just create an empty file and go on to the next step.)

```
<!DOCTYPE HTML PUBLIC "-//W3C//DTD HTML 4.01//EN"
"http://www.w3.org/TR/html4/strict.dtd">
<html>
<head>
    <title>An If Example</title>
</head>
<body>

<script type = "text/javascript" >
var inputNum = prompt("Please enter a number below 100:");

if (inputNum > 99) {
    alert("That number, " + inputNum + ", is not below 100.");
}

</script>
```

```
<p>This is an example from Chapter 6.</p>

</body>
</html>
```

3. Save the file with a different file name. I might suggest multilevel.htm.

4. Within the newly saved file, enter the following code. Note that I've put the changes from the earlier example in bold:

```
<!DOCTYPE HTML PUBLIC "-//W3C//DTD HTML 4.01//EN"
"http://www.w3.org/TR/html4/strict.dtd">
<html>
<head>
    <title>A Multi-Level Example</title>

</head>
<body>

<script type = "text/javascript" >
var inputNum = prompt("Please enter a number between 50 and 100:");

if (isNaN(inputNum)) {
    if (inputNum.match(/one|two|three|four|five|six|seven|eight|nine|ten/)) {
        alert("While this is a number, it's not really a number to me.");
    } else {
        alert(inputNum + " doesn't appear to be a number.");
    }
}
else if ((inputNum > 99) || (inputNum < 51)) {
    alert("That number, " + inputNum + ", is not between 50 and 100.");
}

</script>

<p>This is an example from Chapter 6.</p>

</body>
</html>
```

5. We'll need to test all these conditions now, so here goes. Visit the page in a Web browser. You'll be prompted to enter a number. For this first test, enter the word *four*, as follows:

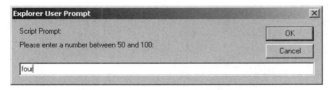

6. Click OK. The first *if* condition will match and then the nested *if* will examine the input. The input matches the string "four", resulting in this dialog box:

7. Click OK to clear the dialog box. Reload the page. Now enter the phrase *pizza*, like so.

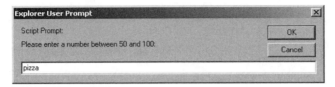

8. Click OK. Like the previous load of the page, the first condition (*isNaN()*) will match. However, since the phrase *pizza* is not matched, the *else* condition of the nested *if* will match, resulting in this dialog box:

9. Click OK to clear the dialog box and once again reload the page. This time, enter the number *4* into the prompt, as follows:

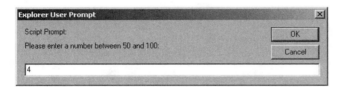

10. Click OK. Now the first *if* condition will fail because the number 4 really is a number. Therefore, the *else if* condition will be evaluated. Because the number 4 is less than 51 and not greater than 99, the *else if* condition will be a match and will therefore display this alert:

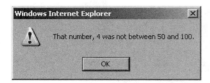

11. Good testing would dictate that we also test a number above 99. Please feel free to do so, if you wish. When you're ready, simply click OK to clear the dialog box and reload the page once more. This time, enter the number *64*, like this:

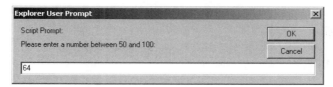

12. When you click OK, you won't receive any alerts because the number 64 is between 50 and 100 and therefore doesn't match any of the test conditions.

The code within the procedure was explained through this and previous procedures, with the exception of the regular expression contained in the nested *if*. That statement was:

```
if (inputNum.match(/one|two|three|four|five|six|seven|eight|nine|ten/) {
```

The regular expression is used with the *match()* function (or property) of the *inputNum* variable. The *match()* function accepts a regular expression as its argument. In this case, the argument is

```
/one|two|three|four|five|six|seven|eight|nine|ten/
```

The expression is delineated with two forward slashes (/), one on each end. After that, the regular expression looks for any one of the strings *one*, *two*, *three*, *four*, *five*, *six*, *seven*, *eight*, *nine*, or *ten*. The pipe character (|) between each string indicates a logical *OR*, meaning that this regular expression will match any one of those strings, but not more than one.

It's interesting to note that while this regular expression is terribly simple, it's also terribly flawed. For this regular expression to be better, it would need to mark or anchor the position of the matching strings. As it stands right now, the string *sixty* would match just as the word *six* matches.

My hope here wasn't to show a perfect regular expression, but rather just to expose you to them so that when you need to work with them you won't run away screaming.

Ternary Conditionals

Another style of conditional construct is called a *ternary conditional*. This type of conditional uses the *?* operator to create a compact *if/else* construct. The basic structure of a ternary conditional expression is quite simple

```
(name == "steve") ? "Hello Steve" : "Hello Unknown Person";
```

This statement might read as follows, "If name is steve, then "Hello Steve", else "Hello Unknown Person".

Such an expression might be used in a statement like this:

```
var greeting = (name == "steve") ? "Hello Steve" : "Hello Unknown Person";
alert(greeting);
```

This code sets the variable *greeting* to the value from the outcome of the ternary test. If the value of the *name* variable is "steve", then the *greeting* variable gets the string value "Hello Steve"; otherwise, the *greeting* variable gets the string value "Hello Unknown Person". Here's that same code in the traditional *if/else* form:

```
if (name == "steve") {
    var greeting = "Hello Steve";
}
else {
    var greeting = "Hello Unknown Person";
}

alert(greeting);
```

The ternary construct can sometimes be confusing if you've never seen it used before. There's no shame in sticking to the traditional *if/else* syntax if you think it will help the read-ability of your programs in the future—especially if the person reading them doesn't know about the ternary construction!

Switch

The *switch* statement is an easy and efficient way to test a variable for several values and then execute code based on whichever case matches. Using an *if* statement can be cumbersome; the *switch* statement can be useful at such times.

Consider the example of a Web site that needs to execute certain code based on the language that the user chooses. For this exercise, assume that the visitor has chosen his or her language through a form. (Chapter 14, "Browsers and JavaScript," examines a method for detecting the default language of the visitor's browser.)

If this site needed to execute code for several languages, we could use a giant set of *if/else if/else* conditionals. Assuming a variable called *languageChoice* with the value of the chosen language, it might look like this:

```
if (languageChoice == "en") {
    // Language is English, execute code for English.
}
else if (languageChoice == "de") {
    // Language is German, execute code for German.
}
else if (languageChoice == "pt") {
    // Language is Portuguese, execute code for Portuguese.
}
else {
    // Language not chosen, use Swedish.
}
```

This code works OK with just a few languages, but carry this out to 20 or more languages and add in more code to be executed for each condition, and it quickly becomes a maze. Here's the same code within a *switch*:

```
switch(languageChoice) {
    case "en":
        // Language is English, execute code for English.
        break;
    case "de":
        // Language is German, execute code for German.
        break;
    case "pt":
        // Language is Portuguese, execute code for Portuguese.
        break;
    default:
        // Language not chosen, use Swedish.
}
// Back to code outside the switch statement
```

The *switch* statement looks for each language case and then executes code for that case. The *break* statement indicates the end of the code that executes when a matching case is found. The *break* statement causes the code execution to break out of the *switch* statement entirely and continue executing after the closing brace of the *switch* statement.

For example, if the variable *languageChoice* was *de* and the *break* statement was missing, then the code for German would be executed, but so would the rest of the code for the other languages until a *break* statement or the end of the *switch* statement was encountered.

You'll almost always use the *break* statement with each case in a *switch* statement. However, part of the elegance of the *switch* statement comes when you have multiple cases that should execute the same code. Consider an example where the visitor chooses which country or region he or she is from. On such a site, visitors from the United States, Canada, and Great Britain might want their page to be displayed in English, even though people in these three countries spell (and pronounce) many words differently. Here's an example *switch* statement for this:

```
switch(countryChoice) {
    case "US":
    case "Canada":
    case "Great Britain":
        // Language is English, execute code for English
        break;
    case "Germany":
        // Language is German, execute code for German.
        break;
    case "Portugal":
        // Language is Portuguese, execute code for Portuguese.
        break;
    default:
```

```
            // Locale not chosen, use Swedish.
}
// Back to code outside the loop
```

> **Note** As my friends from Montreal would point out and as I would recommend, visitors from any country should be able to choose another language that the site supports, such as French. Ignore that factor for this example, but take it into account when designing your site.

If the visitor has chosen Canada as their country, the case for Canada will match, thus executing the code for English. Thanks to the *break* statement, JavaScript will then break out of the *switch* statement and execute the first line of code following the *switch* statement.

Looping with *while*

The *while* statement creates a loop where code is executed as long as some condition is true. This section examines the *while* statement and the related *do...while* statement.

The *while* Statement

A *while* loop executes the code contained within its braces until a condition is met. Here's an example:

```
var count = 0;
while (count < 10) {
    // Do something in here.
    // Multiple lines are fine.
    // Don't forget to increment the counter:
    count++;
}
```

There are two important aspects of *while* loops that you should always keep in mind. I'll list them here and then discuss each in turn:

- The code contained within a *while* statement might never execute, depending on the starting value of the variable or condition being tested.

- Always be sure that the condition being tested by the *while* statement is changed within the loop.

Making Sure the Code Executes At Least Once

In the code example, the variable *count* is initially set to the number 0. The *while* statement then runs as follows: The evaluation of the *while* statement examines the value of the *count* variable to see if it is less than 10. Because it is, the code within the braces executes.

(However, if the value of the *count* variable were *not* less than 10, then the code within the *while* statement's braces would never execute—not even once.

In JavaScript, the *do...while* loop executes code once, no matter what the initial condition is. The *do...while* loop is discussed a little later in this chapter.

Changing the Condition

As previously stated, the evaluation of the *while* statement in our example examines the variable to see if it's less than 10. If *count* is less than 10, the code within the *while* loop executes.

One of the lines of code within the *while* loop increments the *count* variable using the ++ unary operator as follows:

```
count++;
```

When the code within the *while* statement finishes executing, the evaluation takes place all over again. Without the code to increment the *count* variable, *count* would always be less than 10, so you would have an endless loop on your hands—not what you want.

> **Tip** When using a generic counter variable, as I have in the example, it's usually not important where you increment that variable so long as it's within the *while* statement's braces or within the *while* statement test. Here's an example: *while (i++ < 10)*.

The moral of this story is to make sure that you increment or change whatever condition that you evaluate in the *while* statement.

The *do...while* Statement

Unlike the *while* statement, the *do...while* statement executes the code contained in its braces at least once. The *while* statement might read like this: "While the condition is met, run this code." On the other hand, the *do...while* statement might read like this: "Do (or run) this code while the condition is met." Consider this code:

```
<!DOCTYPE HTML PUBLIC "-//W3C//DTD HTML 4.01//EN"
"http://www.w3.org/TR/html4/strict.dtd">
<html>
<head>
    <title>Do While</title>
</head>
<body>
<script type = "text/javascript">
var count = 0;
do {
    alert("Count is " + count);
```

```
    count++;
}
while (count < 3);

</script>
</body>
</html>
```

When this code executes, three dialog boxes appear. During the first run, the *count* variable holds a value of zero because it's still set to the initial value, and the dialog box indicates that, as shown in Figure 6-4.

FIGURE 6-4 The count is zero during the first execution.

After running once, the *count* variable gets incremented. When the *while* statement is evaluated, *count* is still less than 3, so the code is executed again. This results in the next dialog box, shown in Figure 6-5.

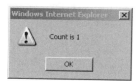

FIGURE 6-5 When running, the code increments the counter and shows the result of the next execution.

The same process occurs again. The *count* variable is incremented and the *while* condition is evaluated. The value of *count* is still less than 3, so the code within the braces runs again, showing another dialog box, as shown in Figure 6-6.

FIGURE 6-6 The count variable after another run.

Experiment with *while* and *do...while* statements until you're comfortable with the differences between them.

Using *for* Loops

A *for* loop is frequently used in the same way as a *while* loop, namely, to execute code a certain number of times. The *for* loop has two cousins in JavaScript, the *for...in* and *for each...in* loops. Each of these loop types will be examined in this section.

The *for* Loop

A *for* loop is used to create a loop where the conditions are initialized, evaluated, and changed in a compact form. I'll begin with an example:

```
for (var count = 0; count < 10; count++) {
    // Execute code here
}
```

A *for* statement has three clauses in parentheses. The first clause sets the initial expression. In the above example, the following code is the first (initialization) clause:

```
var count = 0;
```

The next clause of a *for* statement specifies the test expression, represented by the following code from the example:

```
count < 10;
```

The final expression is usually used to increment the counter used for the test. In the code example, this expression, is the final clause within the parentheses:

```
count++
```

> **Note** The last expression in a *for* loop construct does not require a semicolon.

Here's an example that you can try. It uses a *for* loop to iterate over an array.

Using a *for* loop with an array

1. Using Visual Studio, Eclipse, or another editor, edit the file forloop.htm in the Chapter06 sample files folder.

2. Within the page, add the following code shown in bold:

```
<!DOCTYPE HTML PUBLIC "-//W3C//DTD HTML 4.01//EN"
"http://www.w3.org/TR/html4/strict.dtd">
<html>
<head>
    <title>For Loop Example</title>
</head>
```

```
<body>
<script type = "text/javascript" >

var myArray = ["Vega","Deneb","Altair"];
for (var count = 0; count < myArray.length; count++ ) {
    alert(myArray[count]);
}

</script>
</body>
</html>
```

3. Save the page and view it in a Web browser. You'll receive three successive *alert()* dialog boxes:

As you can see, the code iterates through each of the values within the *myArray* array. I'd like to highlight some of the code from this example. You learned how to create an array in Chapter 4, but here it is again for completeness. Recall that arrays in JavaScript are indexed by integer values beginning at 0. This knowledge will come in handy in a little while. Here's the pertinent line from the code example:

```
var myArray = ["Vega","Deneb","Altair"];
```

The *for* loop first creates and initializes the *count* variable, and then checks whether the *count* variable is less than the length of the *myArray* array, and finally the value of the *count* variable is incremented. Within the *for* loop itself, an alert is shown, using the value of the *count* variable to iterate through the indexes of the *myArray* array. Here's the code:

```
for (var count = 0; count < myArray.length; count++ ) {
    alert(myArray[count]);
}
```

Obtaining the length of the *myArray* array illustrates the use of an object function property, *length*. There'll be more about objects in Chapter 8, "Objects in JavaScript."

The *for...in* Loop

The for...in loop iterates through the properties of an object, returning the names of the properties themselves. Here's an example:

```
for (var myProp in myObject) {
    alert(myProp + " = " + myObject[myProp]);

}
```

In this code, the variable *myProp* gets set to a new property of *myObject* each time the loop is executed. Here's a more complete example that you can do:

Using a *for...in* loop

1. Using Visual Studio, Eclipse, or another editor, edit the file forinloop.htm in the Chapter06 sample files folder.

2. Within the page, add the following code shown in bold:

```
<!DOCTYPE HTML PUBLIC "-//W3C//DTD HTML 4.01//EN"
"http://www.w3.org/TR/html4/strict.dtd">
<html>
<head>
    <title>For In Loop Example</title>
</head>
<body>
<script type = "text/javascript">
    var star = new Object;

    star.name = "Polaris";
    star.type = "Double/Cepheid";
    star.constellation = "Ursa Minor";

    for (var starProp in star) {
        alert(starProp + " = " + star[starProp]);
    }
</script>

</body>
</html>
```

3. Save the file and view it in a Web browser. You'll receive three dialog boxes:

As you can see from the code in the example, the variable *starProp* receives the name of the property, while using *starProp* as the index of the *star* object yields the value of that property.

> **Tip** You'll sometimes see *for...in* loops used to iterate through an array in much the same way that you saw in the previous section. However, using *for...in* to iterate through an array can have mixed results. One of the more visible problems of this approach is that a *for...in* loop doesn't return the properties in any particular order. This behavior can be troublesome, especially when you want to write text to a Web page with JavaScript! If you have a simple array through which you want to loop, use the *for* loop rather than the *for...in* loop.

The *for each...in* Loop

A newer construct available in JavaScript 1.6 is the *for each...in* loop. Because it's new, this construct is not yet supported in all browsers—notably, it's not supported in Windows Internet Explorer 7 and earlier. It is supported in Firefox 2, though.

Where the *for...in* construct returns the name of the property, the *for each...in* loop returns the value of the property. The syntax is essentially the same, but with the obvious addition of the word *each*:

```
for each (var myValue in myObject) {
    alert(myValue " is in the object.");
}
```

Replacing the *for...in* loop from the earlier walk-through example with a *for each...in* loop would result in this code (the new code is in bold):

```
<!DOCTYPE HTML PUBLIC "-//W3C//DTD HTML 4.01//EN" "http://www.w3.org/TR/html4/strict.dtd">
<html>
<head>
    <title>For Each In Loop Example</title>
</head>
```

```
<body>
<script type = "text/javascript">


    var star = new Object;

    star.name = "Polaris";
    star.type = "Double/Cepheid";
    star.constellation = "Ursa Minor";

    for each (var starValue in star) {
        alert(starValue + " is in the star object.");
    }
</script>

</body>
</html>
```

Viewing the page in Windows Internet Explorer results in an error screen (or maybe just a blank screen). Viewing the page in Firefox 2, however, reveals the correct behavior. One of the three dialog boxes that results is shown in Figure 6-7.

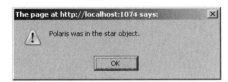

FIGURE 6-7 Iterating through an object using the *for each...in* loop

You may want to refrain from using *for each...in* loops because this construct is not yet supported in Windows Internet Explorer.

Validating Forms with Conditionals

Earlier in this chapter, we used the *prompt()* function to obtain input from the user. Using the *prompt()* function is somewhat uncommon, and it's fast becoming even less common thanks to the function being blocked in Windows Internet Explorer 7. This section previews using Web forms with JavaScript. An entire chapter is devoted to this subject, though, as you'll see in Chapter 11.

Using an *if else ... if else* conditional to validate input is a common task, so let's do that.

Validating input with a conditional statement

1. As you've been doing, open Visual Studio, Eclipse, or another editor and create a new Web page. Call this one form1example.htm.

2. Within the page, enter the following markup and add the code shown in bold:

```
<!DOCTYPE HTML PUBLIC "-//W3C//DTD HTML 4.01//EN"
"http://www.w3.org/TR/html4/strict.dtd">
<html>
<head>

    <title>Just Your Basic Form</title>
    <script type = "text/javascript">
    function alertName() {
        var name = document.forms[0].nametext.value;
        if (name == "steve") {
            alert("Hello Steve.  Welcome to Machine");
        }
        else if (name == "nancy") {
            alert("Hello Tim.");
        }
        else {
            alert("Hello " + name);
        }
        return true;
    } //end function

    </script>
</head>
<body>
<form id="myform" action="#" onsubmit="return alertName();">
<p>Username: <input id="nametext" name="username" type="text" /></p>
<p><input type="submit" /></p>
</form>
</body>
</html>
```

3. Save the page and view it in a Web browser. You should get a page like this:

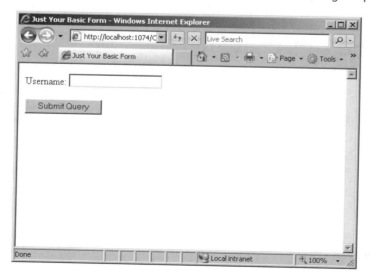

4. Within the form, enter the name "steve", without the quotes, being sure to use lowercase. Click Submit Query and you'll receive a dialog box like this:

5. Click OK, and now type in the name "nancy", again without the quotes and in lowercase. When you click Submit Query, you'll receive a dialog box like this:

> In case you're wondering, Tim's nickname is Nancy, so this dialog box actually does make sense. It's also correct per the code above.

6. Click OK to clear the dialog box. Enter in the name "someone else" and click Submit Query. You'll receive this dialog box:

7. Click OK to clear this dialog box.

You've now created a basic Web form, accessed that form using JavaScript, and used a conditional to take an action based on that user input. Don't worry if everything used in this example doesn't quite make sense yet. The main goal of the example was not to introduce new things without explaining them, but rather to give some context to the conditionals that you've learned in this chapter.

The first example in Chapter 11 will show how to ensure that required fields are filled in by using JavaScript. Prior to that, Chapter 7, "Working with Functions," will examine the use of functions within JavaScript.

Exercises

1. Use a *prompt()* function to collect a person's name. Use a *switch* statement to execute a dialog box displaying the phrase "Welcome *<the inputted name>*" if the name entered is yours, "Go Away" if the name entered is *Steve*, and "Please Come Back Later *<the inputted name>*" for all other cases.

2. Use a *prompt()* function to collect the current temperature as input by the visitor. If the temperature entered is above 100, tell the visitor to cool down. If the temperature is below 20, tell the visitor to warm up.

3. Use a ternary statement to accomplish the same task as in Exercise 2.

4. Use a *for* loop to count from 1 to 100. When the number is at 99, display an alert dialog box.

5. Use a *while* loop to accomplish the same task as in Exercise 4.

Chapter 7
Working with Functions

After reading this chapter, you'll be able to

- Understand the purpose of functions in JavaScript.

- Define your own functions.

- Call functions and receive data back from them.

- Understand some of the built-in functions in JavaScript.

What's in a Function?

A JavaScript function is a collection of statements, either named or unnamed, that can be called from elsewhere within a JavaScript program. Functions can accept arguments or input values that are passed into the function. Within a function, those arguments passed into the function can be acted upon and then passed back out of the function through a *return* value.

Functions are perfect for when you have something that needs to happen multiple times within a program. Rather than defining the same code multiple times on the page, you can use a function (which is really just like a mini-program inside a program) to perform that action. Even if you have bits of code that are very similar—but not identical—throughout the program, you might be able to abstract them into a single function.

A good example of abstracting similar code is a function to verify that required form fields have been filled in. You can write JavaScript code to verify each individual named field in the form, or you could use a function. Chapter 11, "Using JavaScript with Web Forms," will show an example of building a specific function and then showing how to abstract it.

You've already seen functions at work through examples in earlier chapters. A function is defined with the keyword *function*, usually followed by the name of the function and then parentheses with optional arguments or parameters to be used within it. Use braces to hold the statements to be executed as part of the function:

```
function functionName() {
    // Statements go here;
}
```

> **Tip** When a function is defined, as you see with this basic function definition, it's important to note that the code isn't actually executed until the function is invoked or called. You'll see how to call a function shortly.

Function Arguments

Arguments passed to a function go within the parentheses of the function definition. Here's a brief example of a function argument:

```
function myFunction(argument1, argument2) {
    // Do something with argument1 and argument 2 in the code
}
```

Calling or invoking the function is as simple as:

```
myFunction(val1,val2);
```

When invoked, the function is given an array simply called *arguments,* which holds the arguments sent into the array. This can be helpful when you don't know the number of arguments being sent in. Here's an example:

```
function myFunction() {
    var firstArg = arguments[0];
    var secondArg = arguments[1];
}
```

Better still, you could get the length of the *arguments* array and loop through each, as follows:

```
function myFunction() {
    for (var i = 0; i < arguments.length; i++) {
        // Do something with each argument (i)
    }
}
```

Here's a fuller example showing the results from a simple use of the *arguments* array:

```
<!DOCTYPE HTML PUBLIC "-//W3C//DTD HTML 4.01//EN" "http://www.w3.org/TR/html4/strict.dtd">
<html>
<head>
    <title>Arguments Array</title>
</head>
<body>
<script type="text/javascript">
function myFunction() {
    var firstArg = arguments[0];
    var secondArg = arguments[1];
    alert("firstArg is: " + firstArg);
    alert("secondArg is: " + secondArg);
}
myFunction("hello","world");
</script>
</body>
</html>
```

When the code executes, it displays two alerts, as depicted in Figures 7-1 and 7-2.

FIGURE 7-1 Using the *arguments* array within a function to access the first argument

FIGURE 7-2 Using the *arguments* array within a function to access the second argument

Obviously, using the *arguments* array in this way can be extrapolated to any number of arguments, not just the two shown here.

Variable Scoping Revisited

Function arguments are frequently variable names and shouldn't be named the same as the variables that are used to call or invoke the function. I use the purposefully vague conjunction "shouldn't" here because there's really no reason why you *couldn't* name the variables the same within the function as they're named in the function invocation, other than it can create some confusing code and confusing scoping, as you'll see.

Chapter 4, "Working with Variables and Data," contained a section on variable scoping, including an exercise dealing with scoping inside and outside functions. The relevant code from one of the variable scoping examples in Chapter 4 looked like this:

```
<head>
    <title>Scoping Example</title>
    <script type = "text/javascript." >
    var aNewVariable = "is global.";
    function doSomething(incomingBits) {
        alert("Global variable within the function: " + aNewVariable);
        alert("Local variable within the function: " + incomingBits);
    }

    </script>

</head>
<body>
<script type = "text/javascript" >

    doSomething("is a local variable");
    alert("Global var outside the function: " + aNewVariable);
    alert("Local var outside the function: " + incomingBits);

</script>
</body>
```

This example showed how globally and locally declared and scoped variables are seen from inside and outside a function. However, it kept the variables logically separate, in that the example didn't use the same variable name and then change its value. Here's an example where using the same variable name might cause confusion. I've found that code I wrote years ago is confusing enough without introducing weird scoping issues, so try to avoid code like this:

```
function addNumbers() {
    firstNum = 4;
    secondNum = 8;
    result = firstNum + secondNum;
    return result;
}
result = 0;
sum = addNumbers();
```

You might have already spotted the problem with this code. The *var* keyword is missing pretty much everywhere. Even though the code explicitly initializes the *result* variable to 0 outside the function, the variable gets modified by the call to the *addNumbers()* function. This in turn modifies the *result* variable, making it 12, the result of adding 4 and 8 inside the function.

If you were to add an alert to display the *result* variable right after the initialization of the *result* variable, it would show 0. And if you added another alert to display the *result* variable after the call to the *addNumbers()* function, it now would show 12. I'll leave it to you as an exercise later to add these alerts in the right places.

The bottom line is that your life will be easier if you use different names for variables inside and outside functions and always use the *var* keyword to initialize variables. Depending on the code contained in the function, it may or may not have a *return* value. That *return* value is passed back to the caller, as you'll see in the next section.

Return Values

When a function finishes executing its code, a *return* value can be passed back to the caller. Take a look at Listing 7-1.

LISTING 7-1 A Simple *return* Value Example

```
function multiplyNums(x) {
    return x * 2;
}
var theNumber = 10;
var result = multiplyNums(theNumber);
alert(result);
```

In Listing 7-1, a function, *multiplyNums* is created with an intended input value, which will be set to the variable *x*. The function does one thing—return its argument multiplied by 2, as follows:

```
function multiplyNums(x) {
    return x * 2;
}
```

The code then creates a variable called *theNumber,* as follows:

```
var theNumber = 10;
```

Next, the code creates another variable called *result*. This variable will hold the result of the call to the *multiplyNums* function. The *multiplyNum* function uses the variable *theNumber* as an argument:

```
var result = multiplyNums(theNumber);
```

When run, the code results in a dialog box, like the one shown in Figure 7-3.

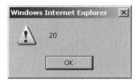

FIGURE 7-3 This alert shows the return value from the function call

Actually, the *return* value can be placed anywhere within a function, not just at the end. It's common to use a *return* within a conditional or after a loop, like this:

```
function myFunction(x) {
    if (x == 1) {
        return true;
    } else {
        return false;
    }
}
```

Be careful where you place the *return* statement, though. Once the function hits the *return* statement, it jumps out and won't execute any code after that. Code like this probably won't do what you want:

```
function myFunction() {
    var count = 0;
    var firstNum = 48;
    return;
    var secondNum = 109;
}
```

This code will never get to the initialization of the variable *secondNum*.

More on Calling Functions

When you call or invoke a function, you'll usually call it with some arguments or at least with empty parentheses, like this:

```
var result = orderFruit();
```

If arguments are required for that function, it might look like this:

```
var result = orderFruit(type,quantity);
```

Omitting the parentheses to call a function may result in actions that are entirely different from what you want. Calling a function without parentheses results in the text of the function being returned, rather than whatever the function was supposed to return. Just as important, the function isn't actually executed.

Here's an example. Listing 7-2 shows some basic JavaScript code.

LISTING 7-2 Invoking a Function

```
<!DOCTYPE html PUBLIC "-//W3C//DTD XHTML 1.0 Transitional//EN" "http://www.w3.org/TR/
xhtml1/DTD/xhtml1-transitional.dtd">
<html xmlns="http://www.w3.org/1999/xhtml" >
<head>
    <title>Order Fruit</title>
    <script type = "text/javascript">
    function orderFruit() {
        var total = 0;
        // Call another function to place order
        return total;
    }
    </script>
</head>
<body>
<script type = "text/javascript">
var result = orderFruit();
alert("The total is " + result);
</script>
</body>
</html>
```

When executed, this code will invoke the *orderFruit()* function. The *orderFruit()* function actually invokes another function (not shown) to place an order. The total is then calculated and sent back to the caller. As written, the code will work fine, resulting in a dialog box like that shown in Figure 7-4.

FIGURE 7-4 Invoking the *orderFruit()* function with parentheses yields the results you'd expect

A slight modification to the code, specifically changing the function call to remove the parentheses, changes the entire result:

```
var result = orderFruit;
```

The result is shown in Figure 7-5.

FIGURE 7-5 Calling *orderFruit* without parentheses probably doesn't turn out the way you'd want

Whether or not a function returns a value or accepts any arguments, it's important to call it using parentheses to actually execute the function's code.

Unnamed Functions (Function Literals)

Functions don't have to be as formally delineated as you've seen in the examples so far in this chapter and throughout the rest of this book. Function literals are beyond the scope of this text, so I won't cover them other than giving a brief definition. With a function literal, also known as an unnamed function, the function itself is defined and tied to a variable, like this:

```
var divNums = function(firstNum,secondNum) { return firstNum / secondNum; };
```

Methods

The easiest way to think about methods is that methods are functions defined as part of an object. It's a bit of an oversimplification, but it'll do for now. You access a method of an object through the dot operator ("."). Built-in objects, such as the *Math*, *Date*, and *String* objects, all have methods that you've seen or will soon see in this book. Things like the *alert()* function are actually just methods of the *window* object and could also be written *window.alert()* rather than just *alert()*.

> **Note** For much of the book, I've used the term *method* and *function* rather interchangeably. I'll continue to do so just to give you a better understanding that the line between these two is rather unspecific for most uses. When a function is used in an object-oriented manner, it's better or clearer to use the term *method*. When not used directly in an object-oriented manner, however, as with the *alert()* function, it's okay to call it a *function*.

Chapter 8, "Objects in JavaScript," covers objects and methods in greater detail.

> ### Defining Your Own Functions vs. Using Built-in Functions
>
> As you've seen throughout the book, there are numerous built-in functions, or methods. In addition to these built-in functions, you frequently will find yourself defining your own functions in JavaScript. Most scripts you write beyond the most trivial ones will involve your own self-defined functions.
>
> There are cases, however, where you might define your own function and then later discover that JavaScript already has an equally good built-in function for that same purpose. If you find that a JavaScript built-in function does the same thing as your own function, it's usually better to use the JavaScript function.

A Look at Dialog Functions

By now, you know all about the *alert()* function in JavaScript because you've seen many examples of it in previous chapters. You've also learned that the *alert()* function is just a method of the *window* object. This section looks at the everyday use of the *alert()* function in JavaScript, as well as two related functions of the *window* object.

> **More Info** The *window* object is important enough to get some additional attention in Chapter 9, "The Browser Object Model." We'll discuss the numerous methods of the *window* object in that chapter.

Although the *window* object has several methods, for now, I'd just like to highlight these three functions (which are technically methods): *alert()*, *confirm()*, and *prompt()*. Because you've already seen too many *alert()* dialog boxes in the book, I won't include another one here (thank me later). Chapter 6, "Controlling Flow with Conditionals and Loops," discussed the use of the *prompt()* function and the fact that as of Microsoft Windows Internet Explorer 7, the *prompt()* function is now blocked by default as a security measure. The *confirm()* function is still available in Windows Internet Explorer, though.

The *confirm()* function displays a modal dialog box with two buttons, OK and Cancel, like the one shown in Figure 7-6. (A modal dialog box prevents other activity or clicks in the browser until the visitor clicks OK or Cancel.)

FIGURE 7-6 The *confirm()* function provides a dialog box for making decisions with JavaScript

If you click OK, the *confirm()* function returns *true*. On the other hand, as you might guess, if you click Cancel, the *confirm()* function returns *false*.

Like *alert()* and *prompt()*, the *confirm()* function creates a modal dialog box on most platforms. This can get annoying if these functions are overused or used in the wrong place. But used properly, to provide important feedback and obtain vital information, these functions can be quite useful.

> **Tip** Don't use the *confirm()* function in place of a Web form to obtain user input. The Web form is much better for navigation and will keep your visitors happier.

The next step-by-step exercise will walk you through using the *confirm()* function to obtain input and make a decision.

Obtaining input with *confirm()*

1. Using Microsoft Visual Studio, Eclipse, or another editor, edit the file confirm.htm in the Chapter07 sample files folder.

2. Within the page, add the code shown below in bold type:

```
<!DOCTYPE HTML PUBLIC "-//W3C//DTD HTML 4.01//EN"
"http://www.w3.org/TR/html4/strict.dtd">
<html>
<head>
    <title>Confirming Something</title>

    <script type = "text/javascript">

    function processConfirm(answer) {
        var result = "";
        if (answer) {
            result = "Excellent.  We'll play a nice game of chess.";
        } else {
            result = "Maybe later then.";
        }
```

```
        return result;
    }
    </script>
</head>
<body>
<script type = "text/javascript">

var confirmAnswer = confirm("Shall we play a game?");
var theAnswer = processConfirm(confirmAnswer);
alert(theAnswer);
</script>
</body>
</html>
```

3. Save the page and view it in a Web browser. You'll be presented with a dialog box like this:

4. Click OK. You'll then see an *alert()* dialog box, like this:

5. Click OK, and then reload the page.

6. You'll once again be shown the original dialog box from the *confirm()* function, asking if you'd like to play a game. This time click Cancel. You'll be presented with a different *alert()* dialog box:

7. Click OK to clear the dialog box.

The code has two major areas, one within the *<head>* and the other within the *<body>*. Within the *<head>* portion of the page, the function *processConfirm(answer)* is created:

```
function processConfirm(answer) {
    var result = "";
    if (answer) {
        result = "Excellent.  We'll play a nice game of chess";
```

```
    } else {
        result = "Maybe later then.";
    }
    return result;
}
```

This function evaluates the value contained in the argument that is held in the variable *answer.* If the value in the *answer* variable evaluates to *true,* as it does if the visitor clicks OK, then the function creates the variable *result* and assigns to *result* a string value of "Excellent. We'll play a nice game of chess." On the other hand, if the value in the *answer* variable evaluates to *false,* as it does if the visitor clicks Cancel, then the function still creates the *result* variable, but now assigns to this variable the value of "Maybe later then." Regardless of what's held in the *answer* variable, the *result* variable is sent back to the caller by the *return* statement within the function. The function could be more succinctly written like so:

```
function processConfirm(answer) {
    if (answer) {
        return "Excellent.  We'll play a nice game of chess.";
    } else {
        return "Maybe later then.";
    }
}
```

And even more succinctly:

```
function processConfirm(answer) {
    var result;
    (answer) ? result = "Excellent.  We'll play a nice game of chess." : result = "Maybe
later then.";
    return result;
}
```

In all likelihood, I would use the last function example to perform this task. However, I've found many a programmer who isn't comfortable with the ternary logic of the last example and so for readability, I'd choose the more explicit of the two:

```
function processConfirm(answer) {
    if (answer) {
        return "Excellent.  We'll play a nice game of chess.";
    } else {
        return "Maybe later then.";
    }
}
```

The JavaScript contained within the *<body>* section of the code creates the confirm dialog box, calls the *processConfirm()* function, and displays the result:

```
var confirmAnswer = confirm("Shall we play a game?");
var theAnswer = processConfirm(confirmAnswer);
alert(theAnswer);
```

Like the *alert()* function, the *confirm()* function accepts a single argument, which is the message to be displayed within the dialog box. Unlike the *alert()* function, with the *confirm()* function it's best to phrase your prompt in the form of a question or other statement that gives the visitor a choice. If the user really doesn't have a choice, then use the *alert()* function instead. An even more succinct version would combine all three lines, like this:

```
alert(processConfirm(confirm("Shall we play a game?")));
```

Exercises

1. Define a function that takes one numeric argument, increments that argument, and then returns it to the caller. Call the function from within the *<body>* of a page and display the result on the screen.

2. Define a function that accepts two numeric parameters. If the value of the first parameter is greater than the second, show an alert to the visitor. If the value of the first parameter is less than or equal to the second, return the sum of both parameters.

3. Add appropriate *alert()* functions to the following code so that you can see the value in the *result* variable both before and after the function call. Here's the code:

```
function addNumbers() {
    firstNum = 4;
    secondNum = 8;
    result = firstNum + secondNum;
    return result;
}
result = 0;
sum = addNumbers();
```

4. Create an array with seven string values, initialized to the names of these stars: Polaris, Aldebaran, Deneb, Vega, Altair, Dubhe, and Regulus. Create an array with seven additional string values, initialized to the names of the constellations in which the stars are found: Ursa Minor, Taurus, Cygnus, Lyra, Aquila, Ursa Major, and Leo. Next, create a function that accepts a single string parameter. Within the function, iterate through the first array searching for the star. When the star is found, return the value contained in that index within the second array. In other words, return the constellation name for that star. Within the *<body>* of the page, use a prompt to gather the name of the star from the visitor and then call the function with that input. Don't forget to include code if the star isn't found. Display the result on the screen.

Chapter 8
Objects in JavaScript

After reading this chapter, you'll be able to

- Understand objects in JavaScript, including object properties, object methods, and classes.
- Create objects.
- Define properties for objects using classes.
- Understand arrays in JavaScript.
- Use several array methods.
- Understand the *Date* object in JavaScript.
- Use the *Date* object to display the current date on a Web page.

Object-Oriented Development

For those who are new to object-oriented programming concepts or may need a bit of a refresher, read on. If you're already comfortable with object-oriented programming, skip ahead to the section called "Creating Objects."

A programming paradigm describes a methodology for solving the problems at hand. There are more than 25 different programming paradigms, some of which you might be hard-pressed to find used in an actual program. Others you might have heard of or even used without knowing it. There's functional programming, event-driven programming, component-oriented programming, structured programming, and many others.

Programming paradigms come and go. Object-oriented programming has been around for many years, however, and doesn't appear to be going away anytime soon, so if you haven't yet learned the basics, then there's no time like the present.

This section can't do much more than scratch the surface of this subject. Specifically, I want to get you familiar with object-oriented technology, so you're comfortable with the subset of object-oriented programming concepts and terminology typically used by a JavaScript programmer.

Objects

Objects are things. In the real world, as opposed to the virtual and sometimes surreal world of computer programming, a ball, a desk, and a car are all objects. An object is something that has describable characteristics, that you can do things to, and that behaves in a particular way. An object in the object-oriented programming paradigm is a combination of code and data that similarly exhibits characteristics and behavior.

Properties

Objects have properties—things defined as attributes about them. Going back to the real world again, a ball has a color property—perhaps red, white, or multicolored. It also has a size property—perhaps it is small like a baseball or bigger like a basketball, or something else entirely. These properties might be represented like this:

```
ball.color
```

```
ball.size
```

Methods

Just as objects can have properties, they also can have methods. Methods define the way an object behaves. A ball might have a roll method, which would calculate how far the ball will roll. In theory, not all objects have methods and not all objects have properties, though in practice all objects have at least one method or one property.

Remember from Chapter 7, "Working with Functions," that a method is just a function that belongs to an object. A method definition that uses a function literal for the roll method might look like this:

```
ball.roll = function() {
    var distance = this.size * this.forceApplied;
}
```

> ### What's *this*?
>
> The *ball.roll* example used something new, the keyword *this*. The keyword *this* refers to the object to which the current function or property belongs. In the context of objects, the keyword *this* refers to the calling object. The keyword *this* can be used to set properties of objects within a function call.
>
> The *this* keyword is a boon to JavaScript developers looking to validate Web forms, as you'll see in Chapter 11, "Using JavaScript with Web Forms."

Classes

Classes define sets of objects that share the same properties and methods. Classes simplify the creation of multiple objects of the same type. Consider this example. Throughout previous chapters, I've used a star object in some examples. Listing 8-1 shows what we'd need for a comprehensive Web page with information about 14 important stars.

LISTING 8-1 Assembling a Star Object

```
var star = {};

star["Polaris"] = new Object;
star["Mizar"] = new Object;
star["Aldebaran"] = new Object;
star["Rigel"] = new Object;
star["Castor"] = new Object;
star["Albireo"] = new Object;
star["Acrux"] = new Object;
star["Gemma"] = new Object;
star["Procyon"] = new Object;
star["Sirius"] = new Object;
star["Rigil Kentaurus"] = new Object;
star["Deneb"] = new Object;
star["Vega"] = new Object;
star["Altair"] = new Object;

star["Polaris"].constellation = "Ursa Minor";
star["Mizar"].constellation = "Ursa Major";
star["Aldebaran"].constellation = "Taurus";
star["Rigel"].constellation = "Orion";
star["Castor"].constellation = "Gemini";
star["Albireo"].constellation = "Cygnus";
star["Acrux"].constellation = "Crux";
star["Gemma"].constellation = "Corona Borealis";
star["Procyon"].constellation = "Canis Minor";
star["Sirius"].constellation = "Canis Major";
star["Rigil Kentaurus"].constellation = "Centaurus";
star["Deneb"].constellation = "Cygnus";
star["Vega"].constellation = "Lyra";
star["Altair"].constellation = "Aquila";

star["Polaris"].type = "Double/Cepheid";
star["Mizar"].type = "Spectroscopic Binary";
star["Aldebaran"].type = "Irregular Variable";
star["Rigel"].type = "Supergiant with Companion";
star["Castor"].type = "Multiple/Spectroscopic";
star["Albireo"].type = "Double";
star["Acrux"].type = "Double";
star["Gemma"].type = "Eclipsing Binary";
star["Procyon"].type = "Double";
star["Sirius"].type = "Double";
star["Rigil Kentaurus"].type = "Double";
star["Deneb"].type = "Supergiant";
```

```
star["Vega"].type = "White Dwarf";
star["Altair"].type = "White Dwarf";

star["Polaris"].spectralClass = "F7";
star["Mizar"].spectralClass = "A1 V";
star["Aldebaran"].spectralClass = "K5 III";
star["Rigel"].spectralClass = "B8 Ia";
star["Castor"].spectralClass = "A1 V";
star["Albireo"].spectralClass = "K3 II";
star["Acrux"].spectralClass = "B1 IV";
star["Gemma"].spectralClass = "A0 V";
star["Procyon"].spectralClass = "F5 IV";
star["Sirius"].spectralClass = "A1 V";
star["Rigil Kentaurus"].spectralClass = "G2 V";
star["Deneb"].spectralClass = "A2 Ia";
star["Vega"].spectralClass = "A0 V";
star["Altair"].spectralClass = "A7 V";

star["Polaris"].mag = 2.0;
star["Mizar"].mag = 2.3;
star["Aldebaran"].mag = 0.85;
star["Rigel"].mag = 0.12;
star["Castor"].mag = 1.58;
star["Albireo"].mag = 3.1;
star["Acrux"].mag = 0.8;
star["Gemma"].mag = 2.23;
star["Procyon"].mag = 0.38;
star["Sirius"].mag = -1.46;
star["Rigil Kentaurus"].mag = -0.01;
star["Deneb"].mag = 1.25;
star["Vega"].mag = 0.03;
star["Altair"].mag = 0.77;
```

As you can see, there's a lot of repeated code in Listing 8-1. Each star is defined and then given four properties: the constellation in which it appears, its type, its spectral class, and its magnitude (represented by the word *mag* in the code listing).

Now consider the code in Listing 8-2. It accomplishes the same thing as the code in Listing 8-1, but with the help of a class.

LISTING 8-2 Assembling a Star Object Using a Class

```
var star = {};

function Star(constell,type,specclass,magnitude) {
    this.constellation = constell;
    this.type = type;
    this.spectralClass = specclass;
    this.mag  = magnitude;
}

star["Polaris"] = new Star("Ursa Minor","Double/Cepheid","F7",2.0);
star["Mizar"] = new Star("Ursa Major","Spectroscopic Binary","A1 V",2.3);
```

```
star["Aldebaran"] = new Star("Taurus","Irregular Variable","K5 III",0.85);
star["Rigel"] = new Star("Orion","Supergiant with Companion","B8 Ia",0.12);
star["Castor"] = new Star("Gemini","Multiple/Spectroscopic","A1 V",1.58);
star["Albireo"] = new Star("Cygnus","Double","K3 II",3.1);
star["Acrux"] = new Star("Crux","Double","B1 IV",0.8);
star["Gemma"] = new Star("Corona Borealis","Eclipsing Binary","A0 V",2.23);
star["Procyon"] = new Star("Canis Minor","Double","F5 IV",0.38);
star["Sirius"] = new Star("Canis Major","Double","A1 V",-1.46);
star["Rigil Kentaurus"] = new Star("Centaurus","Double","G2 V",-0.01);
star["Deneb"] = new Star("Cygnus","Supergiant","A2 Ia",1.25);
star["Vega"] = new Star("Lyra","White Dwarf","A0 V",0.03);
star["Altair"] = new Star("Aquila","White Dwarf","A7 V",0.77);
```

The function, shown here, creates a class for stars as shown in bold in Listing 8-2.

When called, the end result is a new star object:

```
star["Polaris"] = new Star("Ursa Minor","Double/Cepheid","F7",2.0);
```

As you can see, even though the two code listings are functionally equivalent, the code in Listing 8-2 is much shorter and easier to understand. Carrying this forward, imagine an object that had nine properties instead of just the four shown here.

Creating Objects

An object is created in two ways:

- By using the new keyword, as shown here:

  ```
  var star = new Object;
  ```

- Or by using curly braces, as shown here:

  ```
  var star = {};
  ```

Which of these ways you use depends largely on personal preference; they both accomplish the same task.

Adding Properties to Methods

Once an object has been created, you can start assigning to it the properties and methods that it will contain. If you have just one star object, then you could assign properties directly to it, like this:

```
star.name = "Polaris";
star.constellation = "Ursa Minor";
```

The previous section showed how to create multiple related objects with multiple properties and how to use a class to assign those properties efficiently.

Displaying Object Properties

With a *for...in* loop, it's possible to loop through each of the properties in an object. Try it out:

Looping through object properties

1. Using Microsoft Visual Studio, Eclipse, or another editor, edit the file proploop.htm in the Chapter08 sample files folder.

2. Within the page, add the *for* loop shown below in bold type:

```
<!DOCTYPE HTML PUBLIC "-//W3C//DTD HTML 4.01//EN"
"http://www.w3.org/TR/html4/strict.dtd">
<html>
<head>
<title>Properties</title>

<script type = "text/javascript">
    var star = {};

    function Star(constell,type,specclass,magnitude) {
        this.constellation = constell;
        this.type = type;
        this.spectralClass = specclass;
        this.mag  = magnitude;
    }

    star["Polaris"] = new Star("Ursa Minor","Double/Cepheid","F7",2.0);
    star["Mizar"] = new Star("Ursa Major","Spectroscopic Binary","A1 V",2.3);
    star["Aldebaran"] = new Star("Taurus","Irregular Variable","K5 III",0.85);
    star["Rigel"] = new Star("Orion","Supergiant with Companion","B8 Ia",0.12);
    star["Castor"] = new Star("Gemini","Multiple/Spectroscopic","A1 V",1.58);
    star["Albireo"] = new Star("Cygnus","Double","K3 II",3.1);
    star["Acrux"] = new Star("Crux","Double","B1 IV",0.8);
    star["Gemma"] = new Star("Corona Borealis","Eclipsing Binary","A0 V",2.23);
    star["Procyon"] = new Star("Canis Minor","Double","F5 IV",0.38);
    star["Sirius"] = new Star("Canis Major","Double","A1 V",-1.46);
    star["Rigil Kentaurus"] = new Star("Centaurus","Double","G2 V",-0.01);
    star["Deneb"] = new Star("Cygnus","Supergiant","A2 Ia",1.25);
    star["Vega"] = new Star("Lyra","White Dwarf","A0 V",0.03);
    star["Altair"] = new Star("Aquila","White Dwarf","A7 V",0.77);

</script>
</head>
<body>
<script type = "text/javascript" >

for (var propt in star) {
    alert(propt);
}

</script>
</body>
</html>
```

3. View this page in a Web browser. You'll be presented with an *alert()* dialog box for each of the stars in the *star* object, a total of 14 in all. (Yes, it's a lot of clicking. Sorry about that.) Here's an example of the type of dialog box you'll see:

This step-by-step exercise built on the earlier example of using classes to define properties of objects. In this case, a *star* object was created with the following code:

```
var star = {};
```

That object was then given several properties of individual star names with a call to create a new *Star* object (using the class):

```
star["Polaris"] = new Star("Ursa Minor","Double/Cepheid","F7",2.0);
```

Each of the properties of the original *star* object, in this case the names of each star, were then enumerated within the *<body>* of the code itself using a *for...in* loop:

```
for (var propt in star) {
    alert(propt);
}
```

You might be wondering how to get to the actual properties of the stars themselves, like the constellations, magnitudes, types, and spectral class. Chapter 11 will show you how to enumerate through each of these.

Looking for a Property

Sometimes you don't want or need to loop through every property. Sometimes you just want to know if a given property already exists within an object. You can use the *in* operator to test for the property, as in this pseudocode:

```
if (property in object) {
    // do something here
}
```

A more complete example is shown in Listing 8-3, where the *star* object is examined for one of the star names, Polaris, and if found, a new property is added to it.

LISTING 8-3 Looking for a Property

```
var star = {};

function Star(constell,type,specclass,magnitude) {
    this.constellation = constell;
```

```
        this.type = type;
        this.spectralClass = specclass;
        this.mag  = magnitude;
    }

    star["Polaris"] = new Star("Ursa Minor","Double/Cepheid","F7",2.0);
    star["Mizar"] = new Star("Ursa Major","Spectroscopic Binary","A1 V",2.3);
    star["Aldebaran"] = new Star("Taurus","Irregular Variable","K5 III",0.85);
    star["Rigel"] = new Star("Orion","Supergiant with Companion","B8 Ia",0.12);
    star["Castor"] = new Star("Gemini","Multiple/Spectroscopic","A1 V",1.58);
    star["Albireo"] = new Star("Cygnus","Double","K3 II",3.1);
    star["Acrux"] = new Star("Crux","Double","B1 IV",0.8);
    star["Gemma"] = new Star("Corona Borealis","Eclipsing Binary","A0 V",2.23);
    star["Procyon"] = new Star("Canis Minor","Double","F5 IV",0.38);
    star["Sirius"] = new Star("Canis Major","Double","A1 V",-1.46);
    star["Rigil Kentaurus"] = new Star("Centaurus","Double","G2 V",-0.01);
    star["Deneb"] = new Star("Cygnus","Supergiant","A2 Ia",1.25);
    star["Vega"] = new Star("Lyra","White Dwarf","A0 V",0.03);
    star["Altair"] = new Star("Aquila","White Dwarf","A7 V",0.77);

    if ("Polaris" in star) {
        star["Polaris"].aka = "The North Star";
        alert("Polaris found and is also known as " + star["Polaris"].aka);
    }
```

 Note There are other methods for checking property existence that aren't covered in this book. Specifically, the *!==* operator can be used for this purpose.

Adding Methods to Objects

Just as properties were added to self-defined objects, methods also can be added. For example, the class used in earlier examples can be extended to include a method called *show()*, which just presents an *alert()* dialog box. This method could be extended to do whatever you need it to do. For example, look at this code:

```
function Star(constell,type,specclass,magnitude) {
    this.constellation = constell;
    this.type = type;
    this.spectralClass = specclass;
    this.mag  = magnitude;
    this.show = function show() {
        alert("hello, this is a method.");
    }
}
```

Calling or invoking that method looks like this:

```
star["Polaris"].show();
```

Object-oriented programming in JavaScript doesn't end here. More advanced features of the object-oriented programming paradigm like inheritance, superclassing, and prototypes are all possible with JavaScript, but they are beyond the scope of this book. MSDN Magazine published an article about some of the more advanced concepts and that article can be found at http://msdn.microsoft.com/msdnmag/issues/07/05/JavaScript/default.aspx.

More About Arrays

Covered in Chapter 4, "Working with Variables and Data," arrays enable a set of values to be grouped into an object and then accessed through a numbered index value. Chapter 4 gave some examples of ways to define arrays. First, you can use the *new Array( )* explicit constructor as follows:

```
var star = new Array( );
star[0] = "Polaris";
star[1] = "Deneb";
star[2] = "Vega";
star[3] = "Altair";
```

You also can do the same thing using the implicit array constructor (square brackets), like so:

```
var star = ["Polaris", "Deneb", "Vega", "Altair"];
```

The *length* Property

The *length* property of an array returns the number of elements in the array. There's an important distinction to be made between how many elements the array contains and how many have been defined. Here's a simple example. Take the implicit star array definition shown just previously. You can count four star names: Polaris, Deneb, Vega, and Altair. The *length* property returns the same thing:

```
var numStars = star.length;    // star.length is 4.
```

> **Note** It is possible to have elements counted by the *length* property that have not yet been defined or initialized.

Array Methods

To introduce you to some of the methods of the array object, this section looks at a few of those methods. More information can be found within the ECMA-262 specification at *http://www.ecma-international.org/publications/files/ECMA-ST/Ecma-262.pdf*.

Adding and Removing Elements

Elements can be added to an array, either prepended or appended using a few different methods.

Using *concat()* to add elements   The *concat()* method appends elements to the end of the array on which it is invoked. The arguments supplied to *concat()* are appended and a new array is returned, as follows:

```
var myArray = new Array( );
myArray[0] = "first";
myArray[1] = "second";
var newArray = myArray.concat("third");
// newArray is now [first,second,third]
```

You can also concatenate another array, like this:

```
var myFirstArray = [51,67];
var mySecondArray = [18,"hello",125];
var newArray = myFirstArray.concat(mySecondArray)
// newArray is [51,67,18,"hello",125]
```

Adding elements with *concat()*

1. Using Visual Studio, Eclipse, or another editor, edit the file concat.htm in the Chapter08 sample files folder.

2. Within the page, add the code shown below in bold type:

```
<!DOCTYPE HTML PUBLIC "-//W3C//DTD HTML 4.01//EN"
"http://www.w3.org/TR/html4/strict.dtd">
<html>
<head>
    <title>Concat</title>
    <script type = "text/javascript">

    var star = ["Polaris", "Deneb", "Vega", "Altair"];

    for (var i = 0; i < star.length; i++) {
        alert(star[i]);
    }

    </script>
</head>
<body>

</body>
</html>
```

3. Save the page and view it in a Web browser. You'll receive an *alert()* dialog box (like the one shown here) for each of the four star names defined in the star array.

4. Now alter the code to concatenate some additional stars onto the star array. (Yes, I realize that you could just add them directly to the star array, but that's cheating.) Here's the code (the changes are highlighted):

```
<!DOCTYPE HTML PUBLIC "-//W3C//DTD HTML 4.01//EN"
"http://www.w3.org/TR/html4/strict.dtd">
<html>
<head>
    <title>Concat</title>
    <script type = "text/javascript">

    var star = ["Polaris", "Deneb", "Vega", "Altair"];

    var newstars = ["Aldebaran", "Rigel"];
    var morestars = star.concat(newstars);

    for (var i = 0; i < morestars.length; i++) {
        alert(morestars[i]);
    }

    </script>
</head>
<body>

</body>
</html>
```

5. Save and view the page in a Web browser. You'll now receive six *alert()* dialog boxes (sorry!), one for each star, like this one for Aldebaran:

Joining and concatenating with *join*   The *join()* method converts all the elements of an array to a joined string. This method is unlike the *concat()* method, which concatenates but does not perform any type conversions. Here's the code:

```
var star = ["Polaris", "Deneb", "Vega", "Altair"];
var starString = star.join();
```

The *starString* variable would contain Polaris,Deneb,Vega,Altair, as shown in Figure 8-1.

FIGURE 8-1 Using *join()* to join an array.

The *join()* method enables you to specify the join delimiter as well. Instead of just using a comma, you might want to use an asterisk, like this:

```
var star = ["Polaris", "Deneb", "Vega", "Altair"];
var starString = star.join("*");
```

The result would be Polaris*Deneb*Vega*Altair, as shown in Figure 8-2.

FIGURE 8-2 Joining with a different delimiter

> **Tip** The *join()* method is a quick way to see the contents of an array without creating an entire *for* loop structure.

Using *push* and *pop* to add and remove elements   Where *concat()* returns the newly concatenated array, *push()* and *pop()* add and remove elements, but also return the new length of the array to which the method is applied. The methods *push()* and *pop()* operate on the end of the array:

```
var star = ["Polaris", "Deneb", "Vega", "Altair"];
star.push("Aldebaran");
```

This code would result in the *star* object containing five elements: Polaris, Deneb, Vega, Altair, and Aldebaran.

The *pop()* method removes the last element and returns the element that is removed:

```
var star = ["Polaris", "Deneb", "Vega", "Altair"];
var removedElement = star.pop();
```

The *removedElement* variable would contain the string "Altair" because that was the last element of the array. The length of the array would also be shortened (or decremented) by 1.

Using *shift* and *unshift* to add and remove elements   The *push()* and *pop()* methods operate on the end of the array. The *shift()* and *unshift()* methods perform the same function as *push()* and *pop()*, except in reverse. The *unshift()* method adds an element to the beginning of an array:

```
var star = ["Polaris", "Deneb", "Vega", "Altair"];
star.unshift("Aldebaran");
```

The star array would now be:

```
["Aldebaran", "Polaris", "Deneb", "Vega", "Altair"]
```

Now use *shift()* to remove an element from the beginning of an array:

```
var star = ["Polaris", "Deneb", "Vega", "Altair"];

var removedElement = star.shift();
```

The star array would now contain:

```
["Deneb", "Vega", "Altair"]
```

Using *slice* to return parts of an array   The *slice()* method is useful if you need to return specific portions of an array, though care must be taken because unless a copy of the array is made, *slice()* will change the original array. For instance, this code would return and place into the *cutStars* variable the value "Vega,Altair" because Vega and Altair are the third and fourth elements of the star array (remember that arrays start counting from zero). The code is as follows:

```
var star = ["Polaris", "Deneb", "Vega", "Altair"];
var cutStars = star.splice(2,3);
```

Sorting elements with *sort*   It's sometimes helpful to sort the elements of an array. Look at this code:

```
var star = ["Polaris", "Deneb", "Vega", "Altair"];
var sortedStars = star.sort();
```

The result is shown in Figure 8-3, and as you can see, the elements of the star array are now sorted alphabetically, even though they weren't given alphabetically in the code. Note that both the original star array and the *sortedStars* variable contain sorted lists.

FIGURE 8-3 The result of a sorted array using the *sort()* method.

Be careful not to use the *sort()* method to sort numbers. Consider this code:

```
var nums = [11,543,22,111];
var sortedNums = nums.sort();
```

One might expect that the *sortedNums* variable would contain 11,22,111,543, but instead it sorts the values alphabetically, as shown in Figure 8-4.

FIGURE 8-4 Attempting to sort numbers with *sort()* doesn't work—at least not if you want them sorted in numerical order.

The array object has other methods that you should know about, but you might not use them much, depending on the requirements of your Web site. Refer to the ECMA-262 standard for more information. Two such methods that you might encounter are listed in Table 8-1.

TABLE 8-1 Select Methods of the Array Object

Method	Description
reverse()	Reverses the order of the elements
splice()	Inserts or removes elements from an array

Built-in Objects

The JavaScript language makes available several useful objects to assist with tasks common to the JavaScript program. Among these are some that have already been discussed, such as the *Number* object and the *Math* object, covered in Chapter 4.

This section looks at the *Date* object. Both the *Regexp* object and the *String* object will be covered as appropriate when they're used throughout the remainder of the book.

The *Date* Object

The *Date* object includes many methods that are helpful when working with dates in JavaScript—too many, in fact, to attempt to examine in any depth in a beginner-level book such as this, but I'll show you some examples that you'll likely want to incorporate in your projects.

Here's some simple code to return a date for the current time, adjusted for the local time zone and formatted automatically by the *toLocaleDateString()* method:

```
var myDate = new Date( );
alert(myDate.toLocaleDateString());
```

When run, this code might result in a date like that shown in Figure 8-5.

FIGURE 8-5 The *Date* object returns a *date* string, which can be localized using the *toLocaleDateString* method of the *Date* object.

What Date?

Notice the date in Figure 8-5, which is Saturday, June 16, 2001. You may be questioning whether the book was written in 2001. It wasn't. But this illustrates an issue with using dates through JavaScript. The dates returned by any JavaScript function depend on the computer upon which the JavaScript is executed.

It just so happens that I changed the date on my computer to June 16, 2001, to illustrate this point. Whenever you use any of the *Date* object's methods, remember that they'll depend on the time on the visitor's computer. (Incidentally, June 16, 2001, is my wedding date and now I have an easy place to find it as a reference in case I forget. Not that I ever would, of course...)

By itself, the *Date* object can be handed a number of arguments ranging from zero arguments up to seven arguments. When the *Date* object constructor is passed a single string argument, the string is assumed to contain the date. When it is passed a number type of argument, the argument is assumed to be the date in milliseconds since January 1, 1970, and when it is passed seven arguments, they're assumed to be:

```
new Date(year, month, day, hours, minutes, seconds, milliseconds)
```

Note Only *year* and *month* are required arguments; the others are optional.

Remember the following points when using a *Date* object:

- The year should be given with four digits unless you want to specify a year between the year 1900 and the year 2000, in which case you'd simply send in the two-digit year, 0 through 99 and it will be added to 1900. So, 2008 equals the year 2008, but just 98 will be turned into 1998.

- The month is represented by an integer 0 through 11, with 0 being January and 11 being December.

- The day is an integer from 1 to 31.

- Hours are represented by 0 through 23, where 23 represents 11 PM.

- Minutes and seconds are both integers ranging from 0 to 59.

- Milliseconds are an integer from 0 to 999.

Although this step-by-step exercise uses some items that won't be covered until later chapters, because we're looking at the *Date* object now, it's a good time to show you how to write the date and time to a Web page. This seems like a fairly popular thing to do. This exercise shows the whole process, including things that I won't explain right now, but I will later.

Writing the date and time to a Web page

1. Using Visual Studio, Eclipse, or another editor, edit the file writingthedate.htm in the Chapter08 sample files folder.

2. Within the page, add the code shown below in bold type:

```
<!DOCTYPE HTML PUBLIC "-//W3C//DTD HTML 4.01//EN"
"http://www.w3.org/TR/html4/strict.dtd">
<html>
<head>
    <title>the date</title>
</head>
<body>
    <p id="dateField"> </p>
    <script type = "text/javascript">

    var myDate = new Date();
    var dateString = myDate.toLocaleDateString() + " " + myDate.toLocaleTimeString();
    var dateLoc = document.getElementById("dateField");
    dateLoc.innerHTML = "Hello - Page Rendered on " + dateString;
    </script>

</body>
</html>
```

3. When saved and viewed in a Web browser, you should receive a page like this (though obviously the date you see probably will be different from what's shown here).

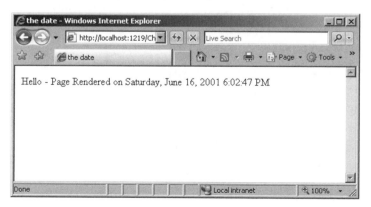

The relevant JavaScript from this exercise is repeated here:

```
var myDate = new Date();
var dateString = myDate.toLocaleDateString() + " " + myDate.toLocaleTimeString();
var dateLoc = document.getElementById("dateField");
dateLoc.innerHTML = "Hello - Page Rendered on " + dateString;
```

The JavaScript related to the *Date* object is really rather simple. It takes advantage of the *toLocaleDateString()* method, which you've already seen, and its cousin, *toLocateTimeString()*, which returns the local time. These two methods are concatenated together with a single space and placed into the *dateString* variable, like this:

```
var dateString = myDate.toLocaleDateString() + " " + myDate.toLocaleTimeString();
```

The remainder of the code writes the contents of the *dateString* variable to the Web page. More information on that aspect of JavaScript is described in Chapter 10, "The Document Object Model."

Other Date-Writing Procedures

The procedure shown in the "Writing the date and time to a Web page" exercise isn't the only way to write the date to the page. There are several others, many of which depend solely on developer preference (in other words, there's no "best" way). One other way to do it is to call *Date()* as a function rather than creating a new *Date* object as was done in the exercise. The key difference is the use of the *new* statement. When called with the word *new*, as in *new Date()*, an object is constructed, whereas when *Date()* is called without the word *new*, it's called as a function. Here is relevant JavaScript for using *Date* as a function:

```
var myDate = Date();
var dateLoc = document.getElementById("dateField");
dateLoc.innerHTML = "Hello - Page Rendered on " + myDate;
```

However, if you call this, you'll notice a subtle difference in the output, as shown here:

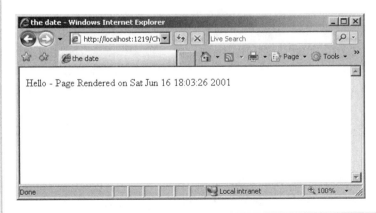

Notice in this screenshot that the word *Saturday* is abbreviated to *Sat,* where the previous screenshot displayed the entire word. The subtle differences in formatting can be important if you are processing the result rather than just displaying it.

Counting down to a certain date in the future

1. Using Visual Studio, Eclipse, or another editor, edit the file countdown.htm in the Chapter08 sample files folder.

2. Add the following code shown in bold type to the page:

```
<!DOCTYPE HTML PUBLIC "-//W3C//DTD HTML 4.01//EN"
"http://www.w3.org/TR/html4/strict.dtd">
<html>
<head>
    <title>the date</title>
</head>
<body>
    <p id="dateField"> </p>
    <script type = "text/javascript">
    var today = new Date();
    var then = new Date();
    // January 1, 2011
    then.setFullYear(2011,0,1);
    var diff = then.getTime() - today.getTime();
    diff = Math.floor(diff / (1000 * 60 * 60 * 24));
    var dateLoc = document.getElementById("dateField");
    dateLoc.innerHTML = "There are " + diff + " days until 1/1/2011";
    </script>

</body>
</html>
```

3. Save the page and view it in a Web browser. Depending on the date on your computer, the number of days represented will be different, but the general look of the page is as it appears here:

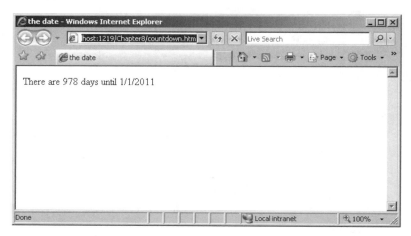

> **Tip** Be careful if using JavaScript dates for anything other than display. Because they are dependent on the visitor's time, you shouldn't rely on them for anything that might be important, like an ordering process.

The exercise you just completed used some additional functions of both the *Math* and *Date* objects, namely *floor()* and *getTime()*. While this book does cover a lot of ground, it's not a complete JavaScript language reference. For that and even more information, refer to MSDN, including this article, *http://msdn2.microsoft.com/en-us/office/aa905433.aspx,* which contains many helpful links to other JavaScript resources.

One final exercise shows how to calculate (or better yet, roughly estimate) the time it takes for a Web page to load in a person's browser.

> **Note** This isn't an entirely accurate procedure because it can't take into account the time it takes for images (or other multimedia items), which are external to the text of the Web page, to load and render. There are also technically a few more bits that will load after the script is finished running. But it's another widget that I've seen on several Web sites, and you might find it useful. At any rate, it shows another example of calculating dates.

Calculating render time

1. Using Visual Studio, Eclipse, or another editor, edit the file render.htm in the Chapter08 sample files folder.

2. Add the following code shown in bold type to the page:

```
<!DOCTYPE html PUBLIC "-//W3C//DTD XHTML 1.0 Transitional//EN"
"http://www.w3.org/TR/xhtml1/DTD/xhtml1-transitional.dtd">
<html>
<head>
    <title>the date</title>
    <script type = "text/javascript">
    var started = new Date();
    var now = started.getTime();
    </script>
</head>
<body>
    <p id="dateField"> </p>
    <script type = "text/javascript">
    var bottom = new Date();
    var diff = (bottom.getTime() - now)/1000;
    var finaltime = diff.toPrecision(5);
    var dateLoc = document.getElementById("dateField");
    dateLoc.innerHTML = "Page rendered in " + finaltime + " seconds.";
    </script>

</body>
</html>
```

3. Save the page and view it in a Web browser. Depending on the speed of your computer, Web server, and the network connection, you might receive a page that indicates that it took 0 seconds for the page to load, like this:

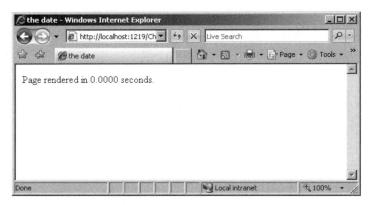

4. If your page takes 0.0000 seconds, as mine did, then you can introduce a delay into the page so you can test it. (I'd never recommend doing this on a live site, however, since I can't think of a reason why you'd want to slow down the rendering of your page! But it can come in handy for testing purposes.) A cheap and easy way to slow the JavaScript executing is a *for* loop:

```
for (var i = 0; i < 1000000; i++) {
   //delay
)
```

(The value I chose, 1000000, is arbitrary. You may need to choose a bigger or smaller number to cause the desired delay.) The final code looks like this:

```
<!DOCTYPE html PUBLIC "-//W3C//DTD XHTML 1.0 Transitional//EN"
"http://www.w3.org/TR/xhtml1/DTD/xhtml1-transitional.dtd">
<html xmlns="http://www.w3.org/1999/xhtml" >
<head>
    <title>the date</title>
    <script type = "text/javascript">
    var started = new Date();
    var now = started.getTime();
    for (var i = 0; i < 1000000; i++) {
       //delay
     }
    </script>
</head>
<body>
    <p id="dateField"> </p>
    <script type = "text/javascript">
    var bottom = new Date();
    var diff = (bottom.getTime() - now)/1000;
    var finaltime = diff.toPrecision(5);
    var dateLoc = document.getElementById("dateField");
```

```
dateLoc.innerHTML = "Page rendered in " + finaltime + " seconds.";
</script>

</body>
</html>
```

5. Save the page and again view it in a Web browser. You should see some delay in the page load, which will cause the value to be a positive number:

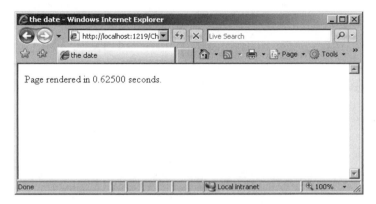

When using this or similar functions to determine the page load times, it's important to place the initial variable near the top of the page or script and then another one near the bottom of the page to calculate a more accurate value—or at least as accurate as possible.

You've now seen just a few of the more than 40 methods of the *Date* object. Many of these have UTC (Coordinated Universal Time) counterparts, meaning that they will get or set the date and time in UTC rather than local time. Table 8-2 lists the methods that return dates. With the exception of *getTime()* and *getTimezoneOffset()*, all these methods have UTC counterparts that are called using the format *getUTCDate()*, *getUTCDay()*, and so on.

TABLE 8-2 The *get* Methods of a *Date* Object

Method	Description
getDate()	Returns the day of the month
getDay()	Returns the day of the week
getFullYear()	Returns the four-digit year
getHours()	Returns the hours of a date
getMilliseconds()	Returns the milliseconds of a date
getMinutes()	Returns the minutes of a date
getMonth()	Returns the month of a date
getSeconds()	Returns the seconds of a date
getTime()	Returns the milliseconds since January 1, 1970
getTimezoneOffset()	Returns the number of minutes calculated as the difference between UTC and local time

Many of the *get...()* methods have siblings prefixed with *set*, as shown in Table 8-3. And like their *get* brethren, most of the *set...()* methods have UTC counterparts, except for *setTime()*.

TABLE 8-3 The *set* Methods of a *Date* Object

Method	Description
setDate()	Sets the day of the month of a date.
setFullYear()	Sets the four-digit year of a date. Also accepts the month and day-of-month integers.
setHours()	Sets the hour of a date.
setMilliseconds()	Sets the milliseconds of a date.
setMinutes()	Sets the minutes of a date.
setMonth()	Sets the month as an integer of a date.
setSeconds()	Sets the seconds of a date.
setTime()	Sets the time using milliseconds since January 1, 1970.

Some other methods include one you've already seen, *toLocaleDateString()*, and others related to it like *toLocaleString()*, *toGMTString()*, *toLocaleTimeString()*, *toString()*, *toDateString()*, *toUTCString()*, and *toTimeString()*. Experiment with these as you see fit. These simple code examples will get you started. Try typing them in the address bar of your browser:

- javascript:var myDate = new Date(); alert(myDate.toLocaleDateString());

- javascript:var myDate = new Date(); alert(myDate.toLocaleString());

- javascript:var myDate = new Date(); alert(myDate.toGMTString());

- javascript:var myDate = new Date(); alert(myDate.toLocaleTimeString());

- javascript:var myDate = new Date(); alert(myDate.toString());

- javascript:var myDate = new Date(); alert(myDate.toDateString());

- javascript:var myDate = new Date(); alert(myDate.toUTCString());

- javascript:var myDate = new Date(); alert(myDate.toTimeString());

Exercises

1. Create code to loop through a simple array of four objects, shown here, and display those in an *alert()* dialog box, one for each element of the array:

   ```
   var star = ["Polaris", "Deneb", "Vega", "Altair"];
   ```

2. Create an object to hold the names of three of your favorite songs. The objects should have properties containing the artist, the song length, and the title for each song.

3. The first step-by-step exercise in this chapter used a list of stars and a class to populate those objects, shown here:

```
function Star(constell,type,specclass,magnitude) {
    this.constellation = constell;
    this.type = type;
    this.spectralClass = specclass;
    this.mag  = magnitude;
}
star["Polaris"] = new Star("Ursa Minor","Double/Cepheid","F7",2.0);
star["Mizar"] = new Star("Ursa Major","Spectroscopic Binary","A1 V",2.3);
star["Aldebaran"] = new Star("Taurus","Irregular Variable","K5 III",0.85);
star["Rigel"] = new Star("Orion","Supergiant with Companion","B8 Ia",0.12);
star["Castor"] = new Star("Gemini","Multiple/Spectroscopic","A1 V",1.58);
star["Albireo"] = new Star("Cygnus","Double","K3 II",3.1);
star["Acrux"] = new Star("Crux","Double","B1 IV",0.8);
star["Gemma"] = new Star("Corona Borealis","Eclipsing Binary","A0 V",2.23);
star["Procyon"] = new Star("Canis Minor","Double","F5 IV",0.38);
star["Sirius"] = new Star("Canis Major","Double","A1 V",-1.46);
star["Rigil Kentaurus"] = new Star("Centaurus","Double","G2 V",-0.01);
star["Deneb"] = new Star("Cygnus","Supergiant","A2 Ia",1.25);
star["Vega"] = new Star("Lyra","White Dwarf","A0 V",0.03);
star["Altair"] = new Star("Aquila","White Dwarf","A7 V",0.77);
```

The code then used a simple *for* loop to move through each of the star objects and display the names of the stars, as shown here:

```
for (var propt in star) {
    alert(propt);
}
```

Your task is to modify this code to display one single dialog box with all the star names rather than displaying one for each star.

Chapter 9
The Browser Object Model

Up until now, we've been looking mainly at JavaScript in the abstract. This chapter starts to touch on JavaScript as it's really applied in the wild.

After reading this chapter, you'll be able to

- Understand the different objects available as part of the window object.
- Use the navigator object to view properties of the visitor's browser.
- Obtain information about the visitor's screen, including available height and width.
- Use JavaScript to detect whether or not Java is enabled in the browser.
- Parse the query string sent by the browser.

Introducing the Browser

I feel rather sheepish about writing this, but it's important, so I'm going to say it anyway: *the browser is central to JavaScript programming*. Projects like Rhino (*http://www.mozilla.org/rhino/*) aim to change that, but in general understanding the browser and the environment that it provides is a key to writing good JavaScript code that works well on multiple browsers on multiple platforms. This section introduces you to the Browser Object Model.

The Browser Hierarchy

The Browser Object Model creates a treelike hierarchy of objects, many of which provide properties and methods for the JavaScript programmer. The browser itself is represented by one object, called the *window* object. The *window* object is the parent of several child objects. The children of the *window* object are as follows:

- *document*
- *frames*
- *history*
- *location*
- *navigator*
- *self/window/parent*
- *screen*

That first child of the *window* object, *document*, is somewhat special because it has several child and even grandchild objects of its own. The *document* object, along with some of its children and their place in the browser hierarchy, are illustrated in Figure 9-1.

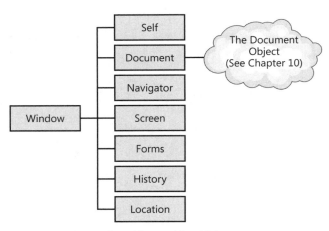

FIGURE 9-1 The *window* object and its children

The *document* object will get its own chapter, Chapter 10, aptly titled "The Document Object Model (DOM)." As for the other children of the *window* object, they will be discussed throughout the remainder of this chapter.

Events

Briefly described in Chapter 1, "JavaScript Is More than You Might Think," events are used in many areas of JavaScript programming, not least with Web forms. An event can be triggered when a button or link is clicked, when the mouse is moved into or out of an area, or when the page itself loads. Chapter 14, "Browsers and JavaScript," goes into details about events related to the *window* object, while more information about form events can be found in Chapter 11, "Using JavaScript with Web Forms."

A Sense of Self

The *window* object represents the global object presented to the currently open window within the browser. The *window* object has several properties, methods, and child objects. You've already used some of the methods, such as *alert()* and *prompt()*. Since the *window* object is the global object, you don't need to preface its properties and methods with *window*. Rather, you can just call them directly, as you've seen with calls to the *alert()* method in examples throughout the book.

Direct descendants of the *window* object don't require the *window.* prefix, but once you're dealing with objects beyond the *window* object's direct descendants, then you'll need to precede them with the object name. For example, the *document* object is a direct descendant of the *window* object and therefore doesn't need to be prefixed with *window.*, but any descendants of the *document* object need to have the *document.* prefix. For instance, look at this example:

```
alert("something");  // note no window. prefix.
document.forms[0]  // note the document. prefix but still no window. prefix
```

In addition to the child objects discussed previously (*document*, *frames*, *history*, and so on), the *window* object has properties and methods. Among these are the *self* property, which refers to the *window* object itself (and gave me the idea for the title for this section). Table 9-1 lists some of the properties of the *window* object. Many of these will be examined further through usage examples throughout the book.

TABLE 9-1 Select Properties of the *window* Object

Property	Description
closed	Set to true when the window has been closed
defaultStatus	Used to set the text that appears by default in the status bar of a browser
name	The name of the window as set when the window is first opened
opener	A reference to the window that created this window
parent	Frequently used with frames to refer to the window that created this window or is one level up from the frame itself
screenLeft	Defines the position of the left edge of the window within the visitor's screen
screenTop	Defines the position of the top of the window within the visitor's screen
status	Frequently used to set the text in the status bar when a visitor hovers over an element such as a link
top	Refers to the highest parent window

The *window* object also has methods that are of interest. Table 9-2 gives some of the methods of the *window* object along with brief descriptions. Like the *window* object's properties, many of these methods will be used throughout the remainder of the book.

TABLE 9-2 Select *window* Object Methods

Method	Description
addEventListener()	Cross-browser (except for Microsoft Windows Internet Explorer) event handler method. See Chapter 14 for more information.
attachEvent()	The version of *addEventListener()* in Windows Internet Explorer. See Chapter 14 for more information.
blur()	Changes the focus of keyboard input away from the browser window.

TABLE 9-2 **Select *window* Object Methods**

Method	Description
focus()	Changes the focus of keyboard input to the browser window.
close()	Close the browser window.
detachEvent()	The version of *removeEventListener()* in Windows Internet Explorer.
removeEventListener()	Cross-browser (except for Microsoft Windows Internet Explorer) event handler removal method.
open()	Opens a window.
print()	Causes the browser's print function to be invoked; behaves just as though someone clicked Print in the browser.

Some methods of the *window* object deal with moving and resizing the window. These are described in Table 9-3.

TABLE 9-3 ***window* Object Methods for Moving and Resizing**

Method	Description
moveBy()	Used to move the window to a relative location
moveTo()	Used to move the window to a specific location
resizeBy()	Used to change the size of the window by a relative amount
resizeTo()	Used to change the size of the window to a certain size

Timers are found in some JavaScript applications and will be discussed in Chapter 14. The *window* object methods related to timers are

- clearInterval()
- clearTimeout()
- setInterval()
- setTimeout()

The remainder of the chapter looks more closely at some of the children of the *window* object.

Getting Information About the Screen

The *screen* object provides a way to get information about the visitor's screen. This information might be used to determine what images to display or how large the page can be. However, a good Cascading Style Sheet (CSS) design should gracefully handle screens of all sizes.

Note You may see child objects of the *window* object sometimes referred to as *properties* of the *window* object—for example, the *screen* property rather than the *screen* object.

The available properties of the *screen* object are

- *availHeight*
- *availWidth*
- *colorDepth*
- *height*
- *pixelDepth*
- *width*

You might be wondering what the difference is between the *availHeight/availWidth* and *height/width* properties. The *availHeight/availWidth* properties return the available height and width (no kidding!) of the screen minus the space used by things like the taskbar in Microsoft Windows, whereas the height and width properties return the gross height and width. This might make some more sense with an example, so here goes.

Looking at the visitor's screen height and width

1. Using Microsoft Visual Studio, Eclipse, or another editor, edit the file screen.htm in the Chapter09 sample files folder.

2. Within the page, add the code shown below in bold type:

```
<!DOCTYPE HTML PUBLIC "-//W3C//DTD HTML 4.01//EN"
"http://www.w3.org/TR/html4/strict.dtd">
<html>
<head>
    <title>Screen</title>

</head>
<body>

    <script type = "text/javascript" >
        alert("Available Height: " + screen.availHeight);
        alert("Total Height: " + screen.height);
        alert("Available Width: " + screen.availWidth);
        alert("Total Width: " + screen.width);
    </script>

</body>
</html>
```

3. Save and view the page in a Web browser. You'll receive four *alert()* dialog boxes, one for each of the properties called. The sample screenshots shown here reflect an 800 × 600 pixel display.

As you can see from these screenshots, the total width and height are 800 pixels and 600 pixels, respectively. However, while the available width remains 800, the available height is reduced to 570 from 600 because of the taskbar in Windows XP. It's interesting to note that if the taskbar is set to hide automatically, the available height will reflect that fact and not subtract the space that the taskbar takes up. Also, if the taskbar consumes multiple rows, that also will be reflected in the available height (reducing it).

Using the *navigator* Object

The *navigator* object provides several properties that assist in the detection of various elements of the visitor's browser and environment. One of the most popular things to do with JavaScript is simply to detect which browser the visitor is using. Well, this section isn't about that—but it could be. See the sidebar "Browser Detection" for more information.

Problems with Browser Detection

For a long time, Web sites used the *navigator* object to detect which browser the visitor was using. (Well, a long time in Internet years—which could be several years or as short as a few months, depending on the technology you're talking about.) This was done to use only JavaScript functions that were compatible with whatever browser was being used to view a site. Although simple browser detection had its uses, some poorly designed sites used this technique as a lazy means to lock out visitors that had particular browsers.

One problem with this, however, lies in the fact that the information sent by a browser can be easily spoofed. The User Agent Switcher add-on for Firefox is one such method to alter this information, thus rendering browser detection with the *navigator* object useless.

I've said it before in this book and I'll say it now (and probably will repeat it again later): Never rely on anything sent from the visitor's browser to your Web site. Always verify. Assuming that the browser is Microsoft Internet Explorer 6 just because it says so is not sufficient. Chapter 14 shows a better method for detecting whether or not the browser is capable of handling the JavaScript on your Web site.

A second problem with using the *navigator* object for browser detection is with so many browsers out there, a Web developer would simply spend too much time keeping track of which browsers might support which functions and then trying to account for each one of those browsers in the code.

All is not lost for the *navigator* object though—it still has some usefulness, as you'll soon see.

Let's walk through the properties of the *navigator* object, along with their values.

Looking at the *navigator* object

1. Using Microsoft Visual Studio, Eclipse, or another editor, edit the file naviprops.htm in the Chapter09 sample files folder.

2. Within the page, add the code shown below in bold type (don't forget to add the *onload* event handler in the *<body>* tag):

```
<!DOCTYPE HTML PUBLIC "-//W3C//DTD HTML 4.01//EN"
"http://www.w3.org/TR/html4/strict.dtd">
<html>
<head>
    <title>The navigator Object</title>
    <script type = "text/javascript" >
```

```
            function showProps() {
                var body = document.getElementsByTagName("body")[0];
                for (var prop in navigator) {
                    var elem = document.createElement("p");
                    var text = document.createTextNode(prop + ": " + navigator[prop]);
                    elem.appendChild(text);
                    body.appendChild(elem);
                }
            }
        </script>
    </head>
    <body onload="showProps()">

    </body>
    </html>
```

3. Save and view the page in a Web browser of your choice. If you chose Firefox, you'll see a page like this:

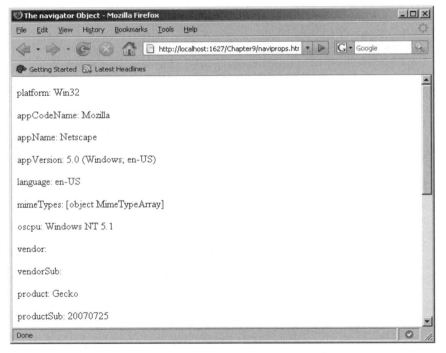

4. If you chose Windows Internet Explorer, the page will look similar to this; however, note the difference in the available properties:

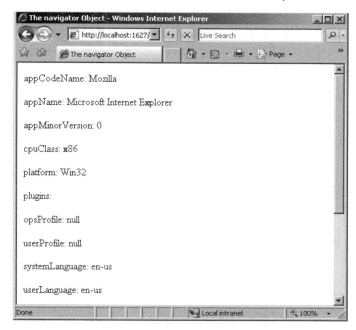

I just couldn't bring myself to use yet another *alert()* dialog box for this exercise, so I had to use some functions that I haven't yet introduced. Never fear, though—the elements in this example will be introduced in Chapter 10 and Chapter 14.

The code for this exercise uses a function that uses the *document* object model to create Hypertext Markup Language (HTML) elements within the Web page. A *for* loop is used to iterate through each of the properties presented by the *navigator* object:

```
function showProps() {
    var body = document.getElementsByTagName("body")[0];
    for (var prop in navigator) {
        var elem = document.createElement("p");
        var text = document.createTextNode(prop + ": " + navigator[prop]);
        elem.appendChild(text);
        body.appendChild(elem);
    }
}
```

The *<body>* tag uses the *onload* event (events are another aspect of the *window* object) to automatically run the JavaScript *showProps()* function:

```
<body onload="showProps()">
```

The *onload* event will be discussed further in Chapter 14.

If the JavaScript you're using doesn't work for a certain version of a Web browser, you could implement a workaround based on using the *navigator* object to detect the browser, with the understanding that this isn't reliable and really shouldn't be done as standard practice. But sometimes it just needs to be done.

If your site uses Java, you can use the *navigator* object to check whether Java is enabled. Here's how:

Using the *navigator* object to detect Java

1. Using Microsoft Visual Studio, Eclipse, or another editor, edit the file javatest.htm in the Chapter09 sample files folder.

2. Within the page, add the code shown below in bold type:

```
<!DOCTYPE HTML PUBLIC "-//W3C//DTD HTML 4.01//EN"
"http://www.w3.org/TR/html4/strict.dtd">
<html>
<head>
    <title>Java Test</title>
    <script type = "text/javascript" >
        if (navigator.javaEnabled()) {
            alert("Java is enabled");
        } else {
            alert("Java is not enabled");
        }
    </script>
</head>

<body>

</body>
</html>
```

3. Save the page and view it in a Web browser. By default, Java is enabled in Windows Internet Explorer, so you should see a dialog box like this:

4. Switch to Firefox, if you have it available, and disable Java (in the Windows version of Firefox, you can do this by selecting Options on the Tools menu and then clicking Content.) When you disable Java and refresh the page, you'll see a dialog box like this:

The *location* Object

The *location* object gives you access to the currently loaded Uniform Resource Identifier (URI), including any information on the query string, the protocol in use, and other related components. For example, a URI might be:

http://www.braingia.org/location.html

If the Web page at that URI happened to contain the JavaScript code presented in the next example to parse the URI, the output would look like that shown in Figure 9-2.

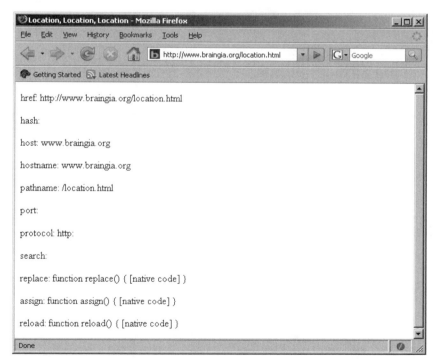

FIGURE 9-2 The *location* object being used to display the various properties

The protocol in this case is *http:*, the host is *www.braingia.org* (as is the host name), and the pathname is *location.html*. Nothing was entered on the query string, so the search value remains empty. The port was the standard port for HTTP traffic, tcp/80, so that too is empty.

Here's a step-by-step exercise to examine the query string.

A look at the *location* object

1. Using Microsoft Visual Studio, Eclipse, or another editor, edit the file location1.htm in the Chapter09 sample files folder.

2. This first bit of HTML and JavaScript creates the page that you saw in Figure 9-2. (Actually, it steals the code from an earlier exercise with the *navigator* object with a slight modification for the *location* object.) We'll build upon it for this exercise, so add the code shown below in bold to the location1.htm page:

```
<!DOCTYPE HTML PUBLIC "-//W3C//DTD HTML 4.01//EN"
"http://www.w3.org/TR/html4/strict.dtd">
<html>
<head>
    <title>Location, Location, Location</title>
    <script type = "text/javascript">
        function showProps() {
            var body = document.getElementsByTagName("body")[0];
            for (var prop in location) {
                var elem = document.createElement("p");
                var text = document.createTextNode(prop + ": " + location[prop]);
                elem.appendChild(text);
                body.appendChild(elem);
            }
        }

    </script>
</head>
<body onload="showProps()">

</body>
</html>
```

3. View the page in a Web browser. If you're viewing it through Visual Studio 2005 and have the local Internet Information Services (IIS) server running, your output might look like this (though obviously it'll be a little different because you're not using the server at *http://www.braingia.org* to serve the file):

4. Modify the URI that you use to call the page to add some query string parameter/value pairs. For example, the URI used for my local environment is *http://localhost:1627/ Chapter9/location1.htm*. Your environment and the location from which you serve the file will likely be different than this. I'm going to modify the URL and add two parameters, *name=Steve* and *country=US*. Feel free to change the value for the *name* parameter to your name and change the *country* value to your home country (if you're not from the United States, that is). The values you choose aren't all that important here—what matters is that you use more than one parameter/value pair. Here's my final URI: *http://localhost:1627/Chapter9/location1.htm?name=Steve&country=US*. Again, yours may differ depending on the server name.

5. When you load the page with the parameters you added, the *search* property will now have a value, as shown here:

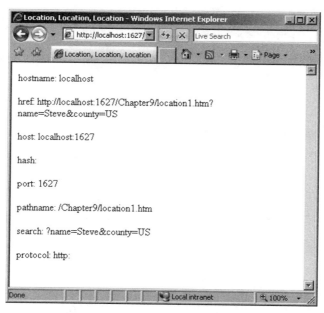

6. Open the location1.htm file again, and save it as location2.htm.

7. Alter the code in location2.htm so that it examines the *search* property, like this (the changes are shown in bold type):

```
<!DOCTYPE HTML PUBLIC "-//W3C//DTD HTML 4.01//EN"
"http://www.w3.org/TR/html4/strict.dtd">
<html>
<head>
    <title>Location, Location, Location</title>
    <script type = "text/javascript">
        function showProps() {
            var body = document.getElementsByTagName("body")[0];
            for (var prop in location) {
                var elem = document.createElement("p");
                var text = document.createTextNode(prop + ": " + location[prop]);
                elem.appendChild(text);
                body.appendChild(elem);
            }
            if (location.search) {
                var querystring = location.search;
                var splits = querystring.split('&');
                for (var i = 0; i < splits.length; i++) {
                    var splitpair = splits[i].split('=');
                    var elem = document.createElement("p");
                    var text = document.createTextNode(splitpair[0] + ": " +
```

```
splitpair[1]);
                        elem.appendChild(text);
                        body.appendChild(elem);
                }
            }
        }

    </script>
</head>
<body onload="showProps()">

</body>
</html>
```

8. Execute this code by pointing your browser to *location2.htm?name=Steve&country=US*
(alter the name and country as appropriate, unless your name is Steve and you live in
the United States). You'll now receive a page that lists the normal properties that you
saw earlier, but also lists (near the bottom) the parameter/value pairs parsed from the
query string:

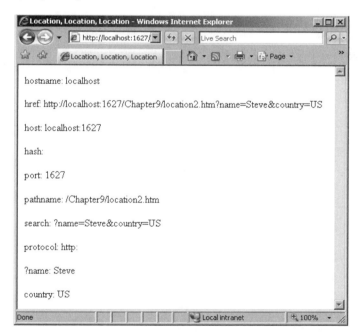

9. Notice, however, that the first parameter, *name*, contains the *?* from the query string,
which is not what you want. There are several ways to solve this problem. One of the
simplest is to use the *substring()* method. Change the *querystring* variable definition
line to read:

```
var querystring = location.search.substring(1);
```

The *substring()* method returns the string starting at the point specified. In this case, the first character of *location.search* (at index 0) is the question mark; therefore, using *substring()* starting at index 1 solves the problem. The final code (with the change shown in bold type) looks like this:

```
<!DOCTYPE HTML PUBLIC "-//W3C//DTD HTML 4.01//EN"
"http://www.w3.org/TR/html4/strict.dtd">
<html>
<head>
    <title>Location, Location, Location</title>
    <script type = "text/javascript">
        function showProps() {
            var body = document.getElementsByTagName("body")[0];
            for (var prop in location) {
                var elem = document.createElement("p");
                var text = document.createTextNode(prop + ": " + location[prop]);
                elem.appendChild(text);
                body.appendChild(elem);
            }
            if (location.search) {
                var querystring = location.search.substring(1);
                var splits = querystring.split('&');
                for (var i = 0; i < splits.length; i++) {
                    var splitpair = splits[i].split('=');
                    var elem = document.createElement("p");
                    var text = document.createTextNode(splitpair[0] + ": " +
splitpair[1]);
                    elem.appendChild(text);
                    body.appendChild(elem);
                }
            }
        }
    </script>
</head>
<body onload="showProps()">

</body>
</html>
```

10. Save this code as location3.htm and run it again. You'll see the results solve the problem of the question mark:

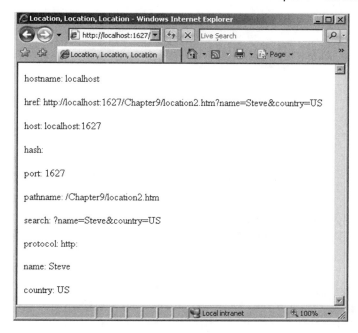

The *history* Object

The *history* object provides ways to move forward and backward through the visitor's browsing history. However, for security reasons, JavaScript cannot access the URIs for sites that the browser visits.

The *back()*, *forward()*, and *go()* methods provide ways to move through the browsing history. It probably goes without saying, but *back* and *forward* move one page backward and forward, respectively. The *go()* method moves to the index value specified as the argument.

Here's some example code for moving backward and forward. This code can be adapted as needed, and examples in later chapters will show more detail on how this kind of code might be used in the wild.

```
<!DOCTYPE HTML PUBLIC "-//W3C//DTD HTML 4.01//EN" "http://www.w3.org/TR/html4/strict.dtd">
<html>
<head>
    <title>History</title>
    <script type = "text/javascript" >
        function moveBack() {
            history.back();
        }
        function moveForward() {
            history.forward();
        }
    </script>
```

```
</head>
<body>
<p><a href="#" onclick="moveBack()">Click to go back</a></p>
<p><a href="#" onclick="moveForward()">Click to go forward</a></p>
</body>
</html>
```

Exercises

1. Use the *availHeight* and *availWidth* methods to determine if a screen is at least 768 pixels high and 1024 pixels wide. If it's not, display an *alert()* dialog box stating the size of the available screen.

2. Alter the step-by-step exercise that used the *location* object to display an *alert()* dialog box based on the values of the query string. Specifically, display the word "Obrigado" if the country is specified as Brazil, and display "Thank you" if the country is Great Britain. Test these conditions.

3. Install the User Agent Switcher add-on to Firefox or a similar add-on to Windows Internet Explorer. Then use the code from the "Looking at the navigator object" exercise earlier in this chapter to experiment with the different values that you find. This exercise will help to show why using the *navigator* object as the sole means of determining compatibility is not recommended. Bonus: Define your own user agent.

Chapter 10
The Document Object Model

After reading this chapter, you'll be able to

- Use the Document Object Model to retrieve elements from a document.

- Create new elements in a document.

- Make changes to elements in a document.

- Remove elements from a document.

The Document Object Model Defined

The Document Object Model (DOM) provides a way to access and alter the contents of Hypertext Markup Language (HTML) documents. The DOM is a standard defined by the World Wide Web Consortium (W3C) and is implemented in various forms and with varying degrees of success by most Internet browsers.

Like many other standards, especially those related to Web programming, the DOM has evolved over the years. It has three specifications, known as *levels* in DOM-speak, with a fourth specification on the way.

The DOM is much more powerful than this chapter or even this book can convey, and there's much more to it than I'll attempt to cover. The DOM can be used for more than just JavaScript programming. Yet my particular focus (namely, JavaScript) pulls me toward writing about how JavaScript can be used with the DOM.

When I refer to the DOM in this chapter (and throughout this book, in fact), I lean heavily toward how it relates to the task at hand rather than the overall concepts or what might be possible with the DOM. For example, I'm going to concentrate on how the DOM represents HTML documents as trees. The DOM does so for HTML and Extensible Markup Language (XML) alike, but since this is a book about JavaScript, it's most important that I convey the DOM's relation to HTML.

For more information on the DOM, refer to the specification itself at the W3C site: http://www.w3.org/DOM/.

DOM Level 0: The Legacy DOM

DOM Level 0 is also known as the legacy DOM. DOM Level 0 was implemented before other formal specifications of the DOM. Once DOM Level 1 was specified, the previous technology related to document scripting was codified (though not really in any formal way by any standards body) as the legacy DOM Level 0. Today, every major browser supports DOM Level 0 components for backwards compatibility. We don't want all those scripts we wrote back in 1998 to break!

The DOM Level 0 concentrated mainly on giving access to form elements, but it incorporated access to links and images. Forms and how to access them with the DOM are covered in Chapter 11, "Using JavaScript with Web Forms." Rather than spending time on examples of DOM Level 0, I'll concentrate on DOM Levels 1 and 2, which are what you're more than likely going to be using when you program JavaScript.

DOM Levels 1 and 2

Level 1 of the DOM was issued as a specification in 1998 and, like the legacy DOM, it too is supported, in various forms, by all the major browsers. Level 2 of the DOM was formally released in 2000. Support of Level 2 DOM varies within browsers. Truthfully, support of all DOM levels varies from browser to browser and from version to version.

Microsoft Windows Internet Explorer claims to support the DOM, but it does so differently than other browsers. As a result, you need to be aware that the DOM feature or function you're using or attempting to use in your JavaScript code might not work in Windows Internet Explorer or might work only in Windows Internet Explorer and nowhere else (and, no, that's not acceptable).

Where applicable, I'll point out the places where browsers implement the DOM differently and some workarounds for such events. Speaking of events, browsers diverge the most from each other in their implementation of the event model.

The DOM as a Tree

The DOM represents HTML documents in a tree-like structure or rather an uprooted tree-like structure because the root of the tree is on top. For example, consider the HTML document shown in Listing 10-1, which will be used to show the tree structure.

LISTING 10-1 A Simple HTML Document

```
<html>
<head>
<title>Hello World</title>
</head>
<body>
<p>Here's some text.</p>
<p>Here's more text.</p>
<p>Link to the <a href="http://www.w3.org">W3</a></p>
</body>
</html>
```

Figure 10-1 shows the HTML from Listing 10-1 when viewed in the tree structure of the DOM.

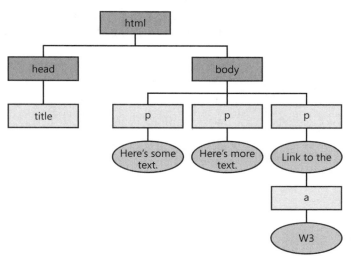

FIGURE 10-1 A simple document represented as a tree structure.

Many HTML elements can have attributes, such as the *href* attribute of the *a* element shown in Listing 10-1. These attributes can be retrieved and set using the DOM, as you'll see later in this chapter.

When working with the DOM, there is a distinction between retrieving elements, setting elements and things related to elements, and removing or deleting elements. The methods for working with DOM elements reflect this distinction.

Working with Nodes

The elements within the tree structure are sometimes referred to as nodes or *node* objects. Nodes at the level below a given node are known as children. For example, in the structure shown in Figure 10-1, the *body* node has three child nodes, all *p* elements, while one of the *p* elements has a child of its own, an *a* element. The *body* node is said to be a parent of the *p* nodes. Any nodes below a given node are known as descendants of that node. The three *p* nodes in Figure 10-1 are known as siblings because they're on the same level.

As there are methods to work with elements of the DOM, there are also methods to work with nodes that reflect the parent/child relationship. Methods such as *appendChild(),* shown later in this chapter, are used to add nodes onto an existing parent.

Retrieving Elements

Retrieving the elements of a document is a central part of using the DOM with JavaScript. This section examines two of the primary methods used to accomplish this: *getElementById()* and *getElementsByTagName()*.

Retrieving by ID

The *getElementById()* method is a workhorse method of the DOM. It retrieves a given element of the HTML document and returns a reference to it. The example from Listing 10-1 could be modified to add an *id* attribute in the *a* element, like this:

```
<html>
<head>
<title>Hello World</title>
<body>
<p>Here's some text.</p>
<p>Here's more text.</p>
<p>Link to the <a id="w3link" href="http://www.w3.org">W3</a></p>
</body>
</html>
```

The *a* element could then be retrieved with the *getElementById()* method, as follows:

```
var a1 = document.getElementById("w3link");
```

The reference for the element with the ID *w3link* would be placed inside the JavaScript variable *a1*.

All HTML elements can be given *id* attributes, making them all retrievable by JavaScript. In this example, the *p* elements could get IDs, thus making them retrievable using the *getElementById()* method too. Take a look at this code:

```
<html>
<head>
<title>Hello World</title>
<body>
<p id="sometext">Here's some text.</p>
<p id="moretext">Here's more text.</p>
<p id="linkp">Link to the <a id="w3link" href="http://www.w3.org">W3</a></p>
</body>
</html>
```

These elements could then be retrieved in the same way, like so:

```
var p1 = document.getElementById("sometext");
var p2 = document.getElementById("moretext");
var plink = document.getElementById("linkp");
```

But what to do with those elements once you retrieve them? In the case of elements like *a*, you can access its attributes, such as the value of the *href*, as in this example, which you can find in the companion code as getelement.htm:

```html
<html>
<head>
    <title>Get By Id</title>
    <script type = "text/javascript" >
    function checkhref() {
        var a1 = document.getElementById("w3link");
        alert(a1.href);
    }
    </script>
</head>
<body onload="checkhref()">
<p id="sometext">Here's some text.</p>
<p id="moretext">Here's more text.</p>
<p id="linkp">Link to the <a id="w3link" href="http://www.w3.org">W3</a></p>
</body>
</html>
```

When viewed, the page containing this code displays a dialog box showing the *href* attribute from the *a* element, like the one in Figure 10-2.

FIGURE 10-2 The *href* attribute retrieved with the help of *getElementById()*

Later in this chapter, you'll see how to change elements and attributes.

A Note on the *innerHTML* Property

One method for changing the text of elements is with the *innerHTML* property. The *innerHTML* property enables fast and simple access to the text in such elements as a *p* element. This property generally works well—so well, in fact, that it's difficult to skip it entirely in this book. So I won't.

The *innerHTML* property has been out of favor in many Web programming circles for some time. The problem with *innerHTML* is that it's not been formally defined as a standard by the W3C, so it's not necessarily supported in all browsers in the way that other DOM-specified objects are. However, with the sometimes hit-and-miss implementations of the actual specification, it's not hard to see why *innerHTML* is still used. The major browsers support *innerHTML* and they do so fairly consistently.

With all this in mind, I'll talk about *innerHTML* in this sidebar, but with the caveat that you should use it sparingly, maybe just for debugging purposes.

Take a look at this example, which is found in the companion code as innerhtml.htm:

```
<!DOCTYPE HTML PUBLIC "-//W3C//DTD HTML 4.01//EN"
"http://www.w3.org/TR/html4/strict.dtd">
<html>
<head>
    <title>Get By Id</title>
    <script type = "text/javascript" >
    function changetext() {
        var p1 = document.getElementById("sometext");
        alert(p1.innerHTML);
        p1.innerHTML = "Changed Text";
    }
    </script>
</head>
<body onload="changetext()">
<p id="sometext">Here's some text.</p>
<p id="moretext">Here's more text.</p>
<p id="linkp">Link to the <a id="w3link" href="http://www.w3.org">W3</a></p>
</body>
</html>
```

Within the function *changetext()*, the element with an ID of *sometext* is retrieved and a reference placed in the variable *p1*, as follows:

```
var p1 = document.getElementById("sometext");
```

Next, the *innerHTML* property is called and sent to an *alert()* dialog box, shown here. Notice not only the *alert()* dialog box, but also the text of the first line in the background window:

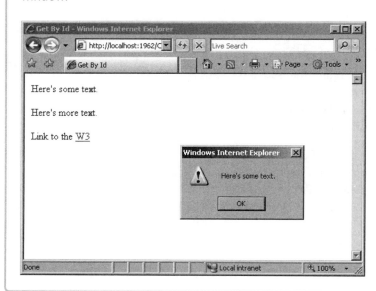

When the user clicks OK, the next line of JavaScript executes, using the *innerHTML* property to change the text of the *p* element, as you see here:

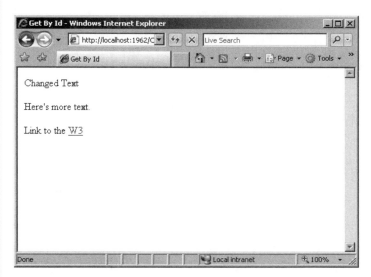

With that, you've seen how to retrieve HTML with *innerHTML* and how to set text with it. Use it at your own risk, and don't be surprised if the JavaScript that uses it mysteriously stops working someday. Then again, maybe we'll all be lucky and *innerHTML* will be formalized into the standard.

Retrieving by Tag Name

The *getElementById()* method works well when you're retrieving one or just a few elements. When you need to retrieve more than one element at a time, however, the *getElementsByTagName()* method might be more appropriate.

The *getElementsByTagName()* method returns all the elements of the given tag in an array or list format. For example, to retrieve all of the images within a document, write the following code:

```
var images = document.getElementsByTagName("img");
```

You could then examine the properties of the images variable by looping through it.

Here's an example with a table. This code changes the background color of each *td* element within the table when the user clicks the Click To Change Colors link. This code is found in the companion code as getbytagname.htm:

```
<!DOCTYPE HTML PUBLIC "-//W3C//DTD HTML 4.01//EN"
"http://www.w3.org/TR/html4/strict.dtd">
<html>
<head>
    <title>Tag Name</title>
    <script type = "text/javascript" >
    function changecolors() {
        var a1 = document.getElementsByTagName("td");
        for (var i = 0; i < a1.length; i++) {
            a1[i].style.background = "#aaabba";
        }
    }

    </script>
</head>
<body>
<table id="mytable" border="1">
<tr><td id="lefttd0">Left column</td><td id="righttd0">Right column</td></tr>
<tr><td id="lefttd1">Left column</td><td id="righttd1">Right column</td></tr>
<tr><td id="lefttd2">Left column</td><td id="righttd2">Right column</td></tr>
</table>
<a href="#" onclick="return changecolors();">Click to Change Colors</a>
</body>
</html>
```

Figure 10-3 shows how this page looks when viewed in a Web browser.

FIGURE 10-3 Using *getElementsByTagName()* to format elements from a table

Clicking the link causes the table elements to change background color, as seen in Figure 10-4.

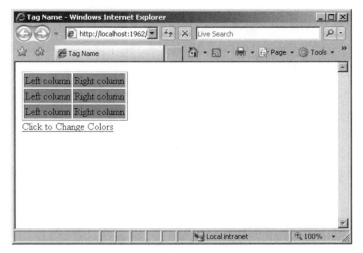

FIGURE 10-4 After a user clicks the link, the table elements change the background color.

Examining the code, the JavaScript in the *<head>* portion of the page creates a function called *changecolors()*:

```
function changecolors() {
```

Inside that function, all *td* elements are retrieved using the *getElementsByTagName()* method. These elements are placed into the *a1* array:

```
var a1 = document.getElementsByTagName("td");
```

This array is then enumerated with a *for* loop. Within the *for* loop, the background style of each element is changed to *#aaabba*, a shade of blue:

```
for (var i = 0; i < a1.length; i++) {
    a1[i].style.background = "#aaabba";
}
```

The use of Cascading Style Sheets (CSS) and JavaScript is shown in Chapter 15, "JavaScript and CSS."

The link itself calls the *changecolors()* function thanks to an *onclick* event:

```
<a href="#" onclick="return changecolors();">Click to Change Colors</a>
```

The *onclick* event, along with *onload* and other events, are covered in detail in Chapter 14, "Browsers and JavaScript."

A common question I've seen is how to color or shade every other row within a table. This too can be done with the help of JavaScript and some CSS, as discussed in Chapter 15.

Working with Attributes

The attributes of elements are both gettable and settable through JavaScript. This section looks at both tasks.

Viewing Attributes

Sometimes, especially when first programming with JavaScript, you might not know what attributes are available. But you don't have to worry about that, thanks to a loop that calls the *getAttribute()* method. Here's a generic function to view all the attributes of a given element:

```
function showattribs(e) {
    var e = document.getElementById("braingialink");
    var elemList = "";
    for (var element in e) {
        var attrib = e.getAttribute(element);
        elemList = elemList + element + ": " + attrib + "\n";
    }
alert(elemList);
}
```

A bit of JavaScript with the *getElementById()* method are all you need to invoke this function, as you'll see in this exercise.

Retrieving element attributes

1. Using Microsoft Visual Studio, Eclipse, or another editor, edit the file showattribs.htm in the Chapter10 sample files folder .

2. Within the page, add the code shown below in bold type:

```
<!DOCTYPE HTML PUBLIC "-//W3C//DTD HTML 4.01//EN"
"http://www.w3.org/TR/html4/strict.dtd">
<html>
<head>
    <title>Show Attribs</title>
    <script type = "text/javascript">
    function showattribs(e) {
        var e = document.getElementById("braingialink");
        var elemList = "";
        for (var element in e) {
            var attrib = e.getAttribute(element);
            elemList = elemList + element + ": " + attrib + "\n";
        }
        alert(elemList);
    }
```

```
      </script>
  </head>
  <body>
  <a onclick="showattribs()" href="http://www.braingia.org" id="braingialink">Steve
  Suehring's
  Web Site</a>
  <script type = "text/javascript" >

  </script>
  </body>
  </html>
```

3. Save the code and view it in a Web browser. You'll see a page like this:

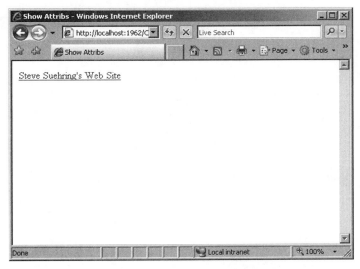

4. Click the link. When you do, the JavaScript function will execute. The function will retrieve the *a* element's attributes and loop through them, appending them onto a variable. Finally, that variable will display in an *alert()* dialog box, like the partial one shown here:

Setting Attributes

You've seen how the *getAttribute()* method retrieves the values in an attribute. You also can set attributes using the *setAttribute()* method.

The *setAttribute()* method takes two arguments or parameters: the attribute to change and the intended value for that attribute. Here's an example of changing the *href* attribute, which can also be found in the companion code as setattrib.htm:

```
<!DOCTYPE HTML PUBLIC "-//W3C//DTD HTML 4.01//EN"
"http://www.w3.org/TR/html4/strict.dtd">
<html>
<head>
    <title>Set Attrib</title>

</head>
<body>
<a onclick="showattribs()" href="http://www.braingia.org" id="braingialink">Steve Suehring's
Web Site</a>
<script type = "text/javascript" >
    var a1 = document.getElementById("braingialink");
    alert(a1.getAttribute("href"));
    a1.setAttribute("href","http://www.microsoft.com");
```

```
    alert(a1.getAttribute("href"));
</script>
</body>
</html>
```

When viewed in a Web browser, an *alert()* dialog box appears with the current value of the *href*, as shown in Figure 10-5.

FIGURE 10-5 The initial value of the href attribute

When the dialog box clears, the *setAttribute()* method executes and the *href* attribute changes, as shown in Figure 10-6.

FIGURE 10-6 The new value of the *href* attribute

Creating Elements

Elements can be added to a document by using the DOM. This section examines some ways to do just that.

Adding Text

At its most basic, the *createElement()* method of the *document* object can be used to create or add an element to a document. Here's some example code:

```
var newelement = document.createElement("p");
```

The element within the variable *newelement* now has a reference to the new element. This element would then need to be appended or added to the document, though usually only after adding text to it. Adding an element onto a document is accomplished using the *appendChild()* method, as follows:

```
document.body.appendChild(newelement);
```

But what good is a *p* element if it doesn't have any text? The *appendChild()* element can help there, too, in conjunction with the *createTextNode()* method as follows:

```
newelement.appendChild(document.createTextNode("Hello World"));
```

The entire three lines can be used any time after the body of the document has been declared. Here's the code in the context of a Web page, also found in the companion code as create.htm:

```
<!DOCTYPE HTML PUBLIC "-//W3C//DTD HTML 4.01//EN"
"http://www.w3.org/TR/html4/strict.dtd">
<html>
<head>
    <title>Create</title>

</head>
<body>
    <script type = "text/javascript" >
    var newelement = document.createElement("p");
    document.body.appendChild(newelement);
    newelement.appendChild(document.createTextNode("Hello World"));
    </script>
</body>
</html>
```

When viewed in a browser, the result is a simple *p* element containing the text "Hello World", as shown in Figure 10-7.

FIGURE 10-7 Using *createElement, createTextNode,* and *appendChild()* to create an element

Adding an Element and Setting an ID

The previous example simply showed how to add an element. When doing so, it's quite common to set some attributes, such as the ID for that element, as well. This code expands upon the previous example to add an *id* attribute (you can find this code in the companion code as createid.htm):

```
<!DOCTYPE HTML PUBLIC "-//W3C//DTD HTML 4.01//EN"
"http://www.w3.org/TR/html4/strict.dtd">
<html>
<head>
    <title>Create</title>

</head>
<body>
    <script type = "text/javascript" >
    var newelement = document.createElement("p");
    newelement.setAttribute("id","newelement");
    document.body.appendChild(newelement);
    newelement.appendChild(document.createTextNode("Hello World"));
    </script>
</body>
</html>
```

Deleting Elements

You can remove nodes from a document using the *removeChild()* method. This section offers an example of this procedure.

Recall the code from the previous section that was used to add an element. Expanding upon that by adding a few *p* elements will make it easier to work with the code in this example, so here goes:

```
<!DOCTYPE HTML PUBLIC "-//W3C//DTD HTML 4.01//EN"
"http://www.w3.org/TR/html4/strict.dtd">
<html>
<head>
    <title>Create</title>

</head>
<body>
    <script type = "text/javascript" >
    for (var i = 0; i < 3; i++) {
        var element = document.createElement("p");
        element.setAttribute("id","element" + i);
        document.body.appendChild(element);
        element.appendChild(document.createTextNode("Hello World, I'm Element " + i + "."));
    }
    </script>
</body>
</html>
```

When viewed in a Web browser, the document creates a page that looks like the one in Figure 10-8.

FIGURE 10-8 Creation of three elements using a *for* loop and the DOM

A few lines of code can now be added to remove one of the newly created elements. You can use *removeChild()* to remove any element from your documents, not just ones that you create. The two lines of code that will be added are:

```
var removeel = document.getElementById("element1");
document.body.removeChild(removeel);
```

For this example, we'll add the lines of code right after the code that creates the elements. In practice, you can place the call to *removeChild()* anywhere, so long as the element has already been created. Here's the final code with the new lines shown in bold type, which you can find within the companion code as removeel.htm:

```
<!DOCTYPE HTML PUBLIC "-//W3C//DTD HTML 4.01//EN"
"http://www.w3.org/TR/html4/strict.dtd">
<html>
<head>
    <title>Create</title>

</head>
<body>
    <script type = "text/javascript" >
    for (var i = 0; i < 3; i++) {
        var element = document.createElement("p");
        element.setAttribute("id","element" + i);
        document.body.appendChild(element);
        element.appendChild(document.createTextNode("Hello World, I'm Element " + i + "."));
    }
    var removeel = document.getElementById("element1");
    document.body.removeChild(removeel);
    </script>
</body>
</html>
```

Figure 10-9 shows the result. The elements are created, but then one is immediately removed.

FIGURE 10-9 Using *removeChild()* to remove an element from a document

Exercises

1. Create a document that contains a paragraph of text that is appended or created using the DOM. Create a link right after this paragraph, linking to the site of your choice, also using the DOM. Make sure that all elements have *id* attributes.

2. Create a document with any elements or use an existing HTML document that contains *id* attributes in its elements. Retrieve two of those elements, make changes to them, and put them back into the document. The type of change you make will depend on the type of element that you choose. For example, if it's an *a* element, you might change the *href*; if it's a *p* element, you might change the text.

3. Create a document using the DOM that contains a table with at least two columns and two rows. Add text within the *table* elements.

Part III

Integrating JavaScript into Design

Chapter 11
Using JavaScript with Web Forms

After reading this chapter, you'll be able to

- Understand how to validate the input to a Web form using JavaScript.

- Work with radio buttons, select boxes, and check boxes, both to get their values and set their state.

- Provide feedback based on validation, both through an *alert()* dialog box and inline within the document.

- Understand the limitations of JavaScript form validation and see an example of validation gone wrong.

JavaScript and Web Forms

JavaScript has been used with Web forms for a long time. JavaScript is commonly used to instantly verify that form fields have been filled in correctly before sending the form to the server. Prior to JavaScript, the form, and everything in it, needed to be sent to the server to make sure that all the required fields were filled in. Even with JavaScript, it is good—no, required—that you still validate on the server side just in case the user has JavaScript disabled or is purposefully doing something malicious.

Remember that *alert()* function that I've been using throughout the earlier chapters to show simple examples? It's back. The *alert()* function is heavily used with form validation, though newer techniques use the DOM (document object model) to display friendlier feedback.

A Web page with a basic form might look like the one in Figure 11-1.

When this form is submitted, the JavaScript code in the background checks to make sure that the Name text box has been filled in. When filled out correctly, with the name "Steve", for example, the page displays the name that was filled in, as shown in Figure 11-2.

When the Name text box is left empty, an *alert()* dialog box indicates that the field was required, as you can see in Figure 11-3.

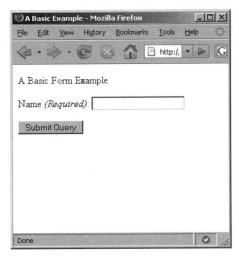

FIGURE 11-1 A basic Web form

FIGURE 11-2 When the Web form has been filled in correctly, the Name text box displays a greeting.

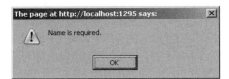

FIGURE 11-3 The form displays an alert when the Name text box is left empty.

The code to do all this is as follows, including the Hypertext Markup Language (HTML):

```
<!DOCTYPE HTML PUBLIC "-//W3C//DTD HTML 4.01//EN"
"http://www.w3.org/TR/html4/strict.dtd">
<html>
<head>
    <title>A Basic Example</title>
    <script type = "text/javascript" >
    function formValid() {
        if (document.forms[0].textname.value.length == 0) {
            alert("Name is required.");
            return false;
        } else {
            alert("Hello " + document.forms[0].textname.value);
            return true;
        }
```

```
    }
    </script>
</head>
<body>
<p>A Basic Form Example</p>
<form action="#" onsubmit="return formValid();">
<p>Name <em>(Required)</em>: <input id="textbox1" name="textname" type="text" /></p>
<p><input id="submitbutton1" type="submit" /></p>
</form>
</body>
</html>
```

The JavaScript within the *<head>* element defines a function called *formValid()* to process the input from the simple form. This code is

```
function formValid() {
    if (document.forms[0].textname.value.length == 0) {
        alert("Name is required.");
        return false;
    } else {
        alert("Hello " + document.forms[0].textname.value);
        return true;
    }
}
```

Within the *formValid()* function, an *if* conditional test uses the *document.forms[]* array. By examining the first index value (0) of that array, the code finds the one and only form on this Web page. The conditional tests whether the length of the *textname.value* property on the form is 0. If it is, then an error is indicated using an *alert()* dialog box. If not, then whatever is in the *textname.value* property is displayed.

The return value is important. When the *onsubmit* or *onclick* event handlers are called and return *false*, the form submission process is stopped. This is why it's important to return *false* if validation fails. Event handling is discussed more in Chapter 14, "Browsers and JavaScript." Note that using *onsubmit* is preferred for validation purposes, as is explained at the end of this chapter.

The example shown used the first index value of the *document.forms[]* list. This is fine if there's only one form on the page. You'll frequently see the form being accessed through its name, and this is shown in the next section.

Obtaining Form Data

Before you can provide feedback based on the form data, you have to get access to it. The previous example showed how to access the form data by using the *document.forms[]* array. This section shows a different method for doing the same, by using the name of the form instead of its index.

Like other elements of an HTML page, the *id* attribute can be set for a form. Here's the previous example with an *id* attribute:

```
<form action="#" id="testform" onsubmit="return formValid();">
<p>Name <em>(Required)</em>: <input id="textbox1" name="textname" type="text" /></p>
<p><input id="submitbutton1" type="submit" /></p>
</form>
```

The form is then accessed using its name rather than its index, as follows:

```
document.forms["testform"]
```

In certain cases, you might not know the index value of the form being accessed. For example, if a form is dynamically created, the most consistent approach is simply to set the form's *id* and then access it through that *id*, rather than trying to figure out (or worse, guess) which index value the form really is within the document.

There's also a nonstandard way to access the form directly through the *document* object itself, like so:

```
document.testform
```

However, you should not use this direct method. It doesn't work consistently, and it's not that much more effort to type it correctly anyway, like this:

```
document.forms["testform"]
```

Working with Form Information

All elements of Web forms can be accessed through the DOM. The exact method for accessing each element differs depending on the type of element. For text boxes and select boxes (also known as drop-downs), the *value* property holds the text that the visitor enters. A different method is used to determine the state of radio buttons and check boxes, though, which this section will also show.

Working with Select Boxes

Select boxes hold groups of options. Here's an example of the HTML used to create a select box. Note that this example uses an event handler, which will be explained in Chapter 14.

```
<form id="starform" action="" onsubmit="return false;" >
Select A Constellation:
<select onchange="displayvalue() name="startype">
<option selected="selected"> </option>
<option value = "Aquila">Aquila</option>
<option value = "Centaurus">Centaurus</option>
```

```
<option value = "Canis Major">Canis Major</option>
<option value = "Canis Minor">Canis Minor</option>
<option value = "Corona Borealis">Corona Borealis</option>
<option value = "Crux">Crux</option>
<option value = "Cygnus">Cygnus</option>
<option value = "Gemini">Gemini</option>
<option value = "Lyra">Lyra</option>
<option value = "Orion">Orion</option>
<option value = "Taurus">Taurus</option>
<option value = "Ursa Major">Ursa Major</option>
<option value = "Ursa Minor">Ursa Minor</option>
</select>
</form>
```

This code produces a select box like the one shown in Figure 11-4.

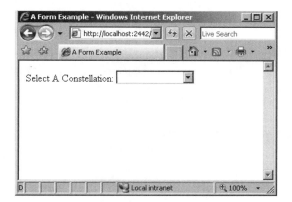

FIGURE 11-4 A select box based on the HTML example

When the user selects an option and submits the form, the value is set to the value of the particular option chosen. For this example, the select box named *startype* holds in its *value* property whatever the visitor chooses. You can access this property as follows:

```
document.forms["starform"].startype.value
```

For this particular example, the select box contains an *onchange* event. The *onchange* event, which you'll find out more about in Chapter 14, causes a function to be called every time a change is noticed within the select box, such as when the user selects an option through the drop-down. In this case, the function is a user-defined function called *displayvalue()*, shown in Listing 11-1.

LISTING 11-1 The Function Called When the Form's *Onchange* Event Is Fired

```
function displayvalue(){
    var selected = document.forms["starform"].startype.value;
    alert("You selected " + selected);
}
```

This bit of JavaScript simply shows the value that's selected from the drop-down. For example, choosing Ursa Minor from the drop-down causes the *alert()* dialog box in Figure 11-5 to be shown.

FIGURE 11-5 Choosing a constellation through a form and then sending an *alert()* dialog box

The HTML for the select box includes an *option* element named *selected*, which indicates which option is shown. In the example, an empty option is selected so that the initial value of the select box is blank:

```
<option selected="selected"> </option>
```

It's also possible through JavaScript and the DOM to choose which option should be selected. Usage of this feature is common on forms with multiple inputs, where one choice automatically leads to preselecting other options.

In the following scenario, we'll build a Web form that a pizza company might use to take orders. The company makes just a few special pizzas: one with vegetables, one with a variety of meats, and one that is Hawaiian style, with ham and pineapple toppings. The company would like a Web page with three buttons to help their pizza makers. The buttons will preselect the main topping on the pizza.

Selecting an option with JavaScript

1. Using Microsoft Visual Studio, Eclipse, or another editor, edit the file pizza.htm in the Chapter11 sample files folder.

2. Within the page, add the code shown below in bold type:

```
<!DOCTYPE HTML PUBLIC "-//W3C//DTD HTML 4.01//EN"
"http://www.w3.org/TR/html4/strict.dtd">
<html>
<head>
    <title>Pizza</title>
    <script type = "text/javascript">
    function flip(pizzatype) {
        if (pizzatype.value == "Veggie Special") {
            document.forms["pizzaform"].topping.value = "veggies";
        } else if (pizzatype.value == "Meat Special") {
            document.forms["pizzaform"].topping.value = "meat";
        } else if (pizzatype.value == "Hawaiian") {
            document.forms["pizzaform"].topping.value = "hampineapple";
        }
    }
    </script>
```

```
</head>
<body>
<form id="pizzaform" action="#" onsubmit="return false;">
<p>
<input type="button" name="veggiespecial" onclick="flip(veggiespecial)"
  value="Veggie Special" />
<input type="button" onclick="flip(meatspecial)" name="meatspecial"
  value="Meat Special" />
<input type="button" onclick="flip(hawaiian)" name="hawaiian"
  value="Hawaiian" />
</p>
Main Topping: <select name="topping">
<option value="cheese" selected="selected">Cheese</option>
<option value="veggies">Veggies</option>
<option value="meat">Meat</option>
<option value="hampineapple">Ham & Pineapples</option>
</select>
</form>
</body>
</html>
```

3. View the page within a Web browser. You'll get a page like this:

4. Choose one of the buttons. (Notice that the select box for Main Topping changes accordingly.)

The heart of the example is the *flip()* function:

```
function flip(pizzatype) {
    if (pizzatype.value == "Veggie Special") {
        document.forms["pizzaform"].topping.value = "veggies";
    } else if (pizzatype.value == "Meat Special") {
        document.forms["pizzaform"].topping.value = "meat";
    } else if (pizzatype.value == "Hawaiian") {
        document.forms["pizzaform"].topping.value = "hampineapple";
    }
}
```

Within this section, the value of the *pizzatype* variable that gets passed into the function is examined. Depending on the value of the *pizzatype* variable, the value of the select box called *topping* changes accordingly.

This example showed how to obtain information from a form and how to set information within a form. While the form doesn't look like much and the pizza company isn't making many pizzas right now, it's growing due to the popularity of its pizzas. Future examples in this chapter will expand on this form.

Working with Check Boxes

The previous example showed select boxes, and you've also already seen text boxes. There's another type of box—check boxes, which allow the user to select multiple items. The pizza ordering scenario explored in the previous section will serve as a good example of this.

Recall that in the initial pizza ordering system, when the pizza order taker selected one of three pizza types, the "Main Topping" select box changed to reflect the main ingredient of the pizza. However, it would be nice to allow more flexibility and more pizza types.

Take a look at Figure 11-6, which shows a new pizza prep form. The order taker can now select from a variety of ingredients in any combination.

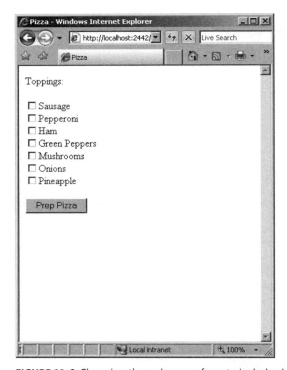

FIGURE 11-6 Changing the order prep form to include check boxes

Selecting the various ingredients and clicking the Prep Pizza button causes the pizza's toppings to be displayed on the screen, as shown in Figure 11-7.

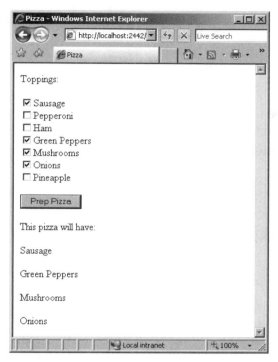

FIGURE 11-7 Ordering a pizza through the new form and adding elements with the DOM.

The code for this functionality is shown in Listing 11-2. Note that some lines continue onto the next line and in such cases, they are sometimes escaped with a backslash character (\).

LISTING 11-2 Using Check Boxes with the Order Form

```
<!DOCTYPE HTML PUBLIC "-//W3C//DTD HTML 4.01//EN"
"http://www.w3.org/TR/html4/strict.dtd">
<html>
<head>
    <title>Pizza</title>
    <script type = "text/javascript">
    function prepza() {
        var checkboxes = document.forms["pizzaform"].toppingcheck.length;
        var newelement = document.createElement("p");
        newelement.setAttribute("id","orderheading");
        document.body.appendChild(newelement);
        newelement.appendChild(document.createTextNode("This pizza will have:"));

        for (var i = 0; i < checkboxes; i++) {
            if (document.forms["pizzaform"].toppingcheck[i].checked) {
                var newelement = document.createElement("p");
```

```
                    newelement.setAttribute("id","newelement" + i);
                    document.body.appendChild(newelement);
                    newelement.appendChild(document.createTextNode( \
                            document.forms["pizzaform"].toppingcheck[i].value));
                }
            }
        }
    </script>
</head>
<body>
<form id="pizzaform" action="#" onsubmit="return false;">
<p>Toppings:</p>
<input type="checkbox" id="topping1" value="Sausage" \
    name="toppingcheck" />Sausage<br/>
<input type="checkbox" id="topping2" value="Pepperoni" \
    name="toppingcheck" />Pepperoni<br/>
<input type="checkbox" id="topping3" value="Ham" \
    name="toppingcheck" />Ham<br/>
<input type="checkbox" id="topping4" value="Green Peppers" \
    name="toppingcheck" />Green Peppers<br/>
<input type="checkbox" id="topping5" value="Mushrooms" \
    name="toppingcheck" />Mushrooms<br/>
<input type="checkbox" id="topping6" value="Onions" \
    name="toppingcheck" />Onions<br/>
<input type="checkbox" id="topping7" value="Pineapple" \
    name="toppingcheck" />Pineapple<br/>

<p><input type="submit" id="formsubmit" \
    name="formsubmit" value="Prep Pizza" onclick="prepza();" /></p>
</form>
</body>
</html>
```

The heart of the page is the function *prepza()*. The first thing *prepza()* does is to gather the number of check boxes contained within the form "pizzaform". These are grouped together in the *toppingcheck* name, as follows:

```
var checkboxes = document.forms["pizzaform"].toppingcheck.length;
```

After setting up a *<p>* element with a heading, a *for* loop is created to walk through the check boxes. Each check box is examined to see if its checked property has been set:

```
if (document.forms["pizzaform"].toppingcheck[i].checked) {
```

If the check box's checked property has indeed been set, a new element is created and placed into the document. The result is the page you saw back in Figure 11-7. (You saw examples of how to create and append elements in Chapter 10, "The Document Object Model.")

Keep this example in mind because one of the exercises at the end of the chapter will ask you to combine this example with functionality to automatically select toppings when a button is pressed, like the select box example cited earlier.

Working with Radio Buttons

Radio buttons create a group of options, only one of which can be selected at any given time. In the context of our pizza restaurant example, visitors might use a radio button to select the type of crust for the pizza—thin, deep dish, or regular. Because a pizza can have only one kind of crust, this is the perfect place to use radio buttons. Adding radio buttons for the crust results in a page like that shown in Figure 11-8.

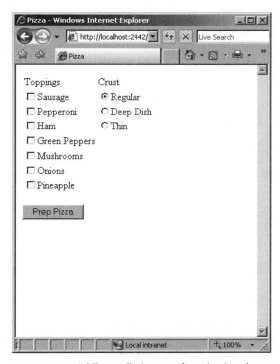

FIGURE 11-8 Adding radio buttons for selecting the crust type

The HTML that adds these radio buttons and a simple table looks like this:

```
<body>
<form id="pizzaform" action="#" onsubmit="return false;">
<table>
<tr><td>Toppings</td><td>Crust</td></tr>
<tr>
<td><input type="checkbox" id="topping1" value="Sausage" \
name="toppingcheck" />Sausage</td>
<td><input type="radio" name="crust" value="Regular" \
checked="checked" id="radio1" />Regular</td>
</tr>
<tr>
<td><input type="checkbox" id="topping2" value="Pepperoni" \
name="toppingcheck" />Pepperoni</td>
```

```
<td><input type="radio" name="crust" value="Deep Dish" \
id="radio2" />Deep Dish</td>
</tr>
<tr>
<td><input type="checkbox" id="topping3" value="Ham" \
name="toppingcheck" />Ham</td>
<td><input type="radio" name="crust" value="Thin" id="radio3" />Thin</td>
</tr>
<tr>
<td><input type="checkbox" id="topping4" value="Green Peppers" \
name="toppingcheck" />Green Peppers</td>
<td></td>
</tr>
<tr>
<td><input type="checkbox" id="topping5" value="Mushrooms" \
name="toppingcheck" />Mushrooms</td>
<td></td>
</tr>
<tr>
<td><input type="checkbox" id="topping6" value="Onions" \
name="toppingcheck" />Onions</td>
<td></td>
</tr>
<tr>
<td><input type="checkbox" id="topping7" value="Pineapple" \
name="toppingcheck" />Pineapple</td>
<td></td>
</tr>
</table>
<p><input type="submit" id="formsubmit" name="formsubmit" \
value="Prep Pizza" onclick="prepza();" /></p>
</form>
</body>
```

The code for processing radio buttons is similar to that for check boxes. The main difference is that radio buttons all share the same name and logical grouping, meaning that they are grouped together and only one can be checked at a time. The code for processing the radio buttons is added to the *prepza()* function, like this:

```
var crusttype = document.forms["pizzaform"].crust;
var crustlength = crusttype.length;
for (var c = 0; c < crustlength; c++) {
    if (crusttype[c].checked) {
        var newelement = document.createElement("p");
        newelement.setAttribute("id","crustelement" + i);
        document.body.appendChild(newelement);
        newelement.appendChild(document.createTextNode(crusttype[c].value + " Crust"));
    }
}
```

Prevalidating Form Data

JavaScript is frequently used to validate that a given form field is filled in correctly. You saw an example of this behavior earlier in this chapter, when a form asked you to fill in a name. If you didn't put anything in the field, then an error appeared. JavaScript is good at prevalidating data to make sure that it reasonably resembles valid input. However, JavaScript is poor at actually validating the data that makes it to your server.

You should never, at any time, assume that what gets to the server is valid. I can't count the number of Web developers that I've heard say, "We have a JavaScript validation on the data, so we don't need to check it on the server." This couldn't be further from the truth. People can and do have JavaScript disabled in their browsers; and people also can send POST-formatted and GET-formatted data to the server-side program without having to follow the navigation. No matter how many client-side tricks you employ, they're just that—tricks. Someone will find a way around them.

The bottom line is that you can and should use JavaScript for prevalidation, a small sanity check that may be helpful to provide quick feedback to the visitor if your code notices something blatantly wrong with the input. But you *must* perform the actual validation of all input on the server side, after users have completely submitted their input.

This section looks at some ways to use JavaScript for prevalidation, but to frame that discussion, I'll illustrate the dangers of using JavaScript as the sole validator for your site.

Hacking JavaScript Validation

This section will use a server-side program to create a catalog order system with three simple elements: a product, a quantity, and a price. The items to be sold are blades of grass from my lawn. My area has had an extremely dry summer, so there's not much lawn left at this point—lots of weeds and sand, but not much of what I would call proper lawn. Because blades of grass from my lawn are so rare, orders will be limited to three blades per household, and the price will be high. I'll limit the order quantity by using some JavaScript code.

I've created a page to sell the blades of grass. When viewed in a browser, the page looks like Figure 11-9.

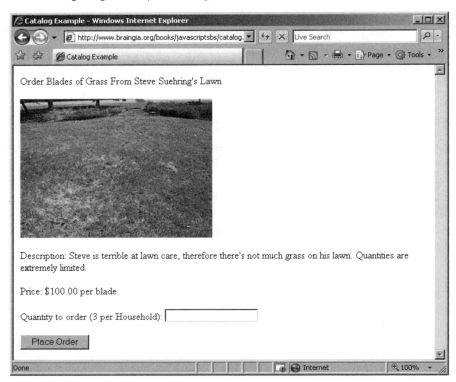

FIGURE 11-9 A small catalog order form

Here's the HTML and JavaScript to produce the page. Note the use of *document.forms* (shown in bold type) to access the quantity filled in within the form. Also, you won't be able to submit the form because the form action, catalog.php, doesn't actually exist. The action of the form isn't that important to this example.

```
<!DOCTYPE HTML PUBLIC "-//W3C//DTD HTML 4.01//EN"
"http://www.w3.org/TR/html4/strict.dtd">
<html>
<head>
<title>Catalog Example</title>
<script type = "text/javascript">
    function formValid() {
        if (document.forms["catalogform"]["quantity"].value > 3) {
            alert("Limit 3 per Household.");
            return false;
        } else {
            return true;
        }
    }
</script>
</head>
```

```
<body>
<form name="catalogform" id="catalogform" action="catalog.php" method="POST">
<p>Order Blades of Grass From Steve Suehring's Lawn</p>
<div id="lawndiv"><img alt="steve suehring's lawn is dead" src="lawn.png"
id="lawnpic"><br/></div>
<p>Description: Steve is terrible at lawn care, therefore there's not much
   grass on his lawn.  Quantities are extremely limited.</p>
<p>Price:  $100.00 per blade</p>
<p>Quantity to order (Limit 3 per Household): <input type="text" name="quantity"></p>
<p><input type="submit" onclick="return formValid();" value="Place Order"></p>
</form>
</body>
</html>
```

Note An improvement you could make to this validation would make sure that the visitor doesn't try to order less than one blade of grass, either!

With JavaScript enabled in my browser, the user's attempt to order a quantity of three or fewer blades of grass is acceptable and follows on through to the server-side script to handle the request and give me an order total, shown in Figure 11-10.

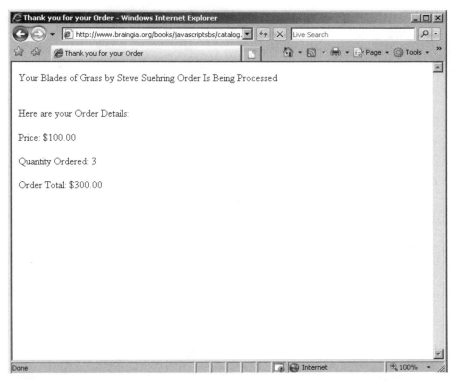

FIGURE 11-10 Ordering a quantity of three blades of grass or fewer gives the expected results, including an order total.

If the user goes back to the page, still with JavaScript enabled, and attempts to order a quantity of four blades of grass, she or he sees an *alert()* dialog box, like the one shown in Figure 11-11.

FIGURE 11-11 An error occurs through JavaScript when I attempt to order more than three blades.

Now imagine that I don't have JavaScript enabled in my browser. There's no noticeable change in the page when I go to the order form, so it looks exactly like the one in Figure 11-9. However, I'm now able to order a quantity of 1500. Simply entering 1500 into the quantity and clicking Place Order results in the server-side Web form happily receiving and processing the order, as shown in Figure 11-12.

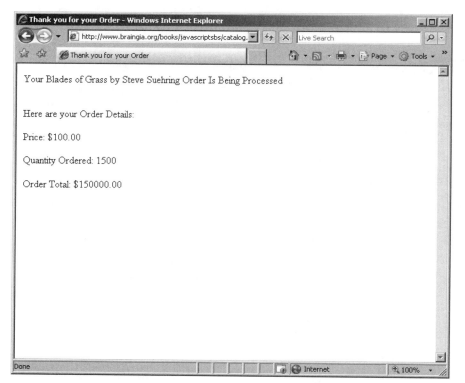

FIGURE 11-12 Because JavaScript was disabled, nothing validated this order before it hit the server.

Because there was no validation on the server side, this input was perfectly valid and the order would be processed. The only problem is that I don't have 1500 blades of grass on my lawn (I counted), so I can't possibly fulfill this order.

You might be tempted to dismiss this scenario as contrived, but it represents an all-too-common occurrence in Web applications. In fact, this example is relatively tame compared to some instances where a site will actually let the visitor change the price of an item during the ordering process and never bother to validate that input, simply "because no one will ever do that." Well, people have done that, and they will—if you don't stop them.

You might be tempted to try to solve the problem by requiring that all visitors have JavaScript enabled in their browsers before they can place an order. This doesn't work. You can attempt to figure out if JavaScript is enabled, but you can never be 100 percent certain.

The only correct way to solve this issue is to validate and enforce these rules on the server side. The back-end script should check the business rule of the quantity limitation. This won't be a problem the vast majority of the time, but it only takes that one time—and then I'd be outside trying to dig up 1500 blades of grass for my customers.

This section helped to show how easy it is to bypass JavaScript validation. The next section shows you how to use JavaScript for prevalidation. JavaScript should be used only for prevalidation and never as the sole means of ensuring that input is clean.

Validating a Text Field

Back in the beginning of this chapter, you saw an example of how to validate a text field. If the field wasn't filled in, an *alert()* dialog box appeared. I'll use this section to show how to provide feedback inline, next to the form field, rather than using an *alert()* dialog box.

Here's the code to achieve this:

```
<!DOCTYPE HTML PUBLIC "-//W3C//DTD HTML 4.01//EN"
"http://www.w3.org/TR/html4/strict.dtd">
<html>
<head>
<title>Catalog Example</title>
<script type = "text/javascript">
    function formValid() {
        if (document.forms["catalogform"]["quantity"].value > 3) {
            var submitbtn = document.forms["catalogform"]["submitbutton"];
            var quantityp = document.getElementById("quantityp");
            var errorel = document.createElement("span");
            errorel.appendChild(document.createTextNode(" Limit 3 per Household"));
            quantityp.appendChild(errorel);
            return false;
        } else {
            return true;
        }
    }
    document.forms["catalogform"].onsubmit = formValid();
</script>
</head>
<body>
<form name="catalogform" onsubmit="return formValid();" id="catalogform" \
```

```
    action="catalog.php" method="POST">
<p>Order Blades of Grass From Steve Suehring's Lawn</p>
<div id="lawndiv"><img alt="steve suehring's lawn is dead" src="lawn.png"
    id="lawnpic"><br/></div>
<p>Description: Steve is terrible at lawn care, therefore there's not much
    grass on his lawn.  Quantities are extremely limited.</p>
<p>Price:   $100.00 per blade</p>
<p id="quantityp">Quantity to order (Limit 3 per Household): <input type="text"
    name="quantity"></p>
<p id="submitp"><input id="submitbutton" type="submit" value="Place Order"></p>
</form>
</body>
</html>
```

Basically this code doesn't do anything that you haven't already seen, with one notable exception. Rather than using the *onclick* event, as in the previous example, this form uses the *onsubmit* event. Using the *onsubmit* event is preferred because it will fire regardless of whether the visitor clicks the Submit button or presses the Enter key on the keyboard. Welcome to JavaScript programming!

The code simply checks whether the form is valid. If the form is not valid, the code builds and appends an HTML span element with the text "Limit 3 per Household", as seen in Figure 11-13, rather than showing an *alert()* dialog box.

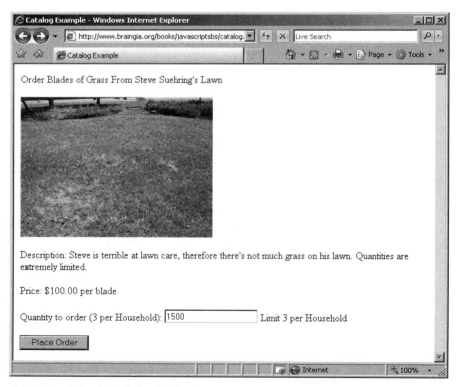

FIGURE 11-13 Providing inline feedback on a Web page rather than an *alert()* dialog box

Exercises

1. Create a Web form that displays an *alert()* dialog box based on a select box input type.

2. Add a set of radio buttons to the pizza form exercise seen earlier in this chapter to accept three pizza sizes: small, medium, and large. Display the results along with the result of the pizza order.

3. Redesign the pizza order system to add the buttons from the original pizza example, enabling the order taker to select the Veggie Special, Meat Special, or Hawaiian pizza types. These buttons should then select the correct topping check boxes for the special type of pizza to be made. For the Veggie Special pizza, select Green Peppers, Mushrooms, and Onions. For the Meat Special pizza, select Sausage, Pepperoni, and Ham; and for the Hawaiian pizza, select Pineapple and Ham.

Chapter 12
Creating and Consuming Cookies

After reading this chapter, you'll be able to

- Understand HTTP cookies.

- Create cookies with JavaScript and send them to the browser.

- Understand how to make a cookie expire in the future.

- Understand how to set the path and domain for a cookie.

- Read cookies from the browser and parse their contents.

A Look at Cookies

Hypertext Transfer Protocol (HTTP) cookies are bits of data that are sent back and forth between a client (usually a browser) and a server. They are used to keep track of everything from the state of an application (such as where you are in the application), to session information, to information about your visit such as your user ID (though there are plenty of reasons why you shouldn't store user IDs or any other personal information).

RFC 2965 describes HTTP cookies in some detail—perhaps even more than you'll want to know for now. You can see the RFC at http://www.rfc-editor.org/cgi-bin/rfcdoctype. pl?loc=RFC&letsgo=2965&type=ftp&file_format=txt.

Cookies and Privacy

For all the privacy problems that some may link to cookies, cookies themselves are in fact quite harmless. At best, they reside in random access memory (RAM) only for the length of time that the visitor keeps the browser open. At worst, they sit as text files on the visitor's hard drive.

Cookies invoke no privacy issues other than what might be stored within them. Yes, it's true that nothing stops Web site operators from storing data within a cookie that shouldn't be there. However, the Web site operator could store that data in other unsafe ways that have nothing to do with cookies. Cookies aren't the problem—the problem is the people who misuse cookies to store data that should otherwise be private.

With all that said, everything you store in a cookie is only as secure as the computer on which it is stored. So I would advise you never to store personally identifiable information within a cookie. Keep your visitors' data safe.

A cookie is usually nothing more than a text file—at least it's easiest and most convenient to think of cookies that way. Cookies contain a few different elements but at heart a cookie is a set of *name/value* pairs, many of which are set by the site operator or developer and are optional.

When visitors come to my Web site, *http://www.braingia.org/,* and go to the blog link, they might end up with a cookie on their computer. The contents of the cookie are something like this:

```
Name: cookie4blog
Content: sess_id02934235
Domain: www.braingia.org
Path: /
Send For: Any type of connection
Expires: Never
```

The browser stores the cookie on the visitor's computer until the cookie expires, which in this case is never. When a repeat visitor comes back to a site, the visitor's browser sends the cookie to the server. The server can then tell that the visitor has been there before and may use some personalized settings from the cookie to customize the visitor's experience.

One of the features of cookies is that they are sent only to servers on the domain for which they were set. So, the cookie shown above is sent by the browser to a server only when the domain the browser is trying to visit matches *www.braingia.org*. Further, a cookie can also have its *Secure* flag set (the one in the example does not). If the *Secure* flag is set, the cookie can only be sent over a Secure Sockets Layer (SSL)–enabled session, such as over a Hypertext Transfer Protocol Secure (HTTPS) connection.

Note Third-party cookies and the subtle ways someone can work around the domain limitation are beyond the scope of this book.

JavaScript can both create and read cookies. The remainder of this chapter looks at both functions.

Creating Cookies with JavaScript

You can use JavaScript to create cookies through the *document.cookie* interface. This section discusses how to create cookies and send them to the site visitor's browser.

Tip When working with cookies, it's important to use simple string values. Avoid spaces and punctuation or other nonalphanumeric characters as they are illegal. Illegal characters need to be escaped or they might cause problems for the cookie, the page, and the browser. And like other problems with JavaScript and Web programming in general, the problems might be subtle and generally difficult to troubleshoot. When in doubt, stick to alphanumerics and rest easier.

A Simple Cookie

At its simplest, a cookie needs a name. This bit of JavaScript creates a cookie and then sends it to the browser:

```
var cookName = "testcookie";
var cookVal = "testvalue";
var myCookie = cookName + "=" + cookVal;
document.cookie = myCookie;
```

When you visit a page with this bit of JavaScript, the JavaScript code sends a cookie named *testcookie* to your browser. The browser may alert you to this fact by displaying a dialog box like the one in Figure 12-1 from Microsoft Windows Internet Explorer. (If you don't see all of the details, click More Info to view the full dialog box.) Assuming that you allow the cookie, the browser then stores the cookie's data (*testvalue*) as well as other information about the cookie for future use.

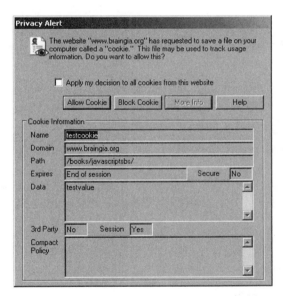

FIGURE 12-1 The privacy notice from Windows Internet Explorer shows the contents of the cookie being sent.

As you can see from the Privacy Alert dialog box, the cookie is being created with the cookie name (*testcookie*) and cookie data (*testvalue*) that were set in the JavaScript code. The values for *Domain, Path, Expires,* and *Secure* are all left at their defaults which depend on the page from which the cookie was sent, but they can be set through JavaScript as well.

When setting a cookie through JavaScript, it gets appended to the end of any existing cookies. This fact will make more sense when you start reading cookies. You should also understand that to specify attributes in a particular cookie, you must concatenate the attribute's *name/value* pair onto the cookie as you build it. The next example will help you to visualize this aspect of working with cookies in JavaScript.

Setting a Cookie's Expiration Date

The example shown earlier created a cookie by building a *name/value* pair, like so:

```
var myCookie = cookName + "=" + cookVal;
```

In essence, the code looks like this (this cookie has only the cookie name and cookie data set):

```
testcookie=testvalue;
```

To add an expiration date, the *expires* attribute needs to be added, so the cookie looks like this:

```
testcookie=testvalue; expires=Wed, 12 Mar 2008 17:51:50 GMT;
```

With this in mind, adding an expiration date is just a matter of concatenating the expiration date onto the end of the cookie to be sent. The format of the expiration date is important. Getting the date formatted correctly for the cookie is handled by a few different JavaScript functions. This is a good place for an exercise so you can practice creating a cookie with an expiration date.

Prior to beginning the exercise, it's a good idea to enable prompting for cookies. This action makes debugging much easier, since each time a cookie is sent to the browser, you'll get prompted, much like the Privacy Notice you saw in Figure 12-1.

In Windows Internet Explorer, select Internet Options from the Tools menu. In the Internet Options dialog box, click the Privacy tab and click Advanced. The Advanced Privacy Settings dialog box appears. Select the Override Automatic Cookie Handling check box. Change the settings for First-Party Cookies and Third-Party Cookies to Prompt, as shown in Figure 12-2, and click OK.

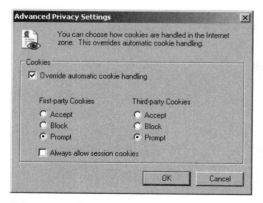

FIGURE 12-2 The advanced privacy settings shown here make troubleshooting cookies easier.

It's a little easier to change the settings in Firefox. In the Microsoft Windows version of Firefox, click Tools and then Options (in the Linux version of Firefox, click Edit and then Preferences). Then, in the Options dialog box, click the Privacy icon and then select Ask Me Every Time from the Keep Until drop-down list as shown in Figure 12-3.

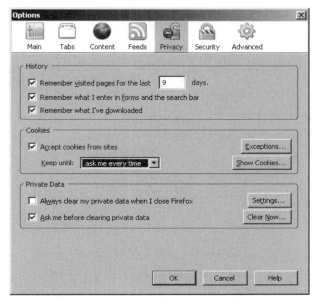

FIGURE 12-3 Changing cookie settings in Firefox

> **Tip** Don't forget to change these settings back to your normal settings when you're finished testing cookie-related issues. The constant prompting can get quite annoying with the number of cookies that most Web sites set.

Adding an expiration date to a cookie

1. Using Microsoft Visual Studio, Eclipse, or another editor, edit the file cookie-expire.htm in the Chapter12 sample files folder Web page called cookie-expire.htm.

2. Within the Web page, add the code shown below in bold type:

```
<!DOCTYPE HTML PUBLIC "-//W3C//DTD HTML 4.01//EN"
"http://www.w3.org/TR/html4/strict.dtd">
<html>
<head>
<title>Hello Cookie</title>
<script type = "text/javascript">
var cookName = "testcookie";
var cookVal = "testvalue";
var myCookie = cookName + "=" + cookVal;
```

```
document.cookie = myCookie;
</script>
</head>
<body>
<p>Hello</p>
</body>
</html>
```

3. View this page in a Web browser. You should receive a prompt like the one shown in Figure 12-1. Click Block (in Windows Internet Explorer) or Disallow (in Firefox) to make sure this cookie does not get saved by the browser. If you accidentally accept the cookie, close your browser and reopen it. Because this was a session cookie, it'll be cleared when you close the browser. Congratulations—you've used JavaScript code to send a cookie to the browser.

4. Modify the code to add lines for the date. This code should appear prior to the *myCookie* variable declaration, like this:

```
var date = new Date();
date.setTime(date.getTime()+604800000)
var expireDate = date.toGMTString();
```

5. Modify the *myCookie* variable declaration to include the new expiration elements:

```
var myCookie = cookName + "=" + cookVal + ";expires=" + expireDate;
```

6. The entire code should now look like this (the added lines are shown in bold type):

```
<!DOCTYPE HTML PUBLIC "-//W3C//DTD HTML 4.01//EN"
"http://www.w3.org/TR/html4/strict.dtd">
<html>
<head>
<title>Hello Cookie</title>
<script type = "text/javascript">
var cookName = "testcookie";
var cookVal = "testvalue";
var date = new Date();
date.setTime(date.getTime()+604800000)
var expireDate = date.toGMTString();
var myCookie = cookName + "=" + cookVal + ";expires=" + expireDate;
document.cookie = myCookie;
</script>
</head>
<body>
<p>Hello</p>
</body>
</html>
```

7. When viewed in a Web browser, the JavaScript code on the page will now send a cookie to the browser with an expiration date of exactly one week from the time of your visit. The Privacy Alert you'll see will look like the screenshot below.

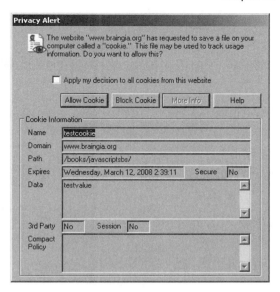

Four lines were added or modified within this exercise that enabled the cookie to have an expiration date rather than existing only for the term of the browser. The first three lines set the date. The first line creates a new date and places it in the *date* variable. Next, the date is set using the *setTime()* method. The parameter for the *setTime()* method is an expression that includes a call to *getTime()*. The *getTime()* method retrieves the current date in milliseconds since 1/1/1970. The value returned by *getTime()* represents the current date, so for the cookie to expire at some point in the future (a week in this case), I calculated the number of seconds in a week (604,800 to be exact) and then multiplied that by 1,000 to convert it to milliseconds. The resulting number (604,800,000) is then added to the *getTime()* value. Finally, this number is converted to a Greenwich Mean Time (GMT) string with the help of the *date* object's *toGMTString()* method.

The *expires* attribute is then appended to the cookie so that it looks like this:

```
testcookie=testvalue;expires=Wed, 12 Mar 2008 02:23:11 GMT
```

Setting the Cookie Path

In the examples shown so far, the JavaScript code will send the cookie to the browser only when the path for the HTTP request matches */books/javascriptsbs/* because that's where I've been serving the pages from for my environment. This path would likely be different in other cases. This path can be changed by adding another option onto the cookie when it's set. A more common scenario is just to set the path to / so that the cookie is available for all requests at the domain.

Like the *expires* option, setting the path means appending a *name/value* pair to the cookie.

Here's an example Web page like the ones shown so far in this chapter, including the previously added code to specify an expiration date and the new path option (shown in bold type):

```
<!DOCTYPE HTML PUBLIC "-//W3C//DTD HTML 4.01//EN"
"http://www.w3.org/TR/html4/strict.dtd">
<html>
<head>
<title>Hello Cookie</title>
<script type = "text/javascript">
var cookName = "testcookie";
var cookVal = "testvalue";
var date = new Date();
date.setTime(date.getTime()+604800000)
var expireDate = date.toGMTString();
var path = ";path=/";
var myCookie = cookName + "=" + cookVal + ";expires=" + expireDate + path;
document.cookie = myCookie;
</script>
</head>
<body>
<p>Hello</p>
</body>
</html>
```

One line was added for the path functionality. The *myCookie* variable was also changed to concatenate the new path variable. With this new code, the resulting cookie now essentially looks like this:

```
testcookie=testvalue;expires=Wed, 12 Mar 2008 02:23:11 GMT;path=/
```

When I view the page that creates this cookie, the Privacy Alert dialog box now looks like Figure 12-4.

Setting the Cookie Domain

Consider the examples shown so far where the *domain* attribute hasn't been set. The domain is by default set to the host and domain for the server that is sending the cookie to the browser (or for the server that sent the page in which the JavaScript code sends the cookie to the browser). In the examples, the domain has been *www.braingia.org*. However, many sites (including *braingia.org*) have multiple hosts from which HTTP content is served. For example, there might be an entirely separate server, maybe called *images.braingia.org*, that serves just the images on *braingia.org*'s pages. It would be nice if you could simply set the domain to *braingia.org* so that the same cookies could be shared across the entire domain.

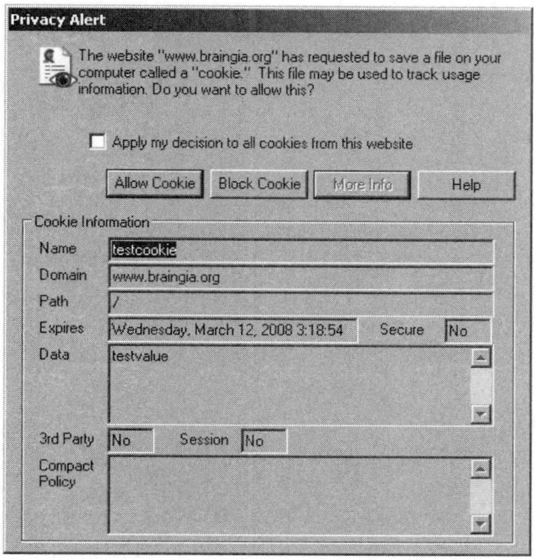

FIGURE 12-4 Setting the path within the cookie

If you think that setting the domain for the cookie is just like setting the path, you're right. Appending the domain option to the cookie will cause the domain to be set to a specific value. Here's an example Web page integrating the path, expiration date, and now the domain. The new code to specify the domain and append the *domain* attribute to the *myCookie* variable is shown in bold type:

```
<!DOCTYPE HTML PUBLIC "-//W3C//DTD HTML 4.01//EN"
"http://www.w3.org/TR/html4/strict.dtd">
<html>
<head>
<title>Hello Cookie</title>
<script type = "text/javascript">
var cookName = "testcookie";
var cookVal = "testvalue";
var date = new Date();
date.setTime(date.getTime()+604800000)
var expireDate = date.toGMTString();
var path = ";path=/";
var domain = ";domain=braingia.org";
var myCookie = cookName + "=" + cookVal + ";expires=" + expireDate + path + domain;
document.cookie = myCookie;
</script>
</head>
<body>
<p>Hello</p>
</body>
</html>
```

When the page is viewed in a browser, the Privacy Alert dialog box appears as shown in Figure 12-5.

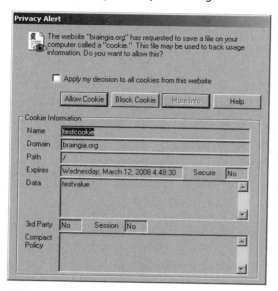

FIGURE 12-5 Setting the cookie's domain so it can be read from anywhere in the *braingia.org* domain

> **Tip** Just as you can make the domain less specific (like this example), you also could make it more specific, so that it might be read only by *images.braingia.org* or by *someotherspecificcomputer.braingia.org*. However, you cannot attempt to set a domain outside the one from which the content is being served. For example, I can't change the domain value to *microsoft.com* in this cookie. The browser will just ignore it.

Working with Secure Cookies

The *secure* flag set with a cookie indicates that the cookie will be sent only when the connection uses SSL, such as an HTTPS connection.

Adding the *secure* flag onto the *myCookie* variable that we've been using throughout the chapter looks like this:

```
var myCookie = cookName + "=" + cookVal + ";expires=" + expireDate + path + domain +
";secure";
```

When the page is viewed in a browser, even over an unencrypted HTTP connection, the JavaScript code sends the cookie, as indicated in the dialog box shown in Figure 12-6. Notice the Secure option value is now Yes, whereas in all the previous screenshots you've seen in this chapter, it's been No.

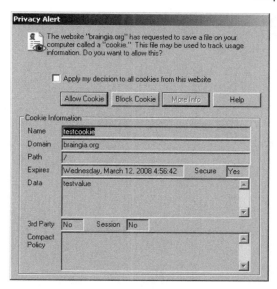

FIGURE 12-6 Setting a cookie's *secure* flag

We've now covered everything you need to know about setting cookies with JavaScript. It's finally time to learn how to read cookies with JavaScript.

Reading Cookies with JavaScript

Until now, we've been looking at code that sends a cookie to the browser when you visit a Web page. When the browser subsequently visits a page whose domain and path match cookies stored on the client computer, the browser sends any matching cookies to the server along with the request for the Web page. The cookie is available to the JavaScript code in the page when the page is delivered to the browser.

Reading cookies with JavaScript involves taking the cookies from the *document.cookie* object and then splitting them into manageable pieces. A call to the *split* method of *document.cookie* does the trick because cookies are delimited by semicolons, similar to the way in which a cookie's attributes are delimited as described in the previous section of the chapter. Here's an example:

```
var incCookies = document.cookie.split(";");
```

With this bit of JavaScript, all the cookies would be split up, waiting to be accessed. With the help of a *for* loop, you could loop through all the cookies available for the domain to find each one's cookie name and cookie data as follows. (Note that this code does not examine the attributes of each cookie other than the cookie name and cookie data.)

```
<!DOCTYPE HTML PUBLIC "-//W3C//DTD HTML 4.01//EN"
"http://www.w3.org/TR/html4/strict.dtd">
<html>
<head>
<title>Reading Cookie</title>
<script type = "text/javascript">
var incCookies = document.cookie.split(";");
for (var c = 0; c < incCookies.length; c++) {
    alert(incCookies[c]);
}
</script>
</head>
<body>
<p>Hello</p>
</body>
</html>
```

This code reads the available cookies for the domain into a variable called *incCookies*. The cookies are split at their semicolon delimiters. For example, I've set three cookies for the *braingia.org* domain. These can be read with the code listed above. The alerts are shown in Figures 12-7, 12-8, and 12-9.

FIGURE 12-7 The first cookie read by the loop

FIGURE 12-8 The second cookie read by the loop

FIGURE 12-9 The final cookie read by the loop

Using the *for* loop, it would then be possible to split the cookies along the equals sign (=) to further divide the cookie name from the cookie data, as in this code:

```
var incCookies = document.cookie.split(";");
for (var c = 0; c < incCookies.length; c++) {
    var pairs = incCookies[c].split("=");
    var cookieName = pairs[0];
    var cookieValue = pairs[1];
    alert("Name: " + cookieName + " - " + "Value: " + cookieValue);
}
```

In this code, each cookie, *incCookie[c]*, is split at the equals sign (=) and placed into a variable called *pairs*. The first index of the *pairs* variable is the name of the cookie; the second index is its data. Take a look at Figure 12-10 for an example of the output.

FIGURE 12-10 Splitting a *name/value* pair to separate the cookie name and cookie data

Removing Cookies

There's no built-in method for removing or deleting cookies, either through JavaScript or by any other means. To remove a cookie, simply blank out its value and set its expiration date to some time in the past.

A previous example used this code to create and set a cookie:

```
var cookName = "testcookie";
var cookVal = "testvalue";
var date = new Date();
date.setTime(date.getTime()+604800000)
var expireDate = date.toGMTString();
var path = ";path=/";
var domain = ";domain=braingia.org";
var myCookie = cookName + "=" + cookVal + ";expires=" + expireDate + path + domain;
document.cookie = myCookie;
```

To delete a cookie, set its expiration date to sometime in the past. Note that the components, such as *name, path,* and *domain,* must match in order for the cookie to be reset. In effect, you want to overwrite the existing cookie with a new one that expired in the past, as follows:

```
var cookName = "testcookie";
var cookVal = "";
var date = new Date();
date.setTime(date.getTime()-60)
```

```
var expireDate = date.toGMTString();
var path = ";path=/";
var domain = ";domain=braingia.org";
var myCookie = cookName + "=" + cookVal + ";expires=" + expireDate + path + domain;
document.cookie = myCookie;
```

This code causes the *testcookie* data to be set to an empty value and the expiration date to be set in the past.

Note When this JavaScript executes, the cookie is deleted immediately from Firefox. However, other browsers may keep the cookie until the browser closes.

Exercises

1. Create a Web page that sends a cookie to the browser. Set the expiration date ahead one day. Verify that the JavaScript code has sent the cookie to the browser, either by viewing it as it gets set or after it's been stored on the computer, possibly by using JavaScript or by viewing the cookies on the computer itself.

2. Create a Web page that sends a cookie, with the cookie's expiration date set ahead one week, and the *secure* flag set. This can be the same page that you created for Exercise 1, but be sure to give the cookie a different name so that you have created two separate cookies, one for each exercise. Also, be sure to enable the *secure* flag for this cookie, not the one from Exercise 1.

3. Create a Web page that attempts to read the cookie with the *secure* flag set. Did you receive the cookie? If not, what would you need to do to receive it?

4. Create a Web page that reads the cookie you created in Exercise 1. Use a *for* loop and an *if* conditional to display an *alert()* dialog box when the cookie with the correct name is found within the loop. Don't display an *alert()* dialog box for any other cookies.

Chapter 13
Working with Images in JavaScript

After reading this chapter, you'll be able to

- Understand both new and old methods for creating rollover images using JavaScript.

- Preload images using JavaScript.

- Create a slideshow of images.

- Enhance image maps using JavaScript.

Working with Image Rollovers

The term *image rollover* refers to changing an image when the mouse is moved over it, giving visual feedback to the visitor as to the location of the mouse on the screen. Though this technique has been largely supplanted by Cascading Style Sheets (CSS)–based solutions, you still can benefit from learning how it can be achieved using JavaScript.

Rollovers take advantage of certain events that relate to mouse movement on a computer. For rollovers, these primarily consist of *onmouseover* and *onmouseout*.

 Note Some of the examples in this chapter take advantage of the older, inline method of including *onmouseover* and *onmouseout* events right in with the Hypertext Markup Language (HTML). This method of coding is no longer recommended; these days, the separation of content from behavior is preferred instead. Therefore, I'll highlight newer ways to do things as well as the old, tried-and-true, works-almost-everywhere methods that have fallen out of favor with Web designers.

Additionally, the rollover effect can now be created, albeit with varying degrees of success, using CSS. This being a JavaScript book, I'm going to show only the JavaScript methods for creating rollovers.

A Simple Rollover

At its most basic, simply placing *onmouseover* and *onmouseout* event handlers within the *img* tag creates the rollover effect. The handlers display images that differ only slightly from each other.

The following HTML creates a rollover effect using the old model:

```
<img id="home" name="img_home" src="box1.png" alt="Home"
onmouseover="window.document.img_home.src='box2.png'"
onmouseout="window.document.img_home.src='box1.png'">
```

The important parts of this *img* tag are the name, *img_home,* and the *onmouseover* and *onmouseout* events. The name enables the image to be accessed easily through the *window.document* object call, and the *onmouseover* and *onmouseout* events make the magic happen. When viewed in a Web browser, the image called box1.png is loaded, as shown in Figure 13-1.

FIGURE 13-1 The initial load of the box1.png graphic through a Web page.

When the mouse is moved over the graphic, the *onmouseover* event is fired and the source of the graphic is changed to box2.png with this code:

```
window.document.img_home.src='box2.png'
```

While the mouse is over the graphic, the image changes to the one shown in Figure 13-2.

FIGURE 13-2 The graphic changes when the mouse moves over it.

When the mouse moves away from the graphic, the image changes back to box1.png, thanks to the *onmouseout* event, which calls this JavaScript:

```
window.document.img_home.src='box1.png'
```

The Better Way

The newer method for creating rollovers with JavaScript is to use the Document Object Model (DOM) along with the *onload* event of the *window* object. The *onload* event of the *window* object will be covered in further detail in Chapter 14, "Browsers and JavaScript." Using this model, when the *onload* event is called (at page load), a JavaScript function is called to populate the *onmouseover* and *onmouseout* events for all the images in the document.

Using the Better Way

Although I call this method "The Better Way," and it does accomplish the goal of unobtrusive scripting, it can be somewhat more cumbersome. It can also be slightly less compatible when used across various browsers and platforms.

The pragmatist in me wants to say that it's acceptable to use the example that was just shown, especially if your Web page has just a few graphics. On the other hand, I feel like I'm teaching bad methods if I tell you to use this older method. Therefore, I'll leave it up to you to choose which method works best for you. If you have a lot of graphics that will require the rollover effect, you'll find that this second method of using a generic function to handle the rollover events is easier to maintain.

The code that reproduces the same behavior as the previous examples is shown in Listing 13-1.

LISTING 13-1 A Different Approach to Rollovers

```
function rollover() {
    var images = document.getElementsByTagName("img");
    for (var i = 0; i < images.length; i++) {
        images[i].onmouseover = mouseOver;
        images[i].onmouseout = mouseOut;
    }
}
function mouseOver() {
    this.src = "box2.png";
}

function mouseOut() {
    this.src = "box1.png";
}
```

This code, coupled with an *onload* event handler in the <body> tag, creates a simple mouseover effect. Here's what the *<body>* tag looks like:

```
<body onload="rollover();">
```

Even though the functionality is the same, the code in Listing 13-1 is not very portable. We'll work to improve that shortly. For now, here's an explanation of the code as it exists in Listing 13-1.

The first thing accomplished within the function is to retrieve all of the *<img>* elements using the *getElementsByTagName()* method of the *document* object. These are placed into a variable called *images*. Next, the code iterates through the *images* variable, which is really a list of all the images in the document. Within the loop, the *onmouseover* and *onmouseout* events are set to a function.

Up until this point, the code is remarkably portable and we won't work too hard to improve it. However, it goes wrong within the functions themselves. Within the *mouseOver* and *mouseOut* event handlers, the *src* attributes are hard-coded to box1.png and box2.png. This is fine if all we have is one image and its accompanying rollover, as in this example. However, once you have a menu full of images, as you would have in the real world, this code breaks. In addition, the *this* keyword is quirky when it is called from another function related to event handling. Therefore, we need to improve the script.

This example code does show the theory of how to implement rollovers. Loop through the images (or retrieve them by ID) and set their *onmouseover* and *onmouseout* events to their own functions, which in turn should set the *src* attribute to the name of the image to use for that event. Now it's your turn to make the function more portable so that you can use it in the future.

This exercise uses six images (three graphics, each of which has a default and a rollover image), but is written to support any number of images. I've included the images used in this exercise on the CD with the book so that you don't have to reinvent the wheel just to make this exercise work!

Creating portable rollovers

1. Using Microsoft Visual Studio, Eclipse, or another editor, edit the file rollover.htm in the Chapter13\rollover sample files folder. This folder includes six images: home_default. png, home_over.png, about_default.png, about_over.png, blog_default.png, and blog_over.png.

2. Within the Web page, add the code shown below in bold type:

```
<!DOCTYPE HTML PUBLIC "-//W3C//DTD HTML 4.01//EN"
"http://www.w3.org/TR/html4/strict.dtd">
<html>
<head>
<title>Rollover</title>
<script type="text/javascript">
function rollover() {
    var images = document.getElementsByTagName("img");
```

```
        for (var i = 0; i < images.length; i++) {
            images[i].onmouseover = function() { this.src = this.id + "_over.png"; }
            images[i].onmouseout = function() { this.src = this.id + "_default.png"; }
        }
    }
    window.onload = rollover;
</script>
</head>
<body>
<p><img id="home" name="img_home" src="home_default.png" alt="Home"></p>
<p><img id="about" name="img_about" src="about_default.png" alt="About"></p>
<p><img id="blog" name="img_blog" src="blog_default.png" alt="Blog"></p>
</body>
</html>
```

3. View the page in a browser. You should see a page similar to this screenshot. If you run into problems, make sure that each of the images is located in the current directory, because that's where the *<img>* tag is looking for them.

4. Roll the mouse over the buttons one at a time. Each of them should change. Here's what the screen looks like when the mouse is over the "About" graphic:

This example shows a better rollover implementation. Like the previous example, this code creates a function and then calls it using the *window.onload* event. Also, like the previous example, this code gathers all the images into a variable called *images* and then loops through each one, adding an *onmouseover* and *onmouseout* event handler to each, as follows:

```
function rollover() {
    var images = document.getElementsByTagName("img");
    for (var i = 0; i < images.length; i++) {
        images[i].onmouseover = function() { this.src = this.id + "_over.png"; }
        images[i].onmouseout = function() { this.src = this.id + "_default.png"; }
    }
}
```

Where this example differs from Listing 13-1 is in the removal of the definitions of the *mouseOver()* and *mouseOut()* functions. With this example, each image's ID is gathered with a call to *this.id* within an anonymous function. That name is then concatenated with the string "_over.png" and "_default.png" for their respective functions.

The *this* keyword will work in these examples, but it can become quite problematic when using more advanced event handlers, as you'll see in Chapter 14. Different browsers point the *this* keyword to different things. So while it's OK to use the *this* keyword as shown (it gets the desired results in all major browsers), be aware that when more advanced event handling is necessary, you shouldn't use it.

It's important with this example to make sure that the filenames and ID attributes match. For example, here's one of the *<img>* tags from the example:

```
<p><img id="about" name="img_about" src="about_default.png" alt="About"></p>
```

Because the filenames are generated in the *onmouseover* and *onmouseout* event handlers based on the element ID's, the file names must be about_default.png and about_over.png for the About graphic, home_default.png and home_over.png for the Home graphic, and so on. That isn't to say that you can't use an entirely different naming convention—the important thing is that the naming convention that you use for your rollover graphics files must match what you have coded in the JavaScript.

Because the first thing that occurs within the *rollover()* function is that all the images on the page are gathered, there's a good chance that the *images* variable list will contain graphics and images that don't have a rollover action. Therefore, a further improvement on this script is to create a conditional to check whether or not the graphic should be a rollover. One of the simplest solutions is to refine the naming convention for rollover graphics to include the word *rollover* in the *<img>* tag's *id* attribute, like this:

```
<p><img id="rollover_about" name="img_about" src="about_default.png" alt="About"></p>
```

Then within the *mouseOver()* and *mouseOut()* functions, which are back because of the way that the *onload* event is called (within the body instead of within *window.onload*), the code checks if the *id* attribute contains the word *rollover*. If it does, then the code continues the rollover action; otherwise, it simply returns. Figure 13-3 shows an example page with four images, three of which have rollover behavior.

FIGURE 13-3 An example with only certain images being rollovers

When the mouse is moved over any of the top three images on the page, the rollover image loads. However, because the ID of the last image doesn't contain the word *rollover*, it doesn't get an *onmouseover* or *onmouseout* event handler. Here's the full code (but note that we still have a little more improvement to make with this script before it's done). This code is included in the sample files in the rollover regexp folder. Note that even though the *mouseOver()* and *mouseOut()* functions are contained in this example, there's no reason why the code couldn't use anonymous functions instead of the named functions as shown in the example.

```
<!DOCTYPE HTML PUBLIC "-//W3C//DTD HTML 4.01//EN"
"http://www.w3.org/TR/html4/strict.dtd">
<html>
<head>
<title>Rollover</title>
<script type="text/javascript">
function rollover() {
    var images = document.getElementsByTagName("img");
    for (var i = 0; i < images.length; i++) {
        images[i].onmouseover = mouseOver;
        images[i].onmouseout = mouseOut;
    }
}
function mouseOver() {
    var roll = new RegExp ("rollover");
    if (this.id.match(roll)) {
```

```
        this.src = this.id + "_over.png";
    } else {
        return;
    }
}

function mouseOut() {
    var roll = new RegExp ("rollover");
    if (this.id.match(roll)) {
        this.src = this.id + "_default.png";
    } else {
        return;
    }
}

</script>
</head>
<body onload="rollover();">
<p><img id="rollover_home" name="img_home" src="rollover_home_default.png"
alt="Home"></p>
<p><img id="rollover_about" name="img_about" src="rollover_about_default.png"
alt="About"></p>
<p><img id="rollover_blog" name="img_blog" src="rollover_blog_default.png"
alt="Blog"></p>
<p><img id="logo" name="img_logo" src="logo.png" alt="Braingia Logo"></p>
</body>
</html>
```

The differences between this code and the earlier code are slight and exist within the *mouseOver()* and *mouseOut()* custom functions. Within those functions, one of which is shown here as an example, a regular expression is built to look for the string *rollover*. This regular expression is then used with the *match()* method to determine if it occurs within the *this.id* attribute. If the string *rollover* appears within *this.id*, the rollover action is set, just as in the previous examples. If the string isn't found, then the function simply returns

```
function mouseOver() {
    var roll = new RegExp ("rollover");
    if (this.id.match(roll)) {
        this.src = this.id + "_over.png";
    } else {
        return;
    }
}
```

Preloading Images

You may have noticed an issue when you first began working with the rollover examples in the previous section. When the rollover image is first loaded, it can take a second to render. This delay occurs because the image has to be loaded through the Web server and network before it is displayed in the browser.

This isn't a huge issue—it's really more of an annoyance when using the application across a super-fast network connection. However in the real world, which is where most of your applications will likely reside, this lag is noticeable, especially for clients who may be running on slow dial-up connections. Luckily, you can preload the images using a bit of JavaScript. Doing so causes the image to load into the browser's cache and thus will be available almost immediately when the visitor moves the mouse over an image.

The basic premise behind preloading an image is to create an *image* object and then call the *src()* method on that object, pointing to the image you'd like to preload. What exactly you do with that object once you've called the *src()* method isn't important. JavaScript will make the call to that image asynchronously, so the rest of the script continues to execute while the image loads in the background.

The asynchronous nature of preloading does have an important implication when preloading multiple images: you must create a new *image* object for each image that you need to preload. If you have a batch of rollover images, as is often the case, each image needs its own object and *src()* method call. The final and best version of the rollover code incorporates preloading and also makes another slight optimization to call the *mouseOver()* and *mouseOut()* functions only when working with a rollover image. This is accomplished by moving the regular expression test into the main function. Listing 13-2 shows the rollover script along with the HTML page for context. This code is included in the sample files in the rollover regexp preload folder.

LISTING 13-2 Preloading and Rollovers

```html
<!DOCTYPE HTML PUBLIC "-//W3C//DTD HTML 4.01//EN"
"http://www.w3.org/TR/html4/strict.dtd">
<html>
<head>
<title>Rollover</title>
<script type="text/javascript">
function rollover() {
    var images = document.getElementsByTagName("img");
    var roll = new RegExp ("rollover");
    var preload = [];
    for (var i = 0; i < images.length; i++) {
        if (images[i].id.match(roll)) {
            preload[i] = new Image();
            preload[i].src = images[i].id + "_over.png";
            images[i].onmouseover = mouseOver;
            images[i].onmouseout = mouseOut;
        }
    }
}
function mouseOver() {
    this.src = this.id + "_over.png";
}

function mouseOut() {
```

```
    this.src = this.id + "_default.png";
}

</script>
</head>
<body onload="rollover();">
<p><img id="rollover_home" name="img_home" src="rollover_home_default.png"
alt="Home"></p>
<p><img id="rollover_about" name="img_about" src="rollover_about_default.png"
    alt="About"></p>
<p><img id="rollover_blog" name="img_blog" src="rollover_blog_default.png"
alt="Blog"></p>
<p><img id="logo" name="img_logo" src="logo.png" alt="Braingia Logo"></p>
</body>
</html>
```

Working with Slideshows

You can use JavaScript to create a slideshow effect where one image is swapped with
another within the browser window. Frequently, the slideshow is done on a timed basis,
where one image comes after another after a certain interval, maybe 5 seconds. A timed
version of a slideshow will be demonstrated in Chapter 14. The version covered here is a
visitor-controlled slideshow—that is, one where the visitor must click buttons to go forward
and backward through the images.

Creating the Show

There are actually several ways to implement slideshow-like functionality through JavaScript.
One method might use a *for* loop to iterate through the images (in fact, the timed slideshow
in Chapter 14 will do just that). Another slideshow variation, illustrated in this section,
features cleanliness and simplicity.

Truthfully, most slideshows are rather simple in design, though admittedly I've seen some
overly complex ones. Listing 13-3 shows the slideshow in its first version, with just forward
capability. I'll then discuss the major portions of the code in more detail.

LISTING 13-3 A Basic (but Slightly Incomplete) Slideshow

```
<!DOCTYPE HTML PUBLIC "-//W3C//DTD HTML 4.01//EN"
"http://www.w3.org/TR/html4/strict.dtd">
<html>
<head>
<title>Slideshow</title>
<script type="text/javascript">
var images = ['home_default.png','about_default.png','blog_default.png','logo.png'];
```

```
function nextimage() {
    var img = document.getElementById("slideimage");
    var imgname = img.name.split("_");
    var index = imgname[1];
    if (index == images.length - 1) {
        index = 0;
    } else {
        index++;
    }
    img.src = images[index];
    img.name = "image_" + index;
}

</script>
</head>
<body>
<p><img id="slideimage" name="image_0" src="home_default.png" alt="Home"></p>
<form name="slideform">
<input type = "button" id="nextbtn" value = "Next" onclick="nextimage()">
</form>
</body>
</html>
```

First, let's discuss the HTML portion of this code because we can do it rather quickly. Here it is:

```
<p><img id="slideimage" name="image_0" src="home_default.png" alt="Home"></p>
<form name="slideform">
<input type = "button" id="nextbtn" value = "Next" onclick="nextimage()">
</form>
```

In this code, an image is displayed and its ID and name are set to specific values that will be used later in the JavaScript. Next, a form button is shown with an *onclick* action set to the *nextimage()* function, which has been defined in JavaScript. That's all there is to the HTML portion of this slideshow.

The JavaScript portion of the code is as follows:

```
var images = ['home_default.png','about_default.png','blog_default.png','logo.png'];
function nextimage() {
    var img = document.getElementById("slideimage");
    var imgname = img.name.split("_");
    var index = imgname[1];
    if (index == images.length - 1) {
        index = 0;
    } else {
        index++;
    }
    img.src = images[index];
    img.name = "image_" + index;
}
```

Within the JavaScript, an array of images is created. These images just contain the names, so the image files must be located in the same directory as the JavaScript being executed. (If not, then the image filenames within this array would need to include the appropriate path.)

The function *nextimage()* is called when the Next button is clicked. Within this function, the actual image from the *<img>* HTML tag is retrieved, thanks to the DOM. Next, the *name* attribute of that image is split so that the function can obtain the number from the *name* attribute. This number is then placed into the *index* variable.

The next portion of the code performs a conditional test that checks whether the *index* value equals the length of the *images* array minus 1. If this condition is true, then we've reached the end of the slideshow, so we'll set the *index* value back to 0 and start over. If we've not yet reached the end of the available images for the slideshow, then the code simply increments the *index* value by 1.

The final two lines of JavaScript set the *src* attribute to the new image and set its name appropriately so that the next time the code goes through the function, the current index can be determined.

Moving Backward

You might think that adding a button to enable backward traversal through the slideshow should just be a matter of copying and pasting the code you just created to implement the Previous button's functionality. In most instances, you'd be right. However, there's the special case of trying to go backward from the first image. The need to contend with that scenario makes using a Previous button a bit more challenging.

This next exercise uses some of the graphics used for previous exercises and examples in this chapter. They may make the slideshow rather boring, so feel free to replace them with whatever other images you have handy. There's no special reason why I have four images for this example either, so feel free to use more. However, be sure to use at least three images so that you can fully test the backward and forward capabilities of JavaScript.

Creating the Previous button

1. Using Visual Studio, Eclipse, or another editor, edit the file slideshow.htm in the Chapter13\slideshow sample files folder.

2. Within that page, add the code shown below in bold type:

```
<!DOCTYPE HTML PUBLIC "-//W3C//DTD HTML 4.01//EN"
"http://www.w3.org/TR/html4/strict.dtd">

<html>
<head>
<title>Slideshow</title>
```

```
<script type="text/javascript">
var images = ['home_default.png','about_default.png','blog_default.png','logo.png'];
function nextimage() {
    var img = document.getElementById("slideimage");
    var imgname = img.name.split("_");
    var index = imgname[1];
    if (index == images.length - 1) {
        index = 0;
    } else {
        index++;
    }
    img.src = images[index];
    img.name = "image_" + index;
}

</script>
</head>
<body>
<p><img id="slideimage" name="image_0" src="home_default.png" alt="Home"></p>
<form name="slideform">
<input type = "button" id="nextbtn" value = "Next" onclick="nextimage()">
</form>
</body>
</html>
```

3. View the page in a Web browser. You should see a page like this:

4. Click Next to scroll through all the images. Notice that the slideshow will wrap back to the first image once it gets to the end.

5. Now alter the code to add a Previous button (the new code is shown in bold type):

```
<!DOCTYPE HTML PUBLIC "-//W3C//DTD HTML 4.01//EN"
"http://www.w3.org/TR/html4/strict.dtd">
<html>
<head>

<title>Slideshow</title>
<script type="text/javascript">
var images = ['home_default.png','about_default.png','blog_default.png','logo.png'];
function nextimage() {
    var img = document.getElementById("slideimage");
    var imgname = img.name.split("_");
    var index = imgname[1];
    if (index == images.length - 1) {
        index = 0;
    } else {
        index++;
    }
    img.src = images[index];
    img.name = "image_" + index;
}

function previmage() {
    var img = document.getElementById("slideimage");
    var imgname = img.name.split("_");
    var index = imgname[1];
    if (index == 0) {
        index = images.length - 1;
    } else {
        index--;
    }
    img.src = images[index];
    img.name = "image_" + index;
}


</script>
</head>
<body>
<p><img id="slideimage" name="image_0" src="home_default.png" alt="Home"></p>
<form name="slideform">
<input type = "button" id="prevbtn" value = "Previous" onclick="previmage()">
<input type = "button" id="nextbtn" value = "Next" onclick="nextimage()">
</form>
</body>
</html>
```

6. View the page in a browser again. You'll see that there's now a Previous button.

7. Test the functionality of the page by using both buttons in any combination to move backward and forward.

This code added a new button within the HTML for the Previous function:

```
<input type = "button" id="prevbtn" value = "Previous" onclick="previmage()">
```

The JavaScript added a new function called *previmage()* to go backward through the images:

```
function previmage() {
    var img = document.getElementById("slideimage");
    var imgname = img.name.split("_");
    var index = imgname[1];
    if (index == 0) {
        index = images.length - 1;
    } else {
        index--;
    }
    img.src = images[index];
    img.name = "image_" + index;
}
```

The code is strikingly similar to the *nextimage()* function, except for the conditional. If the index is 0, then we're at the first image and therefore the function needs to loop back to the last image. Otherwise, just go backward one index.

Working with Image Maps

Image maps are images that have certain areas defined to behave in a certain way, such as linking to another document. Image maps are frequently used in maps to pick out the country or region in which the visitor resides. They also are used within menus, though less so with the advent of CSS.

Unfortunately, I'm not nearly a good enough artist to draw a map of the Earth. Instead, I created a wildly out-of-scale representation of a small bit of the night sky facing north from 44.52 degrees North, -89.58 degrees West, during the summer months. This graphic is included within the code for this chapter and is called nightsky_map_default.gif.

Within the illustration shown in Figure 13-4, there are four constellations: Ursa Minor, Cepheus, Draco, and Cassiopeia.

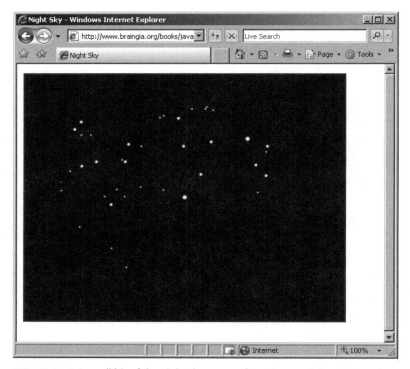

FIGURE 13-4 A small bit of the night sky as seen from Stevens Point, Wisconsin

I've made this graphic into an image map so that when visitors click any of the constellations, they're taken to the Wikipedia page about that constellation. The code for this image map is shown in Listing 13-4 (and is included in the sample files in the Chapter 13\nightsky folder).

LISTING 13-4 An Image Map for the Night Sky Graphic

```
<!DOCTYPE HTML PUBLIC "-//W3C//DTD HTML 4.01//EN"
"http://www.w3.org/TR/html4/strict.dtd">
<html>
<head>
<title>Night Sky</title>
<script type="text/javascript">
</script>
</head>
```

```
<body>
<p><img id="nightsky" name="nightsky" src="nightsky_map_default.gif" isMap useMap =
"#sky" alt="The Night Sky"></p>
<p><map name = "sky">
<area coords = "119,180,264,228" alt="Ursa Minor" shape="RECT"
 href="http://en.wikipedia.org/wiki/Ursa_Minor">
<area coords = "66,68,193,170" alt="Draco" shape="RECT"
 href="http://en.wikipedia.org/wiki/Draco">
<area coords = "36,170,115,246" alt="Draco" shape="RECT"
 href="http://en.wikipedia.org/wiki/Draco">
<area coords = "118,249,174,328" alt="Draco" shape="RECT"
 href="http://en.wikipedia.org/wiki/Draco">
<area coords = "201,47,298,175" alt="Draco" shape="RECT"
 href="http://en.wikipedia.org/wiki/Cepheus_(constellation)">
<area coords = "334,95,389,204" alt="Cassiopeia" shape="RECT"
 href="http://en.wikipedia.org/wiki/Cassiopeia_(constellation)">
</map></p>
</body>
</html>
```

This code creates a simple image map using pixel coordinates to create small rectangular shapes for each constellation and three rectangles to account for the constellation Draco's shape and tail. This code in and of itself is functional and creates a working image map. This map can be enhanced with JavaScript.

The *onmouseover* and *onmouseout* events are available for the *<area>* tag of image maps. Using these events and some JavaScript, you can improve the usability of the image map. For instance, when a visitor moves the mouse over one of the mapped areas, a new image could be loaded that highlights the constellation. This action is merely a variation of the image swapping seen earlier in the chapter. Listing 13-5 shows the code (which is also included in the sample files in the Chapter 13\nightsky folder).

LISTING 13-5 An Image Map with JavaScript Functionality

```
<!DOCTYPE HTML PUBLIC "-//W3C//DTD HTML 4.01//EN"
"http://www.w3.org/TR/html4/strict.dtd">
<html>
<head>
<title>Night Sky</title>
<script type="text/javascript">
function loadconst() {
    var areas = document.getElementsByTagName("area");
    for (var i = 0; i < areas.length; i++) {
        areas[i].onmouseover = mouseOver;
        areas[i].onmouseout = mouseOut;
    }
}
```

```
function mouseOver() {
    document.getElementById("nightsky").src = "nightsky_map_" + this.id + ".gif";
}

function mouseOut() {
    document.getElementById("nightsky").src = "nightsky_map_default.gif";
}

</script>
</head>
<body onload="loadconst()">
<p><img id="nightsky" name="nightsky" src="nightsky_map_default.gif" isMap useMap =
"#sky"
alt="The Night Sky"></p>
<p><map name = "sky">
<area id="ursaminor" coords="119,180,264,228" alt="Ursa Minor" shape="RECT"
 href="http://en.wikipedia.org/wiki/Ursa_Minor">
<area id="draco" coords="66,68,193,170" alt="Draco" shape="RECT"
 href="http://en.wikipedia.org/wiki/Draco">
<area id="draco" coords="36,170,115,246" alt="Draco" shape="RECT"
 href="http://en.wikipedia.org/wiki/Draco">
<area id="draco" coords="118,249,174,328" alt="Draco" shape="RECT"
 href="http://en.wikipedia.org/wiki/Draco">
<area id="cepheus" coords="201,47,298,175" alt="Draco" shape="RECT"
 href="http://en.wikipedia.org/wiki/Cepheus_(constellation)">
<area id="cassie" coords="334,95,389,204" alt="Cassiopeia" shape="RECT"
 href="http://en.wikipedia.org/wiki/Cassiopeia_(constellation)">
</map></p>
</body>
</html>
```

When the page is viewed in a Web browser, the visitor can move the mouse over each constellation and have its outline traced, as shown in Figure 13-5.

As indicated earlier, adding JavaScript to enhance the image map is really just a close offshoot of the rollover code used earlier in this chapter. One notable difference is the retrieval of the *<area>* elements rather than the *<img>* elements:

```
var areas = document.getElementsByTagName("area");
```

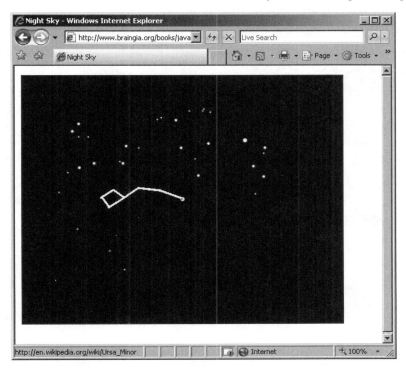

FIGURE 13-5 Adding JavaScript to the image map to implement a rollover

A second difference is how the *mouseOver()* and *mouseOut()* functions set the new image. In the previous rollover example, these were set using the *this* keyword. However, because there's only one image in the image map, that image's ID must be used to set the new *src* attribute. The rollover code achieves that for the *mouseOver()* function:

```
document.getElementById("nightsky").src = "nightsky_map_" + this.id + ".gif";
```

An obvious improvement to this script would be to preload all the rollover images for the image map. (You'll soon be doing this in one of the chapter exercises.)

> **Note**   The HTML used in this example isn't entirely valid according to the HTML 4.01 standard because the *<area>* tags for Draco all use the same *id* value. To make this HTML valid, each tag would need its own *id* value. However, this would complicate the JavaScript because each ID would need to be split or otherwise parsed to make sure that Draco's outline is loaded, or else three different images would need to be loaded or some other workaround found.

Exercises

1. Create a preloaded rollover image, making sure to keep the JavaScript functions separate from the HTML.

2. Look at the slideshow example from earlier in this chapter. When a visitor reaches the end of the slides, he or she is automatically taken back to the beginning, which might be confusing. Therefore, add a prompt to ask the visitor whether he or she would like to start over from the first slide when reaching the end. If the answer is "Yes," return to the beginning; otherwise, stay on the current image.

3. Using the image map example from this chapter (or an image map of your own if you prefer), preload all the images used within the image map so that they don't need to be downloaded when the visitor moves the mouse over the different areas of the map.

Chapter 14
Browsers and JavaScript

After reading this chapter, you'll be able to

- Understand the legacy event model.
- Understand the W3C JavaScript event model.
- Add event handlers to a Web page using JavaScript.
- Open new windows with JavaScript.
- Open new tabs in a Web browser.
- Create a timer using JavaScript.

Understanding Window Events

Event handling has been used a few times in earlier chapters to react to actions that a visitor might perform or that the document itself does when loaded. These events include the *onmouseover()* and *onmouseout()* events used in the previous chapter, along with the *onload()* and *onclick()* events used in other earlier chapters. These events match fairly well across all browsers, but you'll see that other events and event handling are less easy to implement. This section looks at events and their use in JavaScript programming.

The Event Models

The first challenge in understanding events is that there are two distinct models: the model used by Microsoft Windows Internet Explorer and the model defined by the World Wide Web Consortium (W3C). A third model, the legacy Document Object Model 0 (DOM 0) includes the events seen throughout earlier chapters. It is the most compatible model and is supported by all JavaScript-capable browsers. The competing W3C and Windows Internet Explorer event models will be discussed after a brief view of the DOM 0 event model.

Using the DOM 0 Model

The DOM 0 event model is by far the easiest and most compatible one to use for event handling in JavaScript. It is supported in all major Web browsers, and you've already seen in previous chapters how easy it is to work with.

So why not just use the DOM 0 event model everywhere? The reason is simple: it lacks the flexibility needed for more complex event handling. For example, the DOM 0 model can't handle multiple event actions on the same element. With that said, there's nothing wrong with using the legacy event model for simple scripts, as we've done throughout the book so far.

The DOM 0 event model includes several events that can be used on multiple Hypertext Markup Language (HTML) tags. Table 14-1 lists the event name along with its description.

TABLE 14-1 DOM 0 Events

Event Name	Description
onblur()	The element has lost focus (that is, it is not selected by the user).
onchange0	The element has either changed (such as by typing into a text field) or the element has lost focus.
onclick0	The mouse has been clicked on an element.
ondblclick()	The mouse has been double-clicked on an element.
onfocus()	The element has gotten focus.
onkeydown()	A keyboard key has been pressed down (as opposed to released) while the element has focus.
onkeypress()	A keyboard key has been pressed while the element has focus.
onkeyup()	A keyboard key has been released while the element has focus.
onload()	The element has loaded (document, frameset, or image).
onmousedown()	A mouse button has been pressed.
onmousemove()	The mouse has been moved.
onmouseout()	The mouse has been moved off of or away from an element.
onmouseover()	The mouse has moved over an element.
onmouseup()	A mouse button has been released.
onreset()	The form element has been reset, such as when a form reset button is pressed.
onresize()	The window's size has been changed.
onselect()	The text of a form element has been selected.
onsubmit()	The form has been submitted.
onunload()	The document or frameset has been unloaded.

Newer Event Models: W3C and Windows Internet Explorer

The W3C has codified an event model that enables powerful event handling. This model is supported by later versions of all major browsers with the notable exception of Windows Internet Explorer. Since the standard event model and the Windows Internet Explorer event model differ, you must account for each within any JavaScript that intends to use this event style instead of the DOM 0 event model.

Conceptually, both models are similar in the process of event handling. The first step with both models is to register the event. Once the event is registered and gets triggered, the event's function is called. However, the location at which the event occurred is an important area where the models differ.

To understand the difference in event location, picture a document with a *<body>* element and another element within the body, say an *<img>*. If a visitor moves the mouse over the image, should the *onmouseover()* event be handled first within the *<img>,* or should it be handled first in the *<body>*? It's exactly this difference in locating where the event should be processed that creates some divergence in the W3C and Windows Internet Explorer models.

The W3C model supports two forms for locating where the event should be handled: Event Capture and Event Bubbling. With Event Capture, the search for a handler begins at the top level and proceeds downward. In the example given in the last paragraph, handling an event would first be done by the *<body>* and then proceed to the *<img>* element. On the other hand, with Event Bubbling, the element in which the event occurred is searched first for a handler and then the search proceeds upwards from there.

As previously stated, the W3C model—and therefore all browsers that adhere to it (in other words, all browsers except Windows Internet Explorer)—can use both types of event handling techniques. You'll shortly see how. With Windows Internet Explorer, however, only Event Bubbling is used.

With the W3C model, event registration takes place using the *addEventListener()* method. With the Windows Internet Explorer model, *attachEvent()* is used for this purpose. In practical terms, this means that you'll need to use each method within every script you write that uses events, choosing at runtime the one appropriate for the browser in which the script is running.

The basic structure of the *addEventListener()* method is:

```
addEventListener(event,function,capture/bubble);
```

The capture/bubble parameter is a boolean value, where *true* indicates that the event should use top-down capturing and *false* indicates that the event should use bubbling. Here's a typical call to the *addEventListener()* method for a submit button, specifying a function named *myFunction()*, which would be defined elsewhere, and using top-down event capturing:

```
window.addEventListener("submit",myFunction(),true);
```

Performing that same thing using bubbling would be done like this:

```
window.addEventListener("submit",myFunction(),false);
```

The *attachEvent()* method used in the Windows Internet Explorer model doesn't require the third argument because there's no decision whether to use capturing or bubbling. It's all bubbling with the Windows Internet Explorer model.

Here's an example of calling *myFunction()* on the *submit* event using *attachEvent()*:

```
window.attachEvent("submit",myFunction());
```

You might've noticed a subtle difference in the name of the event to which the event handlers were added—*submit,* as opposed to *onsubmit* in the DOM Level 0 model. Many of the events in the DOM Level 2 have changed their names. The names of several DOM Level 0 events and their W3C DOM Level 2 counterparts are shown in Table 14-2. (The Windows Internet Explorer model uses the DOM 0 names.)

TABLE 14-2 DOM 0 and DOM Level 2 Events

DOM 0 Event	DOM 2 Event
onblur()	*blur*
onfocus()	*focus*
onchange()	*change*
onmouseover()	*mouseover*
onmouseout()	*mouseout*
onmousemove()	*mousemove*
onmousedown()	*mousedown*
onmouseup()	*mouseup*
onclick()	*click*
ondblclick()	*dblclick*
onkeydown()	*keydown*
onkeyup()	*keyup*
onkeypress()	*keypress*
onsubmit()	*submit*
onload()	*load*
onunload()	*unload*

Remember the rollover script from the previous chapter? Neither do I, so here it is again for reference:

```
<!DOCTYPE HTML PUBLIC "-//W3C//DTD HTML 4.01//EN" "http://www.w3.org/TR/html4/strict.dtd">
<html>
<head>
<title>Rollover</title>
<script type="text/javascript">
function rollover() {
var images = document.getElementsByTagName("img");
var roll = new RegExp ("rollover");
var preload = [];
for (var i = 0; i < images.length; i++) {
    if (images[i].id.match(roll)) {
        preload[i] = new Image();
        preload[i].src =  images[i].id + "_over.png";
        images[i].onmouseover = function() { this.src = this.id + "_over.png"; }
        images[i].onmouseout = function() { this.src = this.id + "_default.png"; }
    }
}
}
```

```
window.onload = rollover;
</script>
</head>
<body>
<p><img id="rollover_home" name="img_home" src="rollover_home_default.png"
alt="Home"></p>
<p><img id="rollover_about" name="img_about" src="rollover_about_default.png"
alt="About"></p>
<p><img id="rollover_blog" name="img_blog" src="rollover_blog_default.png"
alt="Blog"></p>
<p><img id="logo" name="img_logo" src="logo.png" alt="Braingia Logo"></p>
</body>
</html>
```

The script to create image rollovers, similar to Listing 13-2 in the previous chapter, uses DOM Level 0 to add functions directly to the *onmouseover* and *onmouseout* events. Altering this script to work with the newer DOM Level 2 event model means moving the location where you specify the event listener from the *<body>* element or the *window.onload()* event to a call to *addEventListener()* or *attachEvent()* (as appropriate). It also means getting rid of the *this* keyword, which just doesn't work in the newer model. Also changed are the *mouseover* and *mouseout* events. Listing 14-1 contains the new code.

LISTING 14-1 DOM Level 2 Event Handling Rollovers

```
<!DOCTYPE HTML PUBLIC "-//W3C//DTD HTML 4.01//EN"
"http://www.w3.org/TR/html4/strict.dtd">
<html>
<head>
<title>Rollover</title>
<script type="text/javascript">

function moveOver(imgObj) {
    if (typeof window.addEventListener != "undefined") {
        imgObj.addEventListener("mouseover",function(){imgObj.src = imgObj.id +
"_over.png";}, false);
        imgObj.addEventListener("mouseout", function(){imgObj.src = imgObj.id +
"_default.png";}, false);
    } else {
        imgObj.attachEvent("onmouseover",function(){imgObj.src = imgObj.id +
"_over.png";});
        imgObj.attachEvent("onmouseout", function(){imgObj.src = imgObj.id +
"_default.png";});
    }
}

function rollover() {
var images = document.getElementsByTagName("img");
var roll = new RegExp ("rollover");
var preload = [];
for (var i = 0; i < images.length; i++) {
    if (images[i].id.match(roll)) {
        preload[i] = new Image();
        preload[i].src =  images[i].id + "_over.png";
```

```
            moveOver(images[i]);
        }
    }
}
if (typeof window.addEventListener != "undefined") {
    window.addEventListener("load",rollover,false);
} else {
    window.attachEvent("onload",rollover)
}
</script>
</head>
<body>
<p><img id="rollover_home" name="img_home" src="rollover_home_default.png"
alt="Home"></p>
<p><img id="rollover_about" name="img_about" src="rollover_about_default.png"
alt="About"></p>
<p><img id="rollover_blog" name="img_blog" src="rollover_blog_default.png"
alt="Blog"></p>
<p><img id="logo" name="img_logo" src="logo.png" alt="Braingia Logo"></p>
</body>
</html>
```

The code in Listing 14-1 is strikingly similar to that of Listing 13-2. The notable changes are inside of the *for* loop, which now looks like this:

```
for (var i = 0; i < images.length; i++) {
    if (images[i].id.match(roll)) {
        preload[i] = new Image();
        preload[i].src = images[i].id + "_over.png";
        moveOver(images[i]);
    }
}
```

Inside the loop, the *images[i]* variable, representing the current image, is passed to a new function called *moveOver()*.

The *moveOver()* function accepts a single argument, the *image* object. Because the *this* keyword no longer can be used, the function must explicitly set its variables and attributes on each image object. Each of the events is also altered now to use *addEventListener()* or *attachEvent()* as appropriate for the browser. The function code looks like this:

```
function moveOver(imgObj) {
    if (typeof window.addEventListener != "undefined") {
        imgObj.addEventListener("mouseover",function(){imgObj.src = imgObj.id +
"_over.png";}, false);
        imgObj.addEventListener("mouseout", function(){imgObj.src = imgObj.id +
"_default.png";}, false);
    } else {
        imgObj.attachEvent("onmouseover",function(){imgObj.src = imgObj.id + "_over.png";});
```

```
        imgObj.attachEvent("onmouseout", function(){imgObj.src = imgObj.id + "_default.
png";});
    }
}
```

Of course, the biggest change to the script was to add event listeners for both the W3C and the Windows Internet Explorer model, *addEventListener()* for the W3C model and *attachEvent()* for the Windows Internet Explorer model, as follows:

```
if (typeof window.addEventListener != "undefined") {
    window.addEventListener("load",rollover,false);
} else {
    window.attachEvent("onload",rollover)
}
```

The *if* conditional first tests to see if there is a method of the *window* object called *addEventListener()*. If there is, then the *addEventListener()* method is invoked with three arguments, *load*, *rollover*, and *false*. The *load* argument indicates on which event the listener should be added; the second argument, *rollover*, indicates the function to be executed for the event listener; and the final argument, *false*, indicates that event bubbling should be used for this listener.

If there's no *addEventListener()* method of the window, then the *attachEvent()* method is used. This method receives two arguments: *onload()* for the event, and *rollover*, the name of the function to be called.

Both the W3C and Windows Internet Explorer models include methods for removing event listeners. With the W3C model, this method is called *removeEventListener()* and expects the same three arguments as *addEventListener()*:

```
removeEventListener(event,function,capture/bubble)
```

Removing the *load* event listener placed in Listing 14-1 would look like this:

```
removeEventListener("load",rollover,false);
```

The Windows Internet Explorer model uses *detachEvent()* for this same purpose:

```
detachEvent(event,function);
```

You also may find it necessary to stop event handling from propagating upward or downward after the initial event handler is executed. The *stopPropagation()* method is used for this purpose with the W3C model, while the *cancelBubble()* property is used to stop propagation with the Windows Internet Explorer model. You'll see an example of this behavior in the "Opening, Closing, and Resizing Windows" section later in this chapter.

A Generic Event Handler

Adding event listeners for each event that you need to handle would quickly become much too cumbersome for practical use. Therefore, it quickly becomes necessary to use a generic event handler for this purpose and couple it with the DOM's *getElementsByTagName()* method.

I had written a generic function for this purpose, but then I found an improved version written by John Resig. His original function and discussion can be seen at *http://ejohn. org/projects/flexible-javascript-events/*.

Throughout the remainder of this chapter, you'll see other examples of event handling properties and methods. Event handling is really part of the DOM and not of JavaScript. Therefore, you can find more information about events in DOM 2 at *http://www.w3.org/TR/ DOM-Level-2-Events/*. The Windows Internet Explorer event model is examined in *http:// msdn2.microsoft.com/en-us/library/ms533023.aspx*.

Detecting Things About the Visitor

JavaScript programming often requires browser detection—that is, detecting which browser a visitor to a Web site is using. Prior to the last few years, browser detection had largely been accomplished using the *userAgent* property of the *navigator* object. However, using the *userAgent* property is no longer recommended because visitors can so easily forge it and, in addition, it is incredibly difficult to maintain for every version of every browser.

I personally use five different browsers in various versions, and maintaining an up-to-date list of which browser supports which feature is too cumbersome even for just my browsers. Imagine what it's like trying to maintain JavaScript code that would account for every browser and every version of that browser within it! It's virtually impossible. And this doesn't even take into account when the browser sends a string that the visitor has completely made up (either for malicious or other purposes)!

With this in mind, I'm going to show the *userAgent* property only briefly and then show the newer and much better methods for determining if the JavaScript that you're using will work in the visitor's browser.

This section will also examine other properties of the *navigator* object that are indeed helpful, if not 100 percent reliable.

A Brief Look at the *userAgent* Property

The *userAgent* property is available as part of the *navigator* object and shows information about the user's browser. Within your browser, simply enter:

```
javascript:alert(navigator.userAgent);
```

If you're using Windows Internet Explorer 7, you might see an alert like the one in Figure 14-1.

FIGURE 14-1 The *userAgent* property of the *navigator* object

Other browsers will report themselves differently. For instance, a version of Firefox reports itself as:

```
Mozilla/5.0 (Windows; U; Windows NT 5.1; en-US; rv:1.8.1.7) Gecko/20070914 Firefox/2.0.0.7.
```

This string will change most of the time when a new version of a browser is released. If you tried to track each version of each browser that was released and then tried to track which version of each browser supported which feature of JavaScript, you'd be spending a lot of time (and possibly a lot of your employer's or client's time as well) maintaining that list.

A much better way to track what is and is not supported in the visitor's browser is a technique known as feature testing, discussed in the next section.

Feature Testing

Using feature testing, sometimes referred to as *object detection,* the JavaScript program attempts to detect whether a given feature is supported within the browser visiting the Web page.

Luckily, you don't have to test whether every function and method you want to use are supported in the visitor's browser. The DOM Level 0 model and other legacy functions of JavaScript are so widely supported and their cross-browser implementations are so close that testing for these features isn't necessary. However, the page still must test whether JavaScript is available, because not all browsers and not all visitors have JavaScript support.

The *typeof* operator is the primary mechanism to implement feature testing. In general terms, the code is used as follows:

```
if (typeof featureName != "undefined") {
    // Do Something Fun With That Feature
}
```

To test for the existence of the *getElementById()* method, which would indicate the availability of the more advanced DOM interface, this code might be used:

```
if (typeof document.getElementById != "undefined") {
    alert("getelembyid is supported");
```

```
} else {
    alert("no getelembyid support");
}
```

You may be tempted to skip the use of *typeof* within the test, and you may see examples on the Web where a feature test looks like this:

```
if (document.getElementById) { ... }
```

Unfortunately, this method of feature testing isn't as reliable as the *typeof* test. When *typeof* is not used, the method or property being tested might return *0* or *false* by default, which would make the test fail. Then it would appear that the browser doesn't support that method or property when it actually does. Therefore, testing using *typeof* is the safer, more reliable test.

Another way to accomplish this task that looks a bit cleaner uses the *ternary* operator to set a flag early in the code and use a standard *if* conditional later to check the flag, like so:

```
var getElem = (typeof document.getElementById == "function") ? true : false;
if (getElem) {
    // We know getElementById is supported,
    // so let's use it.
}
```

Keeping JavaScript Away from Older Browsers

One of the most discouraging problems I find when programming for the Web is the continuing presence of older browsers. It's becoming increasingly difficult to write Web pages that have any sort of modern look and feel and still display reasonably well in older browsers.

Backing up a bit, what defines an older browser? Ask three different Web designers and you'll likely get three different answers. To me, an older browser is one that is more than three years old, though I lean towards saying two years rather than three.

By my terms, then, Firefox 1.0 is an older browser, even though a Web page and almost every JavaScript code you'll write will probably display fine in that version of Firefox. A general rule that I've found is that any version of Internet Explorer or Netscape that is earlier than version 5 tends to have many, many quirks that a Web designer needs to take into account.

Considering the depressing fact that even older browsers than this are used sometimes, it's a good idea just to decide that your code might fail in these browsers, but you still can try to make it fail gracefully. However, even that may not always be possible.

I recently installed on my computer a copy of Netscape 3, which, if I remember correctly, was released in 1997. The browser had trouble with most JavaScript fed into it, and it also had problems displaying HTML and Cascading Style Sheets (CSS) on basic Web sites. This was to be expected because that version of Netscape was released well before many of the standards in use today were codified. The point is that no matter how hard you try, you'll likely never get your Web site to fail gracefully in really old versions of browsers. I recommend choosing a minimum browser level to support and designing for that target, keeping in mind that the later the minimum, the more visitors you'll be shutting out of the site. You want to strike a balance between being a welcoming site and being a cutting-edge site.

There are two primary techniques for keeping JavaScript away from older browsers: inserting HTML-style comments into the JavaScript and using the *<noscript> </noscript>* tags.

Using HTML comments around your JavaScript means surrounding them within *<!—* and *—>* marks, as in this example:

```
<script type = "text/javascript">
<!--Begin Comment
var helloelem = document.getElementById("hello");
alert(helloelem.innerHTML);
// End Comment-->
</script>
```

Unfortunately, not every browser will obey HTML comments, so you'll still see errors sometimes. It's becoming less and less common to see this style of commenting or protection in place. As the old browsers slowly get cycled out, this type of kludge isn't really necessary.

When you use the *<noscript> </noscript>* tag pair, whatever falls between the two tags will be displayed when no JavaScript support is detected in the browser.

Here's an example of *<noscript>*:

```
<noscript>
<p>This Web Page Requires JavaScript</p>
</noscript>
```

If visitors whose browsers don't accept JavaScript come to the Web page, they'll see whatever falls between the *<noscript> </noscript>* tag pair. In this example, it's the text "This Web Page Requires JavaScript". Note that execution or parsing of the remainder of the document does not stop at the end tag, so if you have other HTML within the page, it will still be displayed. This provides you with a good opportunity to fail gracefully by providing a text-only page or a site map link.

I recommend keeping the use of *<noscript>* to a minimum, and using it only for those applications where JavaScript is an absolute necessity, rather than when your JavaScript is just for providing behavioral aspects, such as rollovers. JavaScript can easily be overused and sometimes is used incorrectly, thus hindering the user experience rather than enhancing it. There's nothing worse than to have visitors come to your site only to have their browsers crash, lock up, or become otherwise unresponsive because of some unnecessary JavaScript widget.

> **Tip** Remember that there are several legitimate reasons why a visitor might not have JavaScript capability, not the least of which is that she or he is using an accessible browser or text reader. You should strive to allow text capabilities on your site and provide a site map for usability.

Other *navigator* Properties and Methods

The *navigator* object does provide some helpful information to the JavaScript programmer. Chapter 9, "The Browser Object Model," explored the *navigator* object in detail, including how to tell whether Java is enabled in the browser and showing all the properties of this object. Refer to Chapter 9 for this overview.

> **Note** Use the *navigator* object with caution. Sometimes what's reported using the *navigator* object might not be entirely accurate, or worse yet, the navigator object might not even be available at all if JavaScript isn't supported on the visitor's browser. So relying on it for the functionality of your page would definitely be a problem!

Opening, Closing, and Resizing Windows

One of the most maligned uses of JavaScript is its ability to open, close, and resize browser windows. The act of opening a browser window in response to or as part of the *onload* event was one of the most frequent and annoying things that Internet advertisers did (and still do). Browsers like Mozilla Firefox, Opera, and others give their users the ability to block all these annoyances by default without sacrificing usability. Internet Explorer 6 with Service Pack 2 and later has that capability as well.

I have yet to see an automatic pop-up window that actually enhances the usability of a Web site without being intrusive. If you believe that your site requires a component that opens a new window, I recommend rethinking the navigation before creating that component. Not only will your visitors thank you due to your site's simplified navigation and more intuitive use, but your site will tend to work better because it will rely less on JavaScript, which might be disabled.

With all that said, your visitors sometimes might want to open new windows in response to events like the click of a mouse. For example, clicking a link might open a small side window that allows visitors to choose an option from a menu or that displays Help text about the various options.

The *window* object contains several methods helpful for opening, closing, and resizing browser windows. The *open* method, as you might guess, is used to open a new browser window. The basic syntax of the *open()* method is:

```
window.open(url, name, features)
```

The *url* parameter is a string representing the Uniform Resource Locator (URL) to load. If this parameter is left blank, then the page "about:blank" is opened. The *name* parameter is a string representing the name of the window to open. If a window with the same name is already open, then the URL is opened in that named window; otherwise a new window opens.

The *features* parameter is a string of comma-separated options representing the various features that the new window will have, such as, the window's height, width, and whether it will have a scrollbar. Table 14-3 lists some of the features available.

TABLE 14-3 Features Used Within the *open()* method of the *window* object

Feature	Description
directories	Determines whether the personal toolbar or bookmarks toolbar will display in the new window. User-configurable in Firefox.
height	The height in pixels of the new window.
left	The location in pixels from the left edge of the screen where the new window should be placed.
location	Determines whether the location bar will be displayed. This is always displayed in Windows Internet Explorer 7 and can be changed to always be displayed in Firefox, so this option is slowly falling out of use.
menubar	Determines whether the menu bar will appear in the new window.
resizable	Determines whether the window will be resizable by the visitor. Firefox always allows the window to be resized for accessibility (and just general friendliness, too).
scrollbars	Determines whether scrollbars will be displayed.
status	Determines whether the status bar will be displayed in the new window. User-configurable in Firefox.
toolbar	Determines whether the toolbar will appear in the new window.
top	The location in pixels from the top edge of the screen where the new window should be placed.
width	The width in pixels of the new window.

This list is not all-inclusive, though, because browsers support different features and feature names. See *http://msdn2.microsoft.com/en-us/library/ms536651.aspx* for information on Windows Internet Explorer and *http://developer.mozilla.org/en/docs/DOM:window.open* for information on Firefox and the Mozilla family. Some browsers enable the user to control whether these options will have any effect. For example, attempting to hide the location bar from the new window will not work in Windows Internet Explorer 7 or in Firefox, depending on how the user has configured Firefox.

The *close()* method of the *window* object has no parameters. To use *close()*, simply call it like this:

```
window.close()
```

This method doesn't always work reliably, so you should never assume that the window was actually closed. At best you can hope it was.

Window Open and Close: In Action

I work with ICG Media, a Web consulting firm, and I've borrowed some of the code from their purchasing application for this example because it shows a good use of a small pop-up window.

One of the questions you must consider when purchasing dedicated hosting is which operating system to install for the customer. The customer has three choices of operating system: Debian Linux, Red Hat Enterprise Linux, and Windows Server 2003. Figure 14-2 shows what that option page looks like (minus the layout and other elements from the ICG Media Web site).

FIGURE 14-2 Options with a link to open a new window

When the "Which Should I Choose?" link is clicked, it opens a new window of a specific size that contains an explanation of each of the choices. This window is shown in Figure 14-3.

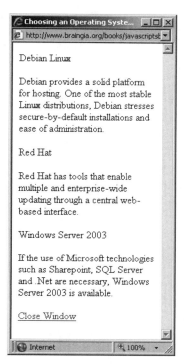

FIGURE 14-3 A new window provides extra information to help the visitor.

The code and markup for the main page is shown in Listing 14-2.

LISTING 14-2 Opening a New Window of a Specific Size

```
<!DOCTYPE HTML PUBLIC "-//W3C//DTD HTML 4.01 Transitional//EN"
"http://www.w3.org/TR/html4/loose.dtd">
<html>
<head>
<title>Options</title>
<script type="text/javascript">
function openwin(e) {
    if (typeof window.open != "undefined") {
        var opened = window.open("http://www.braingia.org/books/" +
            "javascriptsbs/code/c14/os-help.htm","",
            "menubar=no,location=no,toolbar=no,resizable=yes," +
            "scrollbars=yes,status=no,width=240,height=480");
        if (typeof e.preventDefault != "undefined") {
            e.preventDefault();
            e.stopPropagation();
        }
        e.cancelBubble = true;
        return false;
    } else {
        return true;
    }
}
```

```
</script>
</head>
<body>
<form name="option" action="#" method="post">
<p id="ms"><a target="help"
    href="http://www.braingia.org/books/javascriptsbs/code/c14/os-help.htm"
    id="os-helplink">Which Should I Choose?</a></p>
<div>
<input type="radio" name="radiooptions" id="radio1" value="debian">
Debian Linux 4 (Etch)<br/>
<input type="radio" name="radiooptions" id="radio2" value="rhel">
Red Hat Enterprise5<br/>
<input type="radio" name="radiooptions" id="radio3" value="win2003">
Microsoft WindowsServer 2003<br/>
</div>
</form>
<script type = "text/javascript">
var mslink = document.getElementById("os-helplink");
if (window.addEventListener) {
    mslink.addEventListener("click",openwin,false);
} else {
    mslink.attachEvent("onclick",openwin);
}
</script>
</body>
</html>
```

The code and markup for the newly opened explanation window is shown in Listing 14-3.

LISTING 14-3 JavaScript and Markup for the Small Window

```
<!DOCTYPE HTML PUBLIC "-//W3C//DTD HTML 4.01//EN"
"http://www.w3.org/TR/html4/strict.dtd">
<html>
<head>
<title>Choosing an Operating System for Hosting</title>
<script type="text/javascript">
function closewin(e) {
    if (typeof window.close != "undefined") {
        window.close();
    }
}
</script>
</head>
<body>
<div>Debian Linux</div>
<p>Debian provides a solid platform for hosting.  One of the most stable Linux
distributions,
Debian stresses secure-by-default installations and ease of administration.</p>
<div>Red Hat</div>
<p>Red Hat is a good choice for hosting with a Linux environment.  Red Hat has tools
that
```

```
enable multiple and enterprise-wide updating through a central web-based interface.</p>
<div>Windows Server 2003</div>
<p>If the use of Microsoft technologies such as Sharepoint, SQL Server and .Net are
necessary, Windows Server 2003 is available.</p>
<p><a href="#" id="closeme">Close Window</a></p>
<script type = "text/javascript">
var oslink = document.getElementById("closeme");
if (window.addEventListener) {
    oslink.addEventListener("click",closewin,false);
} else {
    oslink.attachEvent("onclick",closewin);
}
</script>
</body>
</html>
```

Let's examine the code in both of these listings.

A Closer Look at the Main Form Page

Listing 14-2 includes a portion of the application's Web form and, more importantly for this discussion, it includes an *<a>* element:

```
<a target="help"
    href="http://www.braingia.org/books/javascriptsbs/code/c14/os-help.htm"
    id="os helplink">Which Should I Choose?</a>
```

The *<a>* element includes a *target* attribute that notably isn't part of the HTML or Extensible Hypertext Markup Language (XHTML) specifications, which is why the DOCTYPE must be transitional for this document. This attribute enables the link to open a new tab in modern browsers. We'll look more at the *target* attribute later, but for now, let's work on JavaScript. As you can see from the *<a>* element, there is no event handler within it and there is also a legitimate *href* attribute. Both of these are important for usability and accessibility, especially when JavaScript isn't available in the visitor's browser.

Within Listing 14-2, the first portion of JavaScript within the *<head>* creates a function to open a new window, reproduced here for reference:

```
function openwin(e) {
    if (typeof window.open != "undefined") {
        var opened = window.open("http://www.braingia.org/books/" +
            "javascriptsbs/code/c14/os-help.htm","",
            "menubar=no,location=no,toolbar=no,resizable=yes," +
            "scrollbars=yes,status=no,width=240,height=480");
        if (typeof e.preventDefault != "undefined") {
            e.preventDefault();
            e.stopPropagation();
        }
```

```
        e.cancelBubble = true;
        return false;
    } else {
        return true;
    }
}
```

The function, called *openwin()*, accepts one argument, which will be the event. The first thing it does is to check whether *window.open()* is available. If it is, then the execution continues. If *window.open()* isn't available, then *true* is returned. The return value is ignored within DOM 2, but if *true* is returned, lower-level event handlers still can use it. In other words, if something goes wrong with DOM 2 event handling, the return value can allow the code to fail gracefully and the link will still work.

If *window.open()* is available, a new variable called *opened* is created and set to the return value from *window.open()*. The *window.open()* method is called with a specific URL that gives the location of the help file to be opened. No name is given to the new window. Finally, several features are requested with this new window, among them that the window should be resizable and have its scrollbars available. The window size is also set with the width and height options.

The window will be opened, but because the link contains an *href* attribute, it will be followed by the browser once it finishes processing the event. You'd like the function to be able to return *false* to prevent the default handling; but there are some conditions under which a browser will still follow the link. Therefore, to prevent both the new window and the existing window from ending up at the same URL, additional code is necessary. In effect, you must prevent the event handling from going further and prevent the default action from occurring. That's what the next portion of code within the *openwin()* function does:

```
if (typeof e.preventDefault != "undefined") {
    e.preventDefault();
    e.stopPropagation();
}
e.cancelBubble = true;
return false;
```

First, the code looks to see if a *preventDefault()* method of the current event is available. The existence of this method indicates that the browser supports the W3C model, and therefore it can be safely called to prevent the default action (sending the browser's current window to the href's URL). A call to *stopPropagation()* is also made to stop further event handling on the link.

If the *preventDefault()* method isn't available, then the browser is probably Windows Internet Explorer. Because *cancelBubble()* is safe to call with Windows Internet Explorer and other browsers, it gets called no matter what.

Finally, *true* is returned just in case none of these event handler methods is available, in which case the return value will cause the default action to occur.

> **Tip** Always include a valid *href* attribute in your links. This attribute will be used if JavaScript isn't available. Not only is its inclusion good practice, but it also enhances usability and accessibility of the page.

One last bit of JavaScript within the main page is located within the *<body>* of the page. That JavaScript adds an event listener to the *<a>* element:

```
var mslink = document.getElementById("os-helplink");
if (window.addEventListener) {
    mslink.addEventListener("click",openwin,false);
} else {
    mslink.attachEvent("onclick",openwin);
}
```

This code is the same format seen earlier in the chapter. This time, the *click()* (for W3C browsers like Firefox and Opera) and *onclick()* (for Windows Internet Explorer) events are used.

A Closer Look at the New Window

The new window contains mostly HTML, but it does contain one event within the Close Window link. That event handler is created with JavaScript in the *<body>*, as you've seen in other examples.

The main function to close the window is contained in this JavaScript:

```
function closewin(e) {
    if (typeof window.close != "undefined") {
        window.close();
    }
}
```

There's not much to this function that you haven't seen already. It is merely a call to *window. close()*, which accepts no arguments. The remainder of the code attempts to stop propagation of the event, which was discussed in the previous section and is of limited usefulness here anyway.

Window Opening Best Practices

While it's possible to open new windows with little more than the window frame, as seen in Figure 14-4, I recommend against doing so except in exceptional cases like the menu example.

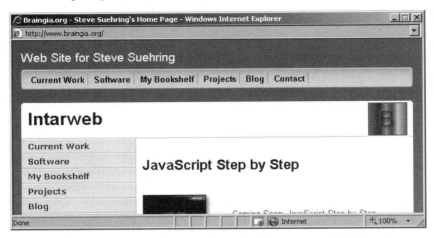

FIGURE 14-4 A window that does not have the menu bar or many of the other features expected in browser windows

Instead, any new windows opened should include the menus and navigational elements and the address bar. Firefox, and increasingly Windows Internet Explorer, don't allow JavaScript to disable things like resizing and the status bar and other user interface components. Those elements are important to enable the visitor to use the site and application in a way that works for them based on their needs rather than the developer's needs. Therefore, as a developer, you'll find it's best to include these and design the page and site in such a way that it won't be affected if user interface elements are used.

In fact, many times *window.open()* is no longer necessary. With the advent of tabbed browsing, *window.open()* has just about seen the end of its useful life. The upcoming section jumps well outside the realm of a JavaScript book to show how to open a new tab without any JavaScript.

No JavaScript Necessary?

Actually, no JavaScript is required to open a new tab, which is really what most developers are looking for anyway. The *target* attribute of *<a>* elements enables new tabs to be opened. Using the *target* attribute is recommended because it won't interfere with the visitor's experience in later browsers like Firefox and Windows Internet Explorer 7. You should be aware that the *target* attribute has been removed from the HTML and XHTML specifications, so any links using the *target* attribute will cause validation to fail unless you use a transitional DOCTYPE Definition, like this one:

```
<!DOCTYPE HTML PUBLIC "-//W3C//DTD HTML 4.01 Transitional//EN"
"http://www.w3.org/TR/html4/loose.dtd">
```

Here's an example of the *target* attribute in action:

```
<a target="Microsoft" href="http://www.microsoft.com" id="mslink">Go To Microsoft</a>
```

Resizing and Moving Windows

JavaScript also enables resizing of the browser window. However, browsers like Firefox include an option to prevent window resizing by JavaScript. For this reason I strongly recommend against resizing windows using JavaScript. It's fine to size them appropriately when opened with JavaScript, as shown earlier in the chapter, but resizing is unfriendly to the visitor and may cause accessibility problems. Therefore, I'll introduce you to the methods and properties only briefly. If you'd like more information on resizing or moving browser windows, refer to *http://support.microsoft.com/kb/287171*.

Chapter 9 included a section titled "Getting Information About the Screen," which showed properties of the window's *screen* object, including *availHeight* and *availWidth*. These properties are sometimes used to assist with changing the size of a browser window. Other helpful properties and methods in the *window* object related to resizing and moving windows are listed in Table 14-4.

TABLE 14-4 Select Properties and Methods Related to Moving and Resizing Windows

Property/Method	Description
moveBy(x,y)	Move the window by the amount of *x* and *y* in pixels
moveTo(x,y)	Move the window to the coordinates specified by *x* and *y*
resizeBy(x,y)	Resize the window by the amount of *x* and *y* in pixels
resizeTo(x,y)	Resize the window to the size specified by *x* and *y*

Timers

JavaScript includes functions called *timers* that (as you might guess) time events or delay execution of code by a given interval.

Four global functions are involved in JavaScript timers:

- setTimeout()
- clearTimeout()
- setInterval()
- clearInterval()

At their most basic, the two timer-related functions for setting the timer [*setTimeout()* and *setInterval()*] expect two arguments: the function to be called or executed, and the interval. With *setTimeout()*, the specified function will be called when the timer expires. With *setInterval()*, the specified function will be called each time the timer expires. The functions return an identifier that can be used to clear or stop the timer with the complementary *clearTimeout()* and *clearInterval()* functions.

Timer-related functions operate in milliseconds rather than seconds. Keep this in mind when using the functions. There's nothing worse than setting an interval of 1, expecting it to execute every second, only to find that it tries to execute 1,000 times a second.

> **Tip** One second is 1,000 milliseconds.

Listing 14-4 shows an example of the *setTimeout()* function set to show an alert after 8 seconds.

LISTING 14-4 An Example of *setTimeout()*

```
<!DOCTYPE HTML PUBLIC "-//W3C//DTD HTML 4.01//EN"
"http://www.w3.org/TR/html4/strict.dtd">
<html>
<head>
<title>timer</title>
<script type="text/javascript">
function sendAlert() {
    alert("Hello");
}
function startTimer() {
    var timerID = window.setTimeout(sendAlert,8000);
}
</script>
</head>
<body onload="startTimer();">
<p>Hello</p>
</body>
</html>
```

The example in Listing 14-4 includes two functions, *sendAlert()* and *startTimer()*. The *startTimer()* function is called with the *onload* event of the page and has one line, to add a *setTimeout()* function. The *setTimeout()* function in this case calls another function called *sendAlert()* after 8 seconds (8,000 milliseconds).

The *timerID* variable contains an internal resource that points to the *setTimeout()* function call. This *timerID* variable could be used to cancel the timer, like this:

```
cancelTimeout(timerID);
```

The *setTimeout()* function can accept raw JavaScript code rather than a function call. However, a function call is the recommended approach. Choosing to include raw JavaScript code rather than a function call can result in JavaScript errors in some browsers.

Exercises

1. Create a Web page that contains an *onclick* event handler connected to a link using a DOM 0 inline event. The event handler should display an alert stating "You Clicked Here".

2. Change the Web page created in Exercise 1 to use the newer style of event handling and connect the same *click/onclick* event to display the alert created in Exercise 1.

3. Create a Web page with a link to *http://www.microsoft.com*. Make that link open in a new tab.

4. Use the Web page created in Step 3 and create another link that opens a new window 250 pixels wide and 300 pixels high that links to *http://www.braingia.org/*.

Chapter 15
JavaScript and CSS

After reading this chapter, you'll be able to

- Understand the basics of Cascading Style Sheets (CSS).
- Understand the relationship between JavaScript and CSS.
- Use JavaScript to change the style of an individual element.
- Use JavaScript to change the style of a group of elements.
- Use JavaScript to provide visual feedback on a Web form using CSS.

What Is CSS?

Cascading Style Sheets (CSS) is a method for specifying the look and feel of a Web page. Items such as color, fonts, and layout can all be applied using CSS.

Figure 15-1 shows a basic Web page. It's fairly boring—or at least the layout is.

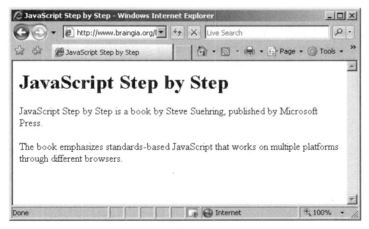

FIGURE 15-1 A basic Web page with no styles applied

Using CSS to add a bit of style enables the text of the page to change the font for the heading and adds some bolding to emphasize a particular portion of the text, as shown in Figure 15-2.

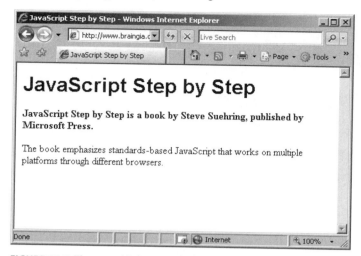

FIGURE 15-2 The same Web page from Figure 15-1 with CSS styles applied to it

Properties and Selectors

The basic structure for CSS is:

```
property: value
```

The *style* property is one of many different properties that can be set. In the example shown in Figure 15-2, the *style* property changed from Figure 15-2 is *font-weight* and the new value is *bold*. A full list of properties and their acceptable values is available on the World Wide Web Consortium (W3C) Web site at *http://www.w3.org/TR/CSS21/propidx.htm*.

CSS style properties are applied to document elements based on the type of element (*<p>*, *<h1>*, *<a>*, and so on), or the *class* or *id* attributes of the element. Collectively, these are known as *selectors*.

A selector tells CSS the element or elements to which the given properties and values will be applied. The basic structure for CSS statements with a selector is:

```
selector { property: value; }
```

For example, the code to apply the Arial font to all *<h1>* elements within the document looks like this:

```
h1 { font-familt: arial; }
```

Using the *class* or *id* attributes enables granular control over the display of elements within the document. For example, the document might have many *<p>* elements, but you want to give only certain *<p>* elements a bold font. Using a *class* attribute with the appropriate CSS gives the *<p>* elements of that class a bold font.

Even more granular control is available with the *id* attribute, which enables the specific element with that ID to have a style applied. This is the case for the example shown in Figure 15-2. Both the text "JavaScript Step by Step is a book by Steve Suehring, published by Microsoft Press" and the "The book emphasizes standards-based JavaScript that works on multiple platforms through different browsers" are enclosed within *<p>* elements. However, the first sentence is given an ID of *tagline*, which then enables it to be given a bold font through CSS.

Here's the Hypertext Markup Language (HTML):

```
<p id="tagline">JavaScript Step by Step is a book by Steve Suehring, published by Microsoft
Press.</p>
```

And the CSS:

```
#tagline { font-weight: bold; }
```

Applying CSS

Several methods exist for applying styles to a document using CSS. These include applying a style directly to an HTML element within the element itself, including a *<style>* element within the *<head>* portion of a document, or including the CSS from an external file, much the same way in which JavaScript is included from external files.

By far the best approach is to use an external CSS file just as the best practice with JavaScript is to use an external JavaScript file. Doing so promotes reusability and greatly simplifies ongoing maintenance of the site. Suppose that you manage a site with hundreds of pages and your boss calls telling you that the new design for the company now requires the font to change for page headings. If the site uses a common external CSS file, the change is quick and easy, and can be accomplished in only one place. If the CSS is contained in each document, then such a change becomes quite time-consuming.

There's much more to the subject of CSS than can really be covered in a JavaScript book. If you're unfamiliar with CSS and would like more information, it can be found at the "CSS Overviews and Tutorials" page on the Microsoft Web site (*http://msdn2.microsoft.com/en-us /library/ms531212.aspx*).

The Relationship Between JavaScript and CSS

JavaScript can manipulate many document styles dynamically. This is accomplished with DOM 2 (which you learned about in Chapter 14, "Browsers and JavaScript"). Using the Document Object Model (DOM) you retrieve an element by its tag name or ID and then set that element's *style* property.

For example, the heading from Figure 15-1 is contained in an *<h1>* element. Give that *<h1>* element an ID that is descriptive, like *heading*, and it can be retrieved using JavaScript's *getElementById()* method. The *style* object is JavaScript's way of altering the style of an element. Here's an example where the style is changed to use a different font:

```
var heading = document.getElementById("heading");
heading.style.fontFamily = "arial";
```

Setting Element Styles by ID

The example already shown in this section uses *getElementById()* and the *style* object to set the style for an element. This is an easy and effective way to change a style.

Styles are set individually using their JavaScript style name, which is usually similar to but not the same as its corresponding CSS property. The name of the JavaScript style property is generally the same as the official CSS style name when the property is a single word, such as *margin*. When the CSS property is a hyphenated word, such as *text-align*, it becomes *textAlign* in JavaScript. Notice the hyphen has been removed and the property now uses CamelCase (that is, separating words using uppercase letters).

Table 15-1 shows selected CSS properties and their JavaScript counterparts.

TABLE 15-1 **CSS and JavaScript Property Names Compared**

CSS Property	JavaScript Property
background	*background*
background-attachment	*backgroundAttachment*
background-color	*backgroundColor*
background-image	*backgroundImage*
background-repeat	*backgroundRepeat*
border	*border*
border-color	*borderColor*
color	*color*
font-family	*fontFamily*
font-size	*fontSize*
font-weight	*fontWeight*
height	*height*
left	*left*
list-style	*listStyle*
list-style-image	*listStyleImage*

TABLE 15-1 CSS and JavaScript Property Names Compared

CSS Property	JavaScript Property
margin	margin
margin-bottom	marginBottom
margin-left	marginLeft
margin-right	marginRight
margin-top	marginTop
padding	padding
padding-bottom	paddingBottom
padding-left	paddingLeft
padding-right	paddingRight
padding-top	paddingTop
position	position
float	styleFloat (in Windows Internet Explorer) cssFloat (in other browsers)
text-align	textAlign
top	top
visibility	visibility
width	width

One common use of JavaScript is form validation. Using CSS with JavaScript can provide visual feedback on the area of the form that is filled out incorrectly. The next exercise shows how this can be achieved.

Using CSS and JavaScript for form validation

1. Using Microsoft Visual Studio, Eclipse, or another editor, edit the file form.htm in the Chapter15 sample files folder.

2. Within that page, add the HTML shown below in bold type:

```
<!DOCTYPE HTML PUBLIC "-//W3C//DTD HTML 4.01//EN"
"http://www.w3.org/TR/html4/strict.dtd">
<html>
<head>
<title>Form Validation</title>
</head>
<body>
<form name="formexample" id="formexample" action="#">
<div id="citydiv">City: <input id="city" name="city"></div>
<div><input id="submit" type="submit"></div>
</form>
</body>
</html>
```

3. View the page in a Web browser. The page should look like this:

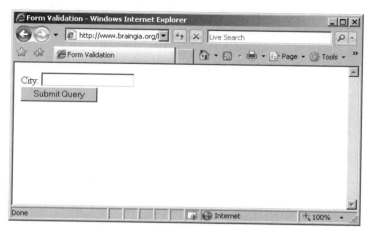

4. Next, create a JavaScript source file in the same location as you saved the form.htm file. Name the JavaScript source file form.js.

5. Within form.js, place the following code. If you like, you can change the value against which *cityField* is being validated to a city other than Stevens Point (my hometown). Save the file.

```
function checkValid() {
    var cityField = document.forms[0]["city"];
    if (cityField.value != "Stevens Point") {
        var cityDiv = document.getElementById("citydiv");
        cityDiv.style.fontWeight = "bold";
        return false;
    } else {
        return true;
    }
}
```

6. Finally, reopen form.htm and alter it to add a reference to the external JavaScript file and to add an *onload()* event to the document. The form.htm file should look like this (I've highlighted the changes in bold):

```
<!DOCTYPE HTML PUBLIC "-//W3C//DTD HTML 4.01//EN"
"http://www.w3.org/TR/html4/strict.dtd">
<html>
<head>
<title>Form Validation</title>
<script type="text/javascript" src="form.js"></script>
</head>
<body>
<form name="formexample" id="formexample" action="#">
<div id="citydiv">City: <input id="city" name="city"></div>
<div><input id="submit" type="submit"></div>
```

```
    </form>
    <script type="text/javascript">
        function init() {
            document.forms[0].onsubmit = function() { return checkValid(this) };
        }
        window.onload = init;
    </script>
    </body>
    </html>
```

7. Reload form.htm in your browser. Within the *City* text field, enter the word "test" and click Submit Query. You should immediately see the background of the text field change to red.

8. Now change the input for the *City* text field to "Stevens Point" (or whatever you used for the value in Step 5) and click Submit Query. The background will change and the field will empty. This is because the form will continue along its submission path, which in this case doesn't do anything.

The code used in this example is merely a variation on code used earlier in the book with the addition of an external JavaScript file to perform the validation and provide the feedback through CSS. Inside the external JavaScript file is the validation code, which first retrieves the *text field* object from the form. Next, this field is examined to see if its value matches "Stevens Point". If the value isn't "Stevens Point", the *font-weight* style property of the text field changes to bold.

Setting Element Styles by Type

While setting the style by ID as shown is already a common method for changing styles with JavaScript, you might also find it necessary to set properties on entire types of elements.

Recall the screenshots shown earlier in this chapter, Figure 15-2 in particular. The HTML for that page is shown in Listing 15-1.

LISTING 15-1 The HTML for Figure 15-2

```
<!DOCTYPE HTML PUBLIC "-//W3C//DTD HTML 4.01//EN"
"http://www.w3.org/TR/html4/strict.dtd">
<html>
<head>
<title>JavaScript Step by Step</title>
<style type="text/css">
h1 { font-familt: arial; }
#tagline { font-weight: bold; }
</style>
</head>
<body>
<h1 id="heading">JavaScript Step by Step</h1>
<p id="tagline">JavaScript Step by Step is a book by Steve Suehring,
```

```
published by Microsoft Press.</p>
<p>The book emphasizes standards-based JavaScript that works on multiple
platforms through different browsers.</p>
</body>
</html>
```

There are two *<p>* elements within Listing 15-1. The first *<p>* element has a style applied to it, *font-weight: bold*. JavaScript can be used to apply additional styles to all *<p>* elements. Consider the code in Listing 15-2, in which JavaScript code (shown in bold type) has been added to change the *<p>* element's font family.

LISTING 15-2 Using JavaScript plus HTML to Change Element Style

```
<!DOCTYPE HTML PUBLIC "-//W3C//DTD HTML 4.01//EN"
"http://www.w3.org/TR/html4/strict.dtd">
<html>
<head>
<title>JavaScript Step by Step</title>
<style type="text/css">
h1 { font-family: arial; }
#tagline { font-weight: bold; }
</style>
</head>
<body>
<h1 id="heading">JavaScript Step by Step</h1>
<p id="tagline">JavaScript Step by Step is a book by Steve Suehring, published by
Microsoft Press.</p>
<p>The book emphasizes standards-based JavaScript that works on multiple platforms
through different browsers.</p>
<script type="text/javascript">
var pElements = document.getElementsByTagName("p");
for (var i = 0; i < pElements.length; i++) {
    pElements[i].style.fontFamily = "arial";
}
</script>
</body>
</html>
```

When viewed in a Web browser, the result is that the two *<p>* elements will be Arial, as depicted in Figure 15-3.

The JavaScript used for this example is rather simple insofar as it uses things that you've already seen throughout the book. First, the *<p>* elements are retrieved using the DOM's *getElementsByTagName()* method. These are then placed into a variable called *pElements*. The *pElements* variable list is iterated using a *for* loop, and each of the elements has its *style. fontFamily* property changed to Arial.

FIGURE 15-3 Using JavaScript to change the font of several elements at once

Retrieving Element Styles with JavaScript

The existing styles applied to a given element are accessible using JavaScript. The method for retrieving the styles is different between Microsoft Windows Internet Explorer and other browsers.

Styles are retrieved using the *getComputedStyle()* method for W3C-compliant browsers and using the *currentStyle()* array for Windows Internet Explorer. The style retrieved is the final style applied, because it is rendered from all possible CSS locations, including external files and CSS styles applied within the document.

Listing 15-3 shows an example of retrieval of the computed CSS *color* property of an element with the ID of *heading*. In this example, the heading is an *<h1>* element:

```
<h1 style="font-family: arial; color: #0000FF;" id="heading">JavaScript Step by Step</h1>
```

In Listing 15-3 an *alert()* dialog box displays the result.

LISTING 15-3 Using JavaScript to Retrieve a CSS *color* Property

```
var heading = document.getElementById("heading");
if (typeof heading.currentStyle != "undefined") {
    var curStyle = heading.currentStyle.color;
else if (typeof window.getComputedStyle != "undefined") {
    var curStyle =
        document.defaultView.getComputedStyle(heading,null).getPropertyValue("color");
}
alert(curStyle);
```

When viewed through a Web browser, the *alert()* dialog box shown in Figure 15-4 is displayed. The *getComputedStyle()* method accepts two parameters, which are the element to retrieve and a pseudo-element. For most cases, you'll use only the element itself, as in the example, so the second parameter can be ignored and set to null, as in the example.

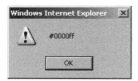

FIGURE 15-4 The currently applied style for an element

 Note Firefox returns *rgb(0, 0, 255)* for this same code to represent the *color* value.

Modifying Style Sheets with JavaScript

The examples given so far in this chapter show how to work with individual style elements through the *style* object. However, you might find that you want to alter the entire style applied to an element—in other words, alter the style sheet as it applies to an element or class of elements. Unfortunately, doing this isn't quite as easy as the previously shown methods for manipulating document styles.

The first hurdle is determining whether the visitor's browser supports retrieval of the existing styles at all. This task is accomplished by using *document.styleSheets*, as follows:

```
if (typeof document.styleSheets != "undefined") {
    // The browser supports retrieval of style sheets.
}
```

The *document.styleSheets* array contains the styles applied to a document, listed in the order applied. This means that external style sheets linked within the document are set in the order in which they appear in the document, beginning with the index 0. Consider this code:

```
<link rel="stylesheet" href="ex1.css" type="text/css" />
<link rel="stylesheet" href="ex2.css" type="text/css" />
```

These style sheets are indexed as *document.styleSheets[0]* and *document.styleSheets[1]*, respectively. Therefore, knowing the order in which style sheets appear in a document is important if you would like to retrieve the styles applied to a given element within the document.

After you've determined whether the browser supports the retrieval of existing styles, you need to overcome the differences between Windows Internet Explorer and W3C-compliant browsers.

Windows Internet Explorer retrieves the rules applied by the given style sheet using the *rules* array, whereas W3C-compliant browsers retrieve the rules using the *cssRules* array. Like the differences between browsers in the event model, you must code around the differences between these browsers in style sheet retrieval. Suppose you have a style rule like this:

```
h1 { font-family: arial; }
```

Listing 15-4 shows an example of retrieving the first style sheet from a document.

LISTING 15-4 Retrieving the Style Sheet Using JavaScript

```
if (typeof document.styleSheets != "undefined") {
    var stylerules;
    if (typeof document.styleSheets[0].rules != "undefined") {
        stylerules = document.styleSheets[0].rules;
    } else {
        stylerules = document.styleSheets[0].cssRules;
    }
}
```

The following code, coupled with Listing 15-4, changes the font of each of the specified elements within that CSS style sheet to a different font:

```
stylerules[0].style.fontFamily = "san-serif";
```

It's quite uncommon to change all the selectors within a style sheet to one setting, though. Therefore, looping through the style sheet to look for the specific selector is helpful, as shown in Listing 15-5.

LISTING 15-5 Looping Through Style Sheets to Find an <h1> Selector

```
for (var i = 0; i < stylerules.length; i++) {
    if (stylerules[i].selectorText.toLowerCase() == "h1") {
        stylerules[i].style.fontFamily = "san-serif";
    }
}
```

Here's a more complete example of this functionality. Assume a simple external CSS style sheet, called ex1.css, exists for this example:

```
h1 { font-family: arial; }
```

Listing 15-6 shows the HTML page that uses the ex1.css style sheet and another called ex2.css:

LISTING 15-6 Changing an Element Style Through the *styleSheets* Array

```
<!DOCTYPE HTML PUBLIC "-//W3C//DTD HTML 4.01//EN"
"http://www.w3.org/TR/html4/strict.dtd">
<html>
<head>
<title>JavaScript Step by Step</title>
<link rel="stylesheet" href="ex1.css" type="text/css" />
<link rel="stylesheet" href="ex2.css" type="text/css" />
<script type="text/javascript">
if (typeof document.styleSheets != "undefined") {
    var stylerules;
    if (typeof document.styleSheets[0].rules != "undefined") {
        stylerules = document.styleSheets[0].rules;
    } else {
        stylerules = document.styleSheets[0].cssRules;
    }

    for (var i = 0; i < stylerules.length; i++) {
        if (stylerules[i].selectorText.toLowerCase() == "h1") {
            stylerules[i].style.fontFamily = "san-serif";
        }
    }
}
</script>
</head>
<body>
<h1 id="heading">JavaScript Step by Step</h1>
<p id="tagline">JavaScript Step by Step is a book by Steve Suehring,
published by Microsoft Press.</p>
<p>The book emphasizes standards-based JavaScript that works on multiple
platforms through different browsers.</p>
</body>
</html>
```

When viewed in a Web browser, the page will show a heading styled with san-serif text. This text was changed with the JavaScript inside the *for* loop in Listing 15-6. The result of this code is seen in Figure 15-5.

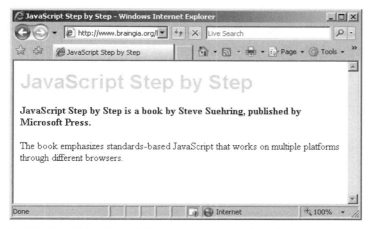

FIGURE 15-5 Using the *styleSheets* array to access the selector

Exercises

1. Create a basic HTML document that uses a style sheet, either within the document itself or through an external file. Make sure the page has at least two *<p>* elements and one *<h1>* element. Give each of the elements ID attributes.

2. Use JavaScript to alter the style of one of the *<p>* elements, changing its *color* property to blue.

3. Use JavaScript to alter the style of all the *<p>* elements to change their visibility to hidden (refer to Table 15-1 for assistance on the property for visibility).

4. Use JavaScript to retrieve the current style for the *<p>* element's visibility and display the current visibility setting using an *alert()* dialog box.

5. Create a Web form that accepts input from a text field. If the text field is not filled in, display an error on the page itself by creating and inserting an element using the DOM.

Chapter 16
JavaScript Error Handling

After reading this chapter, you'll be able to

- Understand error handling using JavaScript methods.

- Handle errors using *try/catch* statements.

- Use *try/catch/finally* statements.

- Handle the *onerror* event for *window* and *image* objects.

An Overview of Error Handling

This chapter looks at two primary, built-in ways of handling error conditions in JavaScript. The *try/catch* statement pair is available in JavaScript. Many languages, such as Microsoft Visual Basic .NET, include this pair of keywords that help the programmer handle error conditions within their code.

Along with *try/catch*, JavaScript offers the *onerror* event, which gives the programmer another tool to perform an action when encountering an error.

Using *try/catch*

The *try/catch* set of statements enables a block of JavaScript to be executed and catches exceptions which the programmer can then handle. The code to do this follows this format:

```
try {
    // Execute some code
}
catch(errorObject) {
    //  Error handling code goes here
}
```

The code within the *try* clause will execute and, should an error be found, processing is immediately handed over to the *catch* clause. Listing 16-1 shows a simple example. (This can be found in the accompanying source code as listing16-1.htm.)

LISTING 16-1 A Basic *try/catch* Example

```
try {
    var numField = document.forms[0]["num"];
    if (isNaN(numField.value)) {
        throw "it's not a number";
```

```
    }
}
catch(errorObject) {
    alert(errorObject);
}
```

If the value of *numField.value* is not a number, a programmer-generated exception is thrown, the text of which reads, "it's not a number". The *catch* clause then executes, and in this case results in the appearance of an *alert()* dialog box. Note the difference between a programmer-generated exception and one that's generated by the JavaScript run-time engine, such as syntax errors. A *try/catch* block won't catch syntax errors, and as such, *try/catch* blocks provide no protection against these types of errors.

When using a *catch* clause, it's common to perform multiple tasks, such as calling another function to log the error or handle the condition in a general fashion. This is particularly helpful in problematic areas of code or in areas where the nature of the code (such as in code that processes user input) can lead to errors.

In this exercise, you'll build a Web form similar to the form that you built in Chapter 15, "JavaScript and CSS." This time, in addition to providing visual feedback within the form's text field, you'll provide a bit of textual feedback.

Using *try/catch* with a Web form

1. Using Microsoft Visual Studio, Eclipse, or another editor, edit the file number.htm in the Chapter16 sample files folder.

2. Within the Web page, add the code shown below in bold type:

```
<!DOCTYPE HTML PUBLIC "-//W3C//DTD HTML 4.01//EN" "http://www.w3.org/TR/html4/
strict.dtd">
<html>
<head>
<title>Try/Catch</title>
<script type="text/javascript" src="number.js"></script>
</head>
<body>
<form name="formexample" id="formexample" action="#">
<div id="citydiv">Enter a Number Between 1 and 100: <input id="num" name="num"> <span
id="feedback"> </span></div>
<div><input id="submit" type="submit"></div>
</form>
<script type="text/javascript">
function init() {
    document.forms[0].onsubmit = function() { return checkValid() };
}
```

```
window.onload = init;
</script>
</body>
</html>
```

3. Create a JavaScript source file called number.js (also found in the source code as number.js).

4. The first task is to convert the error handling code from Chapter 15 to the *try/catch* style and to match the content of this form. A *try/catch* isn't really required here, but this code does provide an easy-to-follow demonstration of this style in action. Within number.js, place the following code. (Although much of this code could be condensed into a single *if* statement, I've written several *if* statements here because we'll expand the code later in this exercise.)

```
function checkValid() {
    try {
        var numField = document.forms[0]["num"];
        if (isNaN(numField.value)) {
            throw numField;
        }
        else if (numField.value > 100) {
            throw numField;
        }
        else if (numField.value < 1) {
            throw numField;
        }
        return true;
    }
    catch(errorObject) {
        errorObject.style.background = "#FF0000";
        return false;
    }
}
```

5. View the page in a Web browser. You should see this window:

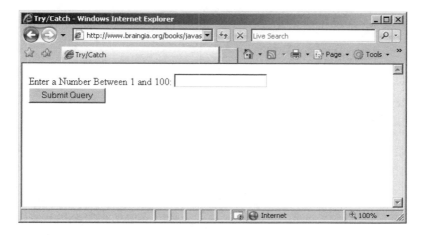

6. Test the functionality of the new *try/catch* clauses. First, enter a number greater than 100 (say, **350**) and click Submit Query. You should see a page like this:

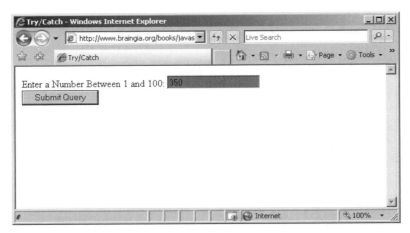

7. Next, enter a phrase rather than a number and click Submit Query again. The form field should remain red.

8. Now enter a number less than 1 and click Submit Query again. The form field should remain red.

9. Finally, enter the number **50** and click Submit Query again. This time the form should submit successfully, which will result in a blank form.

10. Modify the number.js file to add some textual feedback. The final number.js file should look like this:

```
function checkValid() {
    try {
        var numField = document.forms[0]["num"];
        if (isNaN(numField.value)) {
            var err = new Array("It's not a number",numField);
            throw err;
        }
        else if (numField.value > 100) {
            var err = new Array("It's greater than 100",numField);
            throw err;
        }
        else if (numField.value < 1) {
            var err = new Array("It's less than 1",numField);
            throw err;
        }
        return true;
    }
    catch(errorObject) {
        var errorText = document.createTextNode(errorObject[0]);
        var feedback = document.getElementById("feedback");
```

```
        var newspan = document.createElement("span");
        newspan.appendChild(errorText);
        newspan.style.color = "#FF0000";
        newspan.style.fontWeight = "bold";
        newspan.setAttribute("id","feedback");
        var parent = feedback.parentNode;
        var newChild = parent.replaceChild(newspan,feedback);
        errorObject[1].style.background = "#FF0000";
        return false;
    }
}
```

11. Refresh the page in the browser so that a new version of the JavaScript executes. You won't notice any visible changes compared to the first time you loaded the form.

12. Within the form, enter **350** and click Submit Query. Now you'll see a page like the following, with textual feedback next to the form field:

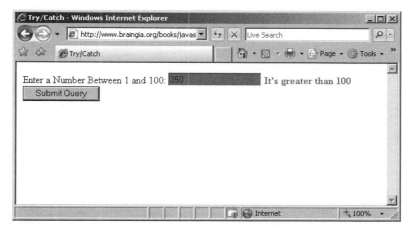

13. Next, enter **-1** into the form and click Submit Query again. You'll see this page:

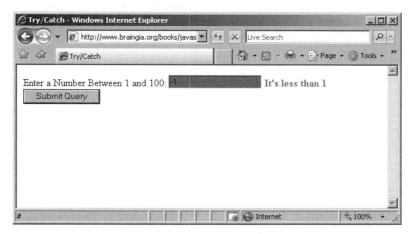

14. Now enter a text phrase into the form and click Submit Query again. You'll see a page like this:

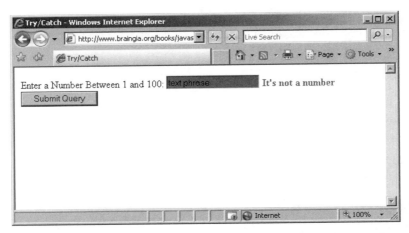

15. Finally, enter a valid number between 1 and 100 (say, **50**) into the form and click Submit Query. The form will submit without error.

This exercise used some of the methods explained in earlier chapters to create a new element and place it into the document to provide feedback. The first portion of the exercise converted the Web form found in Chapter 15 to the *try/catch* style and to the content of this form. Whereas the form found in Chapter 15 asked for a city to be entered, this form looks for a specific range of numbers to demonstrate multiple conditions for feedback.

Each condition throws an error with the *numField* object as its error object. Within the *catch* statement, the background color of *errorObject* changes to red and false is returned to indicate a failed or invalid form. The additional code used an array to join both a textual error and the *form* object (*numField*). This *array* object was then thrown to the *catch* statement. Its first index, 0, is the text for the error and the second index, 1, is the *numField* object, as shown here (pay particular attention to the code in bold):

```
try {
    var numField = document.forms[0]["num"];
    if (isNaN(numField.value)) {
        var err = new Array("It's not a number",numField);
        throw err;
    }
    else if (numField.value > 100) {
        var err = new Array("It's greater than 100",numField);
        throw err;
    }
    else if (numField.value < 1) {
        var err = new Array("It's less than 1",numField);
        throw err;
    }
```

```
    else {
        return true;
    }
}
```

The *catch* statement performs several duties in this exercise. First, it retrieves the *<span>* that will provide feedback to the user:

```
var feedback = document.getElementById("feedback");
```

Following this retrieval, a new text node is created using the text of the error message found in the *errorObject*:

```
var errorText = document.createTextNode(errorObject[0]);
```

A new span element is created so that it can be put into the document later. This span element, known within the code as *newspan,* has the error text appended and is then styled so that it stands out, with a red text color and bold font in this case. This new span is then given an ID of *feedback*, the same as the existing *span* element:

```
var newspan = document.createElement("span");
newspan.appendChild(errorText);
newspan.style.color = "#FF0000";
newspan.style.fontWeight = "bold";
newspan.setAttribute("id","feedback");
```

The *feedback* object has its parent node retrieved so that the *replaceChild()* method can be used. Then the *replaceChild()* method is used on the parent to replace the old *span* element with the new *span* element, as follows:

```
var parent = feedback.parentNode;
var newChild = parent.replaceChild(newspan,feedback);
```

Finally, the background of the text field in the form is colored red and false is returned to cancel submission of the form:

```
errorObject[1].style.background = "#FF0000";
return false;
```

> **Tip** The use of *try/catch* statements in this way helps to abstract the handling of exception cases within code. However, it does not prevent or provide assistance for syntax errors within the code.

Catching Multiple Exceptions

The Mozilla Firefox browser enables the use of multiple exceptions and multiple exception handlers.

For example, consider this code:

```
if (isNaN(numField.value)) {
    throw "NotANumber";
}
else if (numField.value > 100) {
    throw "GreaterThan100";
}
else if (numField.value < 1) {
    throw "LessThan1";
}
```

The *catch* block would then look like this:

```
catch(errorObject if errorObject == "NotANumber") {
    // Perform handling for NaN
}
catch(errorObject if errorObject == "GreaterThan100") {
    // Perform handling for > 100
}
catch(errorObject if errorObject == "LessThan1") {
    // Perform handling for < 1
}
catch(errorObject) {
    // Perform uncaught exception handling
}
```

Each exception is handled by its own exception handler block, and if none of these exceptions occurs, then a generic exception handler is used. Unfortunately, because Microsoft Windows Internet Explorer doesn't support this functionality, it's of limited use.

And Finally...

There is an optional complementary statement in JavaScript that goes along with *try/catch* called *finally*. The *finally* statement contains code that gets executed whether or not the *try* statement's code succeeded or whether the *catch* handler executed. The *finally* block can be used to make sure that some code (such as cleanup code) will execute every time.

Listing 16-2 (found in the source code as listing16-2.htm) shows the *checkValid()* function seen in previous exercises in this chapter with the addition of a *finally* statement:

LISTING 16-2 Adding a *finally* Statement onto the *checkValid()* Function

```
function checkValid() {
    try {
        var numField = document.forms[0]["num"];
        if (isNaN(numField.value)) {
            var err = new Array("It's not a number",numField);
            throw err;
```

```
        }
        else if (numField.value > 100) {
            var err = new Array("It's greater than 100",numField);
            throw err;
        }
        else if (numField.value < 1) {
            var err = new Array("It's less than 1",numField);
            throw err;
        }
        return true;
    }
    catch(errorObject) {
        var errorText = document.createTextNode(errorObject[0]);
        var feedback = document.getElementById("feedback");
        var newspan = document.createElement("span");
        newspan.appendChild(errorText);
        newspan.style.color = "#FF0000";
        newspan.style.fontWeight = "bold";
        newspan.setAttribute("id","feedback");
        var parent = feedback.parentNode;
        var newChild = parent.replaceChild(newspan,feedback);
        errorObject[1].style.background = "#FF0000";
        return false;
    }
    finally {
        alert("This is called on both success and failure.");
    }
}
```

Using the *onerror* Event

You may see the *onerror* event used within programs to provide a means to handle *error* events and conditions, though its use is becoming much less common now that there are less obtrusive ways of handling errors. The *onerror* event can be attached to the *window* and *image* objects.

Attaching *onerror* to the *window* Object

The *onerror* event is assigned a function that is called whenever an error occurs within the JavaScript. The *onerror* event can be helpful during development, though the use of tools like Firebug have lessened the need for it.

The *onerror* event is attached to the *window* object like this:

```
window.onerror = myErrorHandler;
```

The *myErrorHandler* variable refers to a user-defined function to handle the error condition. Three arguments are automatically sent to the error handler by the JavaScript interpreter:

- A textual description of the error

- The Uniform Resource Locator (URL) where the error occurred

- The line on which the error occurred

If the error handler function returns *true*, JavaScript won't handle the error itself, assuming that the error has been taken care of by the error handler.

Listing 16-3 (found in the source code as listing16-3.htm) shows an example of JavaScript and a user-defined handler.

LISTING 16-3 An Example of *onerror* in the *window* Object

```
<!DOCTYPE HTML PUBLIC "-//W3C//DTD HTML 4.01//EN" "http://www.w3.org/TR/html4/
strict.dtd">
<html>
<head>
<title>onerror</title>
</head>
<body>
<div id="mydiv">Hi</div>
<script type="text/javascript">
function init() {
    doSomething();
}
function errorHandler() {
    alert(arguments[0] + " on line " + arguments[2]);
    return true;
}

window.onload = init;
window.onerror = errorHandler;
</script>
</body>
</html>
```

When viewed in a Web browser, an *alert()* dialog box like the one in Figure 16-1 appears.

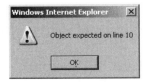

FIGURE 16-1 An error handler using the *onerror* event of the *window* object

Listing 16-3 contains a purposefully undefined function within the *init()* function when the window loads. The JavaScript interpreter in turn throws the error when it finds the undefined function, and because a user-defined function called *errorHandler* is assigned to the *onerror* event, that function gets called. Within the function, an *alert()* dialog box is displayed and *true* is returned so that no further error handling will occur. The *alert()* dialog box displays the first and third indexes of the *arguments* array (*arguments[0]* and *arguments[2]*). The *arguments* array contains the three arguments sent to the error handler.

> ### Avoid Handling Events Obtrusively
>
> The example in Listing 16-3 shows the handling of a JavaScript error in a somewhat obtrusive manner: using an *alert()* dialog box. It's a better practice to handle errors in the background whenever possible rather than using an *alert* dialog box. If the page has a lot of errors, the *alert* dialog boxes can get quite cumbersome for the visitor to have to click through.
>
> If you believe that an error might occur, then you can code around that error and handle it in such a way so as to make the script degrade gracefully, say by substituting a different function, or at worst, by indicating that the page requires JavaScript.

Ignoring Errors

Rather than handling errors with extra error-handling code, you can choose to ignore them entirely. This is accomplished simply by returning *true* from the error handler. Whenever *true* is returned from an error-handling function, the browser will behave as though the error has been handled. So by returning *true,* you're essentially just telling the interpreter to ignore the error.

Take a look at the code in Listing 16-4. It's similar to that in Listing 16-3; however, in Listing 16-4, the only thing that the *errorHandler* function does is return *true* (as shown in bold type). This means that when the *doSomething()* function that's not defined would normally cause an error, it will be silently ignored instead. You can find the code for Listing 16-4 in the accompanying source code as listing16-4.htm.

LISTING 16-4 Code that Silently Ignores an Error

```
<!DOCTYPE HTML PUBLIC "-//W3C//DTD HTML 4.01//EN" "http://www.w3.org/TR/html4/
strict.dtd">
<html>
<head>
<title>onerror</title>
</head>
<body>
<div id="mydiv">Hi</div>
```

```
<script type="text/javascript">
function init() {
    doSomething();
}
function errorHandler() {
    return true;
}

window.onload = init;
window.onerror = errorHandler;
</script>
</body>
</html>
```

You can see this behavior using Firefox with Firebug installed. First, load the code in Listing 16-4 as is. You won't see any errors noted. Then comment the *return true*; statement from within the *errorHandler* function so it looks like this:

```
function errorHandler() {
//    return true;
}
```

When you reload the page, you'll notice an error in the Firebug error console, as shown in Figure 16-2.

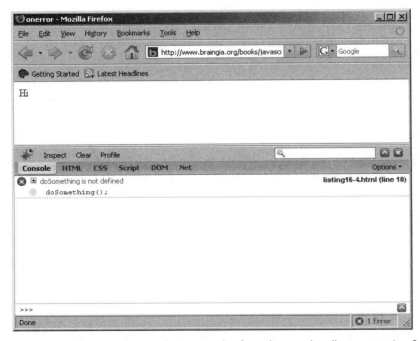

FIGURE 16-2 Commenting out the return value from the error handler causes a JavaScript error that can be viewed using Firebug.

Attaching *onerror* to the *image* Object

An *onerror* event can also be placed directly on *image* objects. When placed inline within the *<img>* tag, these event handlers can be used to handle images that aren't found.

For example, Figure 16-3 shows a page with a missing image.

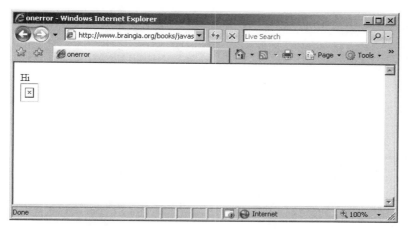

FIGURE 16-3 A missing image that can be avoided using JavaScript

The code for this page is shown in Listing 16-5 (and in the source code as listing16-5.htm).

LISTING 16-5 A Page with a Missing Image

```
<!DOCTYPE HTML PUBLIC "-//W3C//DTD HTML 4.01//EN" "http://www.w3.org/TR/html4/
strict.dtd">
<html>
<head>
<title>onerror</title>
</head>
<body>
<div id="mydiv">Hi</div>
<img src="notfound.png">
</body>
</html>
```

Now consider the code with an inline *onerror* handler. The *onerror* handler points to an image that is found. The content of the image isn't important in this case, but using the *onerror* handler in such a way can help to prevent the "Image Not Found" icon from appearing within your Web pages. Listing 16-6 (also in the source code as listing16-6.htm) shows the new code.

LISTING 16-6 Adding a *onerror()* Handler for the Image

```
<!DOCTYPE HTML PUBLIC "-//W3C//DTD HTML 4.01//EN" "http://www.w3.org/TR/html4/
strict.dtd">
<html>
<head>
<title>onerror</title>
</head>
<body>
<div id="mydiv">Hi</div>
<img src="notfound.png" onerror="this.src='logo.png'; return true">
</body>
</html>
```

When this page is loaded into a Web browser, the image still isn't found. However, in its place, an image called logo.png is retrieved, as shown in Figure 16-4.

FIGURE 16-4 The missing image has been replaced thanks to the *onerror* event handler.

Exercises

1. Use an *onerror* event handler attached to the *window* object to handle errors when a function is undefined.

2. Build a Web form and use a *try/catch* block to catch the case when a city entered into a text field is not "Stockholm". Provide visual feedback that the city was incorrect.

3. Build a Web form and use a *try/catch/finally* block to catch a case when a number is greater than 100. Be sure that visitors are thanked every time that they use the form, no matter what they enter (either valid or invalid values).

Part IV
AJAX and Beyond

Chapter 17
JavaScript and XML

After reading this chapter, you'll be able to

- Examine the functions for opening an Extensible Markup Language (XML) document with JavaScript.

- Display an XML document as a Hypertext Markup Language (HTML) table.

- View a Microsoft Office Excel 2007 XML spreadsheet using JavaScript.

Using XML with JavaScript

XML is a language consisting of tags defined by the user. Because the tags are user-defined, XML is frequently used as a means of exchanging data. An important consideration for the JavaScript programmer is that XML is the *X* in the acronym AJAX (Asynchronous JavaScript and XML). AJAX has become a very popular method for creating interactive Web applications. You'll learn more about AJAX in the next two chapters, Chapter 18, "A Touch of AJAX," and Chapter 19, "A Bit Deeper into AJAX."

XML is an open standard defined by the World Wide Web Consortium (W3C) and is currently in its fourth edition. This section looks briefly at XML as it pertains to JavaScript. More information about XML can be found on the XML Working Group's Web site at *http://www. w3.org/XML/Core/* or on Microsoft's Web site at *http://msdn.microsoft.com/xml/.*

An Example XML Document

XML documents consist of elements within a document structure. These elements have syntax rules of their own, including that they need a start and an end tag. To the Web programmer, the look of a document (text between tags) might be a bit familiar.

Here's an example XML document, also provided as books.xml on the companion CD in the Chapter17 folder:

```
<books>
<book>
    <title>MySQL Bible</title>
    <author>Steve Suehring</author>
    <isbn>9780764549328</isbn>
    <publisher>Wiley Publishing Inc.</publisher>
</book>
<book>
    <title>JavaScript Step by Step</title>
    <author>Steve Suehring</author>
```

```
    <isbn>9780735624498</isbn>
    <publisher>Microsoft Press</publisher>
</book>
</books>
```

The structure of the document as a whole needs to meet certain criteria to qualify as a well-formed document. As seen in the example, each element has its own start tag followed by a corresponding end tag. Elements also can be nested within each other. Many of these rules are similar to HTML rules.

XML documents can contain attributes as well, so the following is also valid:

```
<?xml version="1.0"?>
<book title="JavaScript Step by Step" author="Steve Suehring" isbn="9780735624498"
publisher="Microsoft Press" />
```

Loading an XML Document with JavaScript

XML documents can be loaded and manipulated using JavaScript. This section looks at doing just that.

Importing the Document

XML documents are requested and imported into JavaScript using the *document .implementation.createDocument()* function for browsers that support the W3C model, and the *Microsoft.XMLDOM* object for Microsoft Windows Internet Explorer. Like other incompatibilities, this means that the JavaScript programmer needs to watch and account for such differences when creating code.

For example, the following code creates an object that can be used to load and manipulate an XML document:

```
if (typeof document.implementation.createDocument != "undefined") {
    docObj = document.implementation.createDocument("", "", null);
}
else if (window.ActiveXObject) {
    docObj = new ActiveXObject("Microsoft.XMLDOM");
}
```

The *document.implementation.createDocument()* function accepts three arguments: a namespace Uniform Resource Identifier (URI) to specify the namespace for the document, the root tag name, and a doc type. In practice, you'll find that these arguments are left undefined and null, as in the example.

For Windows Internet Explorer, the *Microsoft.XMLDOM* object must be used for this purpose.

Once the *docObj* object has been created, it can be used to load an XML document. In this example, an XML document called books.xml is loaded:

```
docObj.load("books.xml");
```

Displaying the Document

A function can be attached to the XML document object's *onload* event (for W3C-compliant browsers) and *onreadystatechange* event (for Windows Internet Explorer). The attached function then can be used to process the contents of the XML document. In this section, I'll show how to display the XML document.

Attaching a function to the *load* event of the document is a necessary step for parsing XML. For W3C-compliant browsers, the *onload* event is used. Adding an *onload* event handler called *displayData()* to the previous example would look like this:

```
if (typeof document.implementation.createDocument != "undefined") {
    docObj = document.implementation.createDocument("", "", null);
    docObj.onload = displayData;
}
```

For Windows Internet Explorer, the *readyState* property is examined to check the current state of the document request. If the value of *readyState* is 4, then the document has been loaded and can therefore be processed. For Windows Internet Explorer, a function gets attached to the *onreadystatechange* event. Again, continuing the previous example and attaching a *displayData()* function to the *onreadystatechange* event looks like this:

```
else if (window.ActiveXObject) {
    docObj = new ActiveXObject("Microsoft.XMLDOM");
    docObj.onreadystatechange = function () {
        if (docObj.readyState == 4) displayData()
    };
}
```

The *readyState* property is an integer holding one of five values to indicate the current state of document request being processed. Table 17-1 shows the values and a corresponding description.

TABLE 17-1 The *readyState* Property

Value	Description
0	Uninitialized. Open but has yet to be called.
1	Open. Initialized but not yet sent.
2	Sent. The request has been sent.
3	Receiving. The response is actively being received.
4	Loaded. The response has been fully received.

There will be more about the *readyState* property and the *onreadystatechange* event in Chapter 18. For now, it's sufficient to know that the ready state to be concerned with is number 4. Attempting to use the document or access it while it's loading, such as during ready state 3, will fail.

XML data can sometimes be best visualized in a table or spreadsheet format. Figure 17-1 shows the books.xml file in Excel 2007.

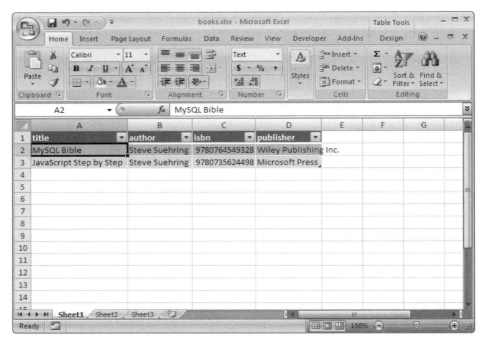

FIGURE 17-1 An XML file represented in a spreadsheet

XML data can sometimes be represented in a spreadsheet, such as the one you've seen here. An HTML table is helpful for representing that same data in a browser. In large part, the display of XML data using JavaScript requires knowledge of the Document Object Model (DOM) but no other special functions or methods beyond loading the document itself, which you've already seen.

Display of the nodes and child nodes within an XML document requires iterating through the document's levels and building the output document. The function shown below does just that, by iterating through a hierarchical XML document to display its data in an HTML table. This code continues the example shown already, where a *docObj* object is created and loaded with an XML document called books.xml:

```
function displayData() {
    var xmlEl = docObj.getElementsByTagName("book");
    var table = document.createElement("table");
```

```
        table.border = "1";
        var tbody = document.createElement("tbody");

        // Append the body to the table
        table.appendChild(tbody);
        var row = document.createElement("tr");

        // Append the row to the body
        tbody.appendChild(row);

        // Create table row
        for (i = 0; i < xmlEl.length; i++) {
            var row = document.createElement("tr");
            // Create the row/td elements
            for (j = 0; j < xmlEl[i].childNodes.length; j++) {
                // Skip it if the type is not 1
                if (xmlEl[i].childNodes[j].nodeType != 1) {
                    continue;
                }

                // Insert the actual text/data from the XML document.
                var td = document.createElement("td");
                var xmlData =
                    document.createTextNode(xmlEl[i].childNodes[j].firstChild.nodeValue);
                td.appendChild(xmlData);
                row.appendChild(td);
            }
            tbody.appendChild(row);
        }
        document.getElementById("xmldata").appendChild(table);
}
```

Putting it all together into a Web page means attaching the functions that load and display the XML file to an event. In Listing 17-1 (included on the companion CD as books.htm), a new function called *getXML* is created and attached to the *onload* event of the *window* object. The code to attach the event is shown in bold type.

LISTING 17-1 Displaying XML Data in an HTML Table

```
<!DOCTYPE HTML PUBLIC "-//W3C//DTD HTML 4.01//EN" "http://www.w3.org/TR/html4/
strict.dtd">
<html>
<head>
<title>Books</title>
</head>
<body>
<div id="xmldata"></div>
<script type="text/javascript">

window.onload = getXML;

function displayData() {
    var xmlEl = docObj.getElementsByTagName("book");
    var table = document.createElement("table");
```

```
    table.border = "1";
    var tbody = document.createElement("tbody");

    // Append the body to the table
    table.appendChild(tbody);

    // Create table row
    for (i = 0; i < xmlEl.length; i++) {
        var row = document.createElement("tr");
        // Create the row/td elements
        for (j = 0; j < xmlEl[i].childNodes.length; j++) {
            // Skip it if the type is not 1
            if (xmlEl[i].childNodes[j].nodeType != 1) {
                continue;
            }

            // Insert the actual text/data from the XML document.
            var td = document.createElement("td");
            var xmlData =
                document.createTextNode(xmlEl[i].childNodes[j].firstChild.nodeValue);
            td.appendChild(xmlData);
            row.appendChild(td);
        }
        tbody.appendChild(row);
    }
    document.getElementById("xmldata").appendChild(table);
}

function getXML() {
    if (typeof document.implementation.createDocument != "undefined") {
        docObj = document.implementation.createDocument("", "", null);
        docObj.onload = displayData;
    }
    else if (window.ActiveXObject) {
        docObj = new ActiveXObject("Microsoft.XMLDOM");
        docObj.onreadystatechange = function () {
            if (docObj.readyState == 4) displayData()
        };
    }
    docObj.load("books.xml");
}

</script>
</body>
</html>
```

When viewed through a Web browser, the table displays the data much like a spreadsheet would, as you can see in Figure 17-2.

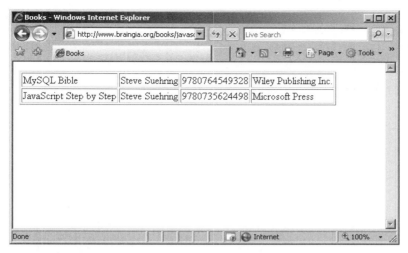

FIGURE 17-2 Representing books.xml in an HTML table

Examining the code from Listing 17-1 reveals a large *for* loop that walks through the XML hierarchy, building table rows as it goes. One item of note is that the loop looks only for *Element* nodes within the XML document using this bit of code:

```
// Skip it if the type is not 1
if (xmlEl[i].childNodes[j].nodeType != 1) {
    continue;
}
```

The *nodeType* of 1 represents an *XML Element* node. If the type of node currently being examined in the loop is not an element, we can move to the next part of the document.

One issue you may notice with the display in Figure 17-2 is that there are no column headings. Adding column headings means the addition of a bit of code.

Adding column headings from an XML document

1. Using Microsoft Visual Studio, Eclipse, or another editor, edit the file books.htm in the Chapter17 sample files folder. (When viewed through a Web browser, books.htm should currently resemble Figure 17-2.)

2. Within books.htm, add the code shown below in bold type to the *displayData()* method:

```
<!DOCTYPE HTML PUBLIC "-//W3C//DTD HTML 4.01//EN" "http://www.w3.org/TR/html4/
strict.dtd">
<html>
<head>
<title>Books</title>
</head>
<body>
```

```
<div id="xmldata"></div>
<script type="text/javascript">

window.onload = getXML;

function displayData() {
    var xmlEl = docObj.getElementsByTagName("book");
    var table = document.createElement("table");
    table.border = "1";
    var tbody = document.createElement("tbody");

    // Append the body to the table
    table.appendChild(tbody);
    var row = document.createElement("tr");

    for (colHead = 0; colHead < xmlEl[0].childNodes.length; colHead++) {
        if (xmlEl[0].childNodes[colHead].nodeType != 1) {
            continue;
        }
        var tableHead = document.createElement("th");
        var colName = document.createTextNode(xmlEl[0].childNodes[colHead].nodeName);
        tableHead.appendChild(colName);
        row.appendChild(tableHead);
    }

    // Append the row to the body
    tbody.appendChild(row);

    // Create table row
    for (i = 0; i < xmlEl.length; i++) {
        var row = document.createElement("tr");
        // Create the row/td elements
        for (j = 0; j < xmlEl[i].childNodes.length; j++) {
            // Skip it if the type is not 1
            if (xmlEl[i].childNodes[j].nodeType != 1) {
                continue;
            }

            // Insert the actual text/data from the XML document.
            var td = document.createElement("td");
            var xmlData =
                document.createTextNode(xmlEl[i].childNodes[j].firstChild.nodeValue);
            td.appendChild(xmlData);
            row.appendChild(td);
        }
        tbody.appendChild(row);
    }
    document.getElementById("xmldata").appendChild(table);
}
function getXML() {
    if (typeof document.implementation.createDocument != "undefined") {
        docObj = document.implementation.createDocument("", "", null);
        docObj.onload = displayData;
    }
```

```
        else if (window.ActiveXObject) {
            docObj = new ActiveXObject("Microsoft.XMLDOM");
            docObj.onreadystatechange = function () {
                if (docObj.readyState == 4) displayData()
            };
        }
        docObj.load("books.xml");
    }

    </script>
    </body>
    </html>
```

8. View the page in a Web browser. It should look like this:

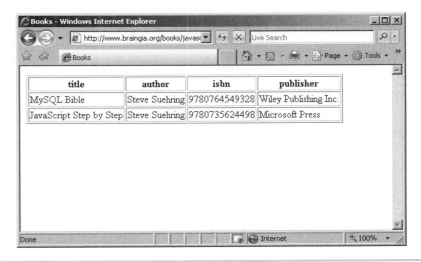

Working with XML Data from Excel 2007

Excel 2007 has several features that make working with XML data rather easy. Both importing and exporting XML data is possible with Excel. In fact, when exporting data from Excel, Excel adds nothing proprietary to the XML document. Here's what the books.xml file looks like when exported from Excel 2007 (included on the companion CD as newbooks.xml):

```
<?xml version="1.0" encoding="UTF-8" standalone="yes"?>
<books xmlns:xsi="http://www.w3.org/2001/XMLSchema-instance">
    <book>
        <title>MySQL Bible</title>
        <author>Steve Suehring</author>
        <isbn>9780764549328</isbn>
        <publisher>Wiley Publishing Inc.</publisher>
    </book>
    <book>
        <title>JavaScript Step by Step</title>
        <author>Steve Suehring</author>
```

```
                        <isbn>9780735624498</isbn>
                        <publisher>Microsoft Press</publisher>
            </book>
</books>
```

Because Excel 2007 is XML-friendly, the *displayData()* function already seen in this chapter works with XML data exported from Excel 2007 without modification. For developers who have worked with proprietary formats in the past, this comes as a welcome surprise.

A Preview of Things to Come

Though XML is indeed the X in the AJAX acronym, there's much more to AJAX than just JavaScript and XML. AJAX can work with data types other than XML, and in Chapter 18, you'll build upon the brief foundation you learned in this chapter to work with AJAX.

In Chapter 19, the integration of JavaScript, AJAX, and Cascading Style Sheets (CSS) will be examined to add presentation onto the retrieval of data using JavaScript.

Exercises

1. Use the code from the book display exercise in this chapter to display the table after a link is clicked rather than when the page loads.

2. Use the code from the book display exercise in this chapter to display the table, but use the DOM to alternate the colors for each row so that every other row has a gray background. Hint: *#aaabba* is the hexadecimal representation of this gray color.

3. True or False: All modern browsers can access an XML document using the same functions.

4. True or False: You can begin working with XML data while it's being loaded with the *readyState* property of Windows Internet Explorer.

Chapter 18
A Touch of AJAX

After reading this chapter, you'll be able to

■ Understand the basics of the Asynchronous JavaScript and XML (AJAX) programming paradigm.

■ Understand the difference between a synchronous and an asynchronous AJAX call.

■ Use AJAX to retrieve data.

■ Use AJAX with different Hypertext Transfer Protocol (HTTP) methods to retrieve responses from a server.

Introduction to AJAX

Asynchronous JavaScript and XML (AJAX) describes the programming paradigm that combines JavaScript and a Web server. AJAX is used to create highly interactive Web applications such as Microsoft Virtual Earth.

Without AJAX, a Web application might make the visitor wait while a response is gathered from the Web server. An AJAX-based application sends requests from the Web browser to the Web server in the background (asynchronously) while the visitor is using the application. This makes the application feel much more responsive to the user.

In an AJAX application, JavaScript processes the response and presents it to the user. When combined with Cascading Style Sheets (CSS) and a good layout, an AJAX application provides excellent usability while also giving the portability that only a Web application can.

As complex as some AJAX applications may seem, the actual process of sending a request and handling the response are really uncomplicated. This chapter looks at how to send and receive requests using a fundamental AJAX object, *XMLHttpRequest*.

One of the central themes in AJAX is using a server-side application to return data. I'll show a brief example of how to create such an application using both Active Server Pages (ASP) and PHP (PHP is a recursive acronym for PHP Hypertext Preprocessor) later in the chapter. However, should you need additional assistance in creating the server-side portion of an AJAX application, you can get help from several sources.

If you're creating a server-side application using Microsoft technologies, the Microsoft Developer Network provides a great resource with many tutorials, including *http://msdn2 .microsoft.com/en-us/library/98wzsc30.aspx*. For an AJAX overview, check out MSDN Magazine (*http://msdn.microsoft.com/msdnmag/issues/07/09/CuttingEdge/*). Microsoft Press also publishes several excellent books on building applications for the Web. One such title is *Microsoft ASP.NET 2.0 Step By Step* (Microsoft Press 2005), and there are many others. Look at *http://www.microsoft.com/mspress* for more information.

If you're developing a server-side application using other technologies such as the LAMP (Linux, Apache, MySQL, Perl/PHP/Python) stack, searching the Web for tutorials is likely the easiest way to get up to speed quickly on development on the platform. The book *Learning Perl* (O'Reilly, 2005) is a great resource to learn the basics of the Perl programming language. PHP's main Web site (*http://www.php.net*) is a good place to start for information on PHP. The same goes for Python (*http://www.python.org*).

The *XMLHttpRequest* Object

The *XMLHttpRequest* object is central to building an AJAX application. While implementations differ, many aspects of JavaScript have been standardized by the ECMAScript standard and through the World Wide Web Consortium (W3C). However, *XMLHttpRequest* has never experienced a standardization process. Even so, with the release of Microsoft Windows Internet Explorer 7, usage of *XMLHttpRequest* is the same across all major browsers.

The *XMLHttpRequest* object was first implemented in Internet Explorer 5. If a visitor is using a browser version earlier than that, applications using *XMLHttpRequest* won't work. In Internet Explorer versions prior to version 7, the *XMLHttpRequest* object was instantiated through the *ActiveXObject* object. This means that applications that need to work with versions of Internet Explorer earlier than version 7 need to instantiate the *XMLHttpRequest* object in a different way, as you'll see. The next section, "Instantiating the *XMLHttpRequest* Object," shows how to test for the existence of *XMLHttpRequest* and how to instantiate it in Internet Explorer 7 and in Internet Explorer versions earlier than version 7.

Instantiating the *XMLHttpRequest* Object

Internet Explorer 7 and all major browsers that support *XMLHttpRequest* instantiate the *XMLHttpRequest* object in the same way:

```
var req = new XMLHttpRequest();
```

Internet Explorer versions earlier than version 7 must use the *ActiveXObject*. However, the exact way to do this varies depending on the version of the XMLHTTP library installed on the client. Therefore, a bit of code juggling needs to be done in order to instantiate an *XMLHttpRequest* object in earlier versions of Internet Explorer.

The code in Listing 18-1 is a cross-browser function to instantiate the *XMLHttpRequest* object across multiple browsers.

LISTING 18-1 Instantiating the *XMLHttpRequest* Object Across Browsers

```
function readyAJAX() {
    try {
        return new XMLHttpRequest();
    } catch(e) {
        try {
            return new ActiveXObject('Msxml2.XMLHTTP');
        } catch(e) {
            try {
                return new ActiveXObject('Microsoft.XMLHTTP');
            } catch(e) {
                return "A newer browser is needed.";
            }
        }
    }
}
```

The function in Listing 18-1 uses multiple levels of *try/catch* blocks to instantiate an *XMLHttpRequest*, whether the visitor is using Internet Explorer or another browser. If the native call to *XMLHttpRequest* fails, it indicates that the visitor is using an Internet Explorer browser older than version 7. In such a case, the error is caught and one of the *ActiveXObject*-based methods for instantiating *XMLHttpRequest* is tried. If none of these methods succeed, the likely reason is that the browser is too old to support *XMLHttpRequest*.

The article "About Native XMLHTTP" on MSDN describes some of the version history and security nuances of the XMLHttpRequest *object in Internet Explorer. This article can be found at* http://msdn2.microsoft.com/en-us/library/ms537505.aspx.

The *readyAJAX()* function shown in Listing 18-1 would be called like this:

```
var requestObj = readyAJAX();
```

The *requestObj* variable now contains the *XMLHttpRequest* object returned by the function, or, if no *XMLHttpRequest* was able to be returned, the *requestObj* variable will contain the string "A newer browser is needed."

Sending an AJAX Request

With a newly created *XMLHttpRequest* object in hand, a request can be sent to the Web server. Sending the request is a combination of using the *open()* and *send()* methods of the *XMLHttpRequest* object.

Describing How the Web Works in 500 Words or Less

The Hypertext Transfer Protocol (HTTP) is the language of the Web. HTTP is currently defined by RFC 2616 and describes a protocol for exchanging information by using requests from clients and responses from servers.

Requests from clients such as Web browsers contain a specific set of headers that define the method used for retrieval, the object to be retrieved, and the protocol version to be used. Other headers contain the Web server host name, languages requested, the name of the browser, and other information that the client deems relevant to the request.

Here's a basic HTTP version 1.1 request:

```
GET / HTTP/1.1
Host: www.braingia.org
```

This request specifies the *GET* method to retrieve the document located at the / directory location using HTTP version 1.1. The second line, commonly called the *Host* header, is *www.braingia.org*. This header tells the Web server which Web site is being requested. Several methods can be used in a request, with the three most common being *GET, POST,* and *HEAD*. HTTP cookies are also exchanged as part of the headers, with cookies being sent in the request and others possibly being received in the response.

When a request like this is received by the Web server for *www.braingia.org,* the Web server sends response headers indicating how it has handled the request. In this case, the Web server sends these response headers:

```
HTTP/1.1 200 OK
Date: Wed, 12 Mar 2008 01:04:34 GMT
Server: Apache/1.3.33 (Debian GNU/Linux) mod_perl/1.29 PHP/4.3.10-22
Transfer-Encoding: chunked
Content-Type: text/html; charset=iso-8859-1
```

The requested document follows the response headers. One of the most important response headers is the first, which indicates the status of the response. In the example, the response is 200, which is synonymous with OK. Other common responses include: 404 (to indicate that the requested document was not found), 302 (to indicate a redirect), and 500 (indicating a server error).

Understanding these basics of HTTP is important for understanding how to build AJAX requests and how to troubleshoot those requests when things go wrong. You can find more information on HTTP, including the various response codes, in RFC 2616 at *ftp://ftp.rfc-editor.org/in-notes/rfc2616.txt.*

There are two fundamentally different ways to send AJAX requests: synchronously and asynchronously. When sent in a synchronous manner, the request will block, effectively preventing further processing or execution of other JavaScript while the script awaits the response from the Web server. This process has obvious disadvantages if the request or response gets lost in transit or is just slow.

Before the request can be sent, it must be built. The open method is used to build the request and has three arguments, the request method (*GET, POST, HEAD,* and others), the Uniform Resource Locator (URL) to which the request will be sent, and *true* or *false*, indicating whether the request will be sent asynchronously or synchronously, respectively.

Assuming that a request object has been retrieved using the *readyAJAX()* function and placed into a variable named *requestObj,* a typical asynchronous call to the open method might look like this:

```
var url = "http://www.braingia.org/getdata.php";
requestObj.open("GET", url, true);
```

That same call sent synchronously looks like this:

```
var url = "http://www.braingia.org/getdata.php";
requestObj.open("GET", url, false);
```

Sending the request is done with the *send* method, as follows:

```
requestObj.send();
```

> **Note** If the parameters sent with the request have any special characters, such as spaces or other characters reserved by the URI RFC, those characters must be escaped using the % notation. This is discussed further within RFC 3986, which can be found at *ftp://ftp.rfc-editor.org/in-notes/ rfc3986.txt* and more information can also be found at *http://msdn2.microsoft.com/en-us/library/ aa226544(sql.80).aspx.*

Processing an AJAX Response

It's easier to work with the response when the request is sent synchronously because the script's execution stops while awaiting the response. This section first looks at synchronous response processing.

The *requestObj* variable provides helpful methods for processing a response, including giving access to the status codes and text of the status sent from the server. Regardless of whether the request is synchronous or asynchronous, the status code should be evaluated to ensure that the response was successful (usually indicated by a status of 200).

The *responseText* method contains the text of the response as received from the Web server.

For example, assume that there is a server application that returns the sum of two numbers. Calling the application to add the numbers 2 and 56 looks like this:

```
http://www.braingia.org/addtwo.php?num1=2&num2=56
```

Here's a synchronous call and response retrieval:

```
requestObj.open("GET", "http://www.braingia.org/addtwo.php?num1=2&num2=56", false);
requestObj.send();
if (requestObj.status == 200) {
    alert(requestObj.responseText);
} else {
    alert(requestObj.statusText);
}
```

In this example, assume that the *requestObj* is built using the *readyAJAX()* function. The *open* method is then called using a *GET* request to the specified URL (*http://www.braingia.org/addtwo.php?num1=2&num2=56*) and the request will be sent synchronously because the last argument to the open method is *false*. The *send* method is then called, which actually sends the request to the Web server.

The status method is called and if it's a 200 response code, indicating success, then the *responseText* is displayed. If the response status code was anything other than 200, the text of the response status is displayed.

Processing an asynchronous response is a bit more complex. When a request is sent asynchronously, the script execution continues. Therefore, it is unpredictable when the script will be notified that the response has been received. The *onreadystatechange* event can trigger code that checks the event's *readyState* property to ascertain the state of the request/response cycle. Recall from Chapter 17, "JavaScript and XML," that the *readyState* property has five states, as shown in Table 18-1.

TABLE 18-1 The *readyState* Property

Value	Description
0	Uninitialized. Open has yet to be called.
1	Open. Initialized but not yet sent.
2	Sent. The request has been sent.
3	Receiving. The response is actively being received.
4	Loaded. The response has been fully received.

For practical purposes, the only state that matters to the JavaScript and AJAX programmer is state 4—Loaded. Attempting to process a response that has a *readyState* value other than 4 results in an error.

An anonymous function is commonly used for handling the *onreadystatechange* event with asynchronous JavaScript. The function checks to see if the *readyState* property has reached 4 and then checks to ensure that the status is 200, indicating success. The code follows this format:

```
requestObj.onreadystatechange = function() {
    if (requestObj.readyState == 4) {
        if (requestObj.status == 200) {
            alert(requestObj.responseText);
        } else {
            alert(requestObj.statusText);
        }
    }
}
```

In this next exercise, you'll create an *XMLHttpRequest* object and send a request to a Web server to retrieve a book title based on its ISBN. For this exercise, you'll need a Web server and Web server code to print the response because requests sent using *XMLHttpRequest* are subject to the JavaScript Same-Origin policy.

The Same-Origin policy requires that requests go only to servers within the same domain from which the calling script is executing. In other words, because I'm executing the script in this exercise directly from my Web server at *http://www.braingia.org,* it will be able to retrieve the response. If you run the script from another Web server, however, the Same-Origin policy will prevent the script from retrieving the response.

One way to get around this security feature is to use an HTTP proxy or to write the server-side program so that it sends a request on behalf of the calling program. Doing so is beyond the scope of this book.

For the upcoming exercise, the script or program running on the server needs to return the phrase "JavaScript Step by Step" when a *GET* request is received with a name/value argument of the following:

```
isbn=9780735624498
```

For example, at its most basic, the server-side program could look like this when implemented inside an ASP page:

```
<%
dim isbn
isbn=Request.QueryString("isbn")
If isbn<>"" Then
    If isbn=="9780735624498" Then       Response.Write("JavaScript Step by Step")
    End If
End If
%>
```

The program looks like this when implemented through PHP:

```php
<?php

$isbn = $_GET['isbn'];

if (! $isbn) {
    print "That request was not understood.";
} else if ($isbn == "9780735624498") {
    print "JavaScript Step by Step";
}

?>
```

Within the following exercise, the URL to which the request will be sent is defined. Replace that URL with the URL where you locate the server-side program. Due to the Same-Origin policy, the server-side program needs to be within the same domain as the page that calls it.

Sending and receiving with *XMLHttpRequest*

1. Create your server-side program to return the book title when an *isbn* argument is received. This can be done in your choice of languages (if you need to, look at the two examples shown earlier).

2. Using Microsoft Visual Studio, Eclipse, or another editor, edit the file isbn.htm in the Chapter17 sample files folder.

3. Within the Web page, add the code shown below in bold type, making sure to replace the *url* variable with the URL where your server-side program is located:

```html
<!DOCTYPE HTML PUBLIC "-//W3C//DTD HTML 4.01//EN"
"http://www.w3.org/TR/html4/strict.dtd">
<html>
<head>
<title>ISBN</title>
</head>
<body>
<div id="data"></div>
<script type="text/javascript">
function readyAJAX() {
    try {
        return new XMLHttpRequest();
    } catch(e) {
        try {
            return new ActiveXObject('Msxml2.XMLHTTP');
        } catch(e) {
            try {
                return new ActiveXObject('Microsoft.XMLHTTP');
            } catch(e) {
                return "A newer browser is needed.";
            }
        }
    }
}
```

```
var requestObj = readyAJAX();
var url = "http://www.braingia.org/isbn.php?isbn=9780735624498";
requestObj.open("GET",url,true);
requestObj.send();
requestObj.onreadystatechange = function() {
    if (requestObj.readyState == 4) {
        if (requestObj.status == 200) {
            alert(requestObj.responseText);
        } else {
            alert(requestObj.statusText);
        }
    }
}
</script>
</body>
</html>
```

4. Save and view the page in a Web browser. You should receive an alert like the one shown here.

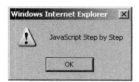

Congratulations! You've now processed your first *XMLHttpRequest*.

Processing XML Responses

The AJAX examples shown so far have all used plain Hypertext Markup Language (HTML) and text responses from the Web server. These responses have been retrieved using the *responseText* method. The server application can also return XML responses, which can be processed natively using the *responseXML* method.

Earlier in this chapter, in the sidebar titled "Describing How the Web Works in 500 Words or Less," an example Web server response was discussed. The server response contained this Content-Type header:

```
Content-Type: text/html; charset=iso-8859-1
```

To retrieve a response using the *responseXML* method, the Web server needs to send a Content-Type of "text/xml" or "application/xml," like this:

```
Content-Type: application/xml
```

When native XML is received as the response, Document Object Model (DOM) methods are used to process the response.

The *responseXML* method has historically been somewhat quirky, meaning that using it can result in unexpected behavior, depending on the browser and operating system. In addition, *responseXML* isn't as widely supported as other JavaScript methods.

Using *responseXML* means combining the *XMLHttpRequest* techniques already seen in this chapter with the XML parsing techniques described in Chapter 17. For example, consider this XML document (let's call it book.xml):

```
<?xml version="1.0" encoding="ISO-8859-1"?>
<book>
<title>JavaScript Step by Step</title>
<isbn>9780735624498</isbn>
</book>
```

Combining *XMLHttpRequest* and XML parsing leads to this code to retrieve and display the ISBN from the book.xml document:

```
var requestObj = readyAJAX();
var url = "http://www.braingia.org/book.xml";
requestObj.open("GET",url,false);
requestObj.send();
if (requestObj.status == 200) {
    var xmldocument = requestObj.responseXML;
    alert(xmldocument.getElementsByTagName("isbn")[0].childNodes[0].nodeValue);
} else {
    alert(requestObj.statusText);
}
```

Working with JSON

JavaScript Object Notation (JSON) is a way to pass data as native JavaScript objects and arrays, rather than encoding that data within XML (or HTML) responses. JSON is a more efficient way to pass data from server to client because it bypasses the DOM parsing and enables the data to be used without needing to be converted to JavaScript objects.

Recall the book.xml document from an earlier example in this chapter. That same data in JSON looks like this:

```
{
"book":
    {
    "title": "JavaScript Step by Step",
    "isbn": "9780735624498"
    }
}
```

Retrieval of an individual element is somewhat easier with JSON than with XML. The *eval()* function is used to parse the response with JSON. For example, this code is used to retrieve and display the book title.

```
var requestObj = readyAJAX();
var url = "http://www.braingia.org/json.php";
requestObj.open("GET",url,false);
requestObj.send();
if (requestObj.status == 200) {
    var xmldocument = eval('(' + requestObj.responseText + ')');
    alert(xmldocument.book.title);
} else {
    alert(requestObj.statusText);
}
```

Using JSON carries with it an inherent security risk because it uses the *eval()* function to parse the response. The *eval()* function essentially executes the JavaScript code received, so it's possible that, if that code were malicious, it would execute in the context of the application being run. It is the developer's responsibility to ensure that the data being used with JSON is clean and free of malicious code that could cause problems when executed using *eval()*.

Processing Headers

The *HTTP HEAD* method returns just the response headers from the server, rather than the headers and the body as would be the case with the *GET* method. The *HEAD* method is sometimes helpful for determining if a given resource has been updated or changed.

One of the HTTP headers frequently sent is the *Expires* header, which indicates when the document should be refreshed by the client instead of read from the client's cache. If the *Expires* header is sent by the server, the *HEAD* method is an efficient way to view and parse it because it retrieves only the response header rather than the entire body of the requested resource.

The *getAllResponseHeaders()* method of the *XMLHttpRequest* object is used to retrieve the response headers, whether using a *HEAD* request or any other type of request such as *GET* or *POST*, as follows:

```
requestObj.getAllResponseHeaders();
```

For example, Listing 18-2 shows retrieval of response headers from my Web site.

LISTING 18-2 Retrieving Headers

```
<!DOCTYPE HTML PUBLIC "-//W3C//DTD HTML 4.01//EN"
"http://www.w3.org/TR/html4/strict.dtd">
<html>
<head>
<title>Response Headers</title>
</head>
<body>
<div id="data"></div>
<script type="text/javascript">
function readyAJAX() {
```

```
    try {
        return new XMLHttpRequest();
    } catch(e) {
        try {
            return new ActiveXObject('Msxml2.XMLHTTP');
        } catch(e) {
            try {
                return new ActiveXObject('Microsoft.XMLHTTP');
            } catch(e) {
                return "A newer browser is needed.";
            }
        }
    }
}
var requestObj = readyAJAX();
var url = "http://www.braingia.org/";
requestObj.open("HEAD",url,true);
requestObj.send();
requestObj.onreadystatechange = function() {
    if (requestObj.readyState == 4) {
        if (requestObj.status == 200) {
            alert(requestObj.getAllResponseHeaders());
        } else {
            alert(requestObj.statusText);
        }
    }
}
</script>
</body>
</html>
```

Note The Same-Origin policy that you ran into during the exercise earlier in the chapter applies equally to the *HEAD* method in Listing 18-2. When writing Listing 18-2, I forgot about the Same-Origin Policy and originally set the *url* variable to *http://www.microsoft.com/*. However, upon receiving an error, I realized the problem and changed the *url* variable to match the domain on which the script was running. Remember to change the *url* variable when attempting to run the code in Listing 18-2.

Using the *POST* Method

Up to this point, the examples shown have used the *GET* and *HEAD* methods to retrieve data from the server. The *POST* method is also a common way to submit queries through HTTP. Using the *POST* method with *XMLHttpRequest* is a bit more complex than either *GET* or *HEAD*. However, the *POST* method offers two specific advantages over the *GET* method.

First, parameters sent using *POST* can be sent over a Secure Sockets Layer (SSL) connection. Compare this to a *GET* request, which sends its parameters directly within the URL, thus possibly making it visible to an eavesdropper. With a *POST* request, the parameters are contained in the body of the request and therefore are subject to the SSL protocol.

Second, the *POST* method enables larger requests to be sent. Some servers limit the amount or size of a *GET* request to a certain number of characters, and while those servers might also limit the size of a *POST* request, the limitation for *POSTs* is almost always much greater.

The HTTP *POST* method requires an additional header to be set within the request. Setting an additional header is accomplished with the *setRequestHeader()* method.

```
requestObj.setRequestHeader(header, value);
```

For example, setting the Content-Type header for a Web form, as would be done for a POST request, looks like this:

```
requestObj.setRequestHeader("Content-type", "application/x-www-form-urlencoded");
```

Recall that when sending an AJAX request using the *GET* method, the URL includes the parameters or *name/value* pairs for the application, like so:

```
http://www.braingia.org/books/javascriptsbs/isbn.php?isbn=9780735624498
```

In this example, the *isbn* parameter is sent using the value 9780735624498. However, when working with *POST* requests, the URL merely contains the document or resource requested and not any parameters. Therefore, the parameters must be sent as part of the *send()* method.

Listing 18-3 presents an AJAX request using the *POST* method, shown in bold type. Two parameters are used—see if you can spot them.

LISTING 18-3 Constructing a *POST* Request

```
<!DOCTYPE HTML PUBLIC "-//W3C//DTD HTML 4.01//EN"
"http://www.w3.org/TR/html4/strict.dtd">
<html>
<head>
<title>Post</title>
</head>
<body>
<div id="xmldata"></div>
<script type="text/javascript">
function readyAJAX() {
    try {
        return new XMLHttpRequest();
    } catch(e) {
        try {
            return new ActiveXObject('Msxml2.XMLHTTP');
        } catch(e) {
```

```
            try {
                return new ActiveXObject('Microsoft.XMLHTTP');
            } catch(e) {
                return "A newer browser is needed.";
            }
        }
    }
}

var requestObj = readyAJAX();
var url = "http://www.braingia.org/books/javascriptsbs/post.php";
var params = "num1=2&num2=2";
requestObj.open("POST",url,true);
requestObj.setRequestHeader("Content-type", "application/x-www-form-urlencoded");
requestObj.send(params);
requestObj.onreadystatechange = function() {
    if (requestObj.readyState == 4) {
        if (requestObj.status == 200) {
            alert(requestObj.responseText);
        } else {
            alert(requestObj.statusText);
        }
    }
}
</script>
</body>
</html>
```

Within the code in Listing 18-3, the parameters are set and placed into a variable called *params*:

```
var params = "num1=2&num2=2";
```

After the request object (*requestObj*) is constructed, the parameters are sent within the *send()* method:

```
requestObj.send(params);
```

Case Study: Live Searching and Updating

Microsoft partner ICG Media, LLC, a computer services company, offers their customers an AJAX application to aid in management of the customer's e-mail filtering solution. Part of that application is a form to search for e-mail addresses that have been either whitelisted or blacklisted.

The whitelist/blacklist search uses AJAX to import an XML file and provide results based on input from the administrator. This application can easily be adapted to provide live search results or live bookmarks. Chapter 19, "A Bit Deeper into AJAX," will use a portion of that application to create a live search form, and the next section will introduce an adaptation of the application to create a live searchable bookmark feed using XML.

I find it necessary to access Web browser bookmarks from multiple computers. With that in mind, here's an AJAX application that provides a Bookmarks page. The bookmarks are managed in an XML file in a central location. Then a Web page is built to retrieve the bookmarks and give a search interface.

The bookmark application is shown in Figure 18-1. Granted, it's only showing 3 bookmarks, but the application works the same with 3 bookmarks or 300, and providing just a few makes it easier to demonstrate.

FIGURE 18-1 A view of the live bookmark application

The search box works by narrowing down the list of viewed bookmarks as text is typed into the text box. For example, typing the letter **m** into the text box immediately shows only those bookmarks that begin with the letter *m,* as depicted in Figure 18-2.

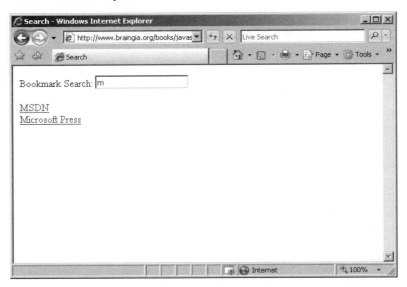

FIGURE 18-2 Typing the letter **m** narrows down the displayed bookmarks to those beginning with *m*.

Further typing, for example adding an **i** to make the characters *mi*, continues to narrow down the available bookmarks, as shown in Figure 18-3.

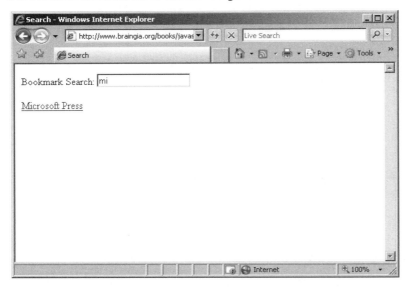

FIGURE 18-3 Adding additional characters to further narrow down the results

When the text is deleted from the text box, the Bookmarks page goes back to its default (as shown in Figure 18-1).

The XML for this application is shown here:

```
<?xml version="1.0" encoding="UTF-8" standalone="yes"?>
<bookmarks xmlns:xsi="http://www.w3.org/2001/XMLSchema-instance">
    <bookmark>
```

```
            <title>Steve Suehring's Home Page</title>
            <url>http://www.braingia.org/</url>
      </bookmark>
      <bookmark>
            <title>MSDN</title>
            <url>http://msdn.microsoft.com/</url>
      </bookmark>
      <bookmark>
            <title>Microsoft Press</title>
            <url>http://www.microsoft.com/mspress</url>
      </bookmark>
</bookmarks>
```

The application itself, along with the Web page, is shown here:

```
<!DOCTYPE HTML PUBLIC "-//W3C//DTD HTML 4.01//EN"
"http://www.w3.org/TR/html4/strict.dtd">
<html>
<head>
<title>Search</title>
</head>
<body>
<form name="nameform" id="nameform" action="" method="post">
Bookmark Search: <input id="textname" type="text" name="textname">
</form>
<div id="data"></div>
<script type="text/javascript">

function textsearch() {
    var textName = document.getElementById("textname");
    var dataNode = document.getElementById("data");
    while (dataNode.hasChildNodes()) {
        dataNode.removeChild(dataNode.firstChild);
    }
    listName(textName.value);
}

function readyAJAX() {
    try {
        return new XMLHttpRequest();
    } catch(e) {
        try {
            return new ActiveXObject('Msxml2.XMLHTTP');
        } catch(e) {
            try {
                return new ActiveXObject('Microsoft.XMLHTTP');
            } catch(e) {
                return "A newer browser is needed.";
            }
        }
    }
}
function listName(text) {
    var xmlEl = AJAXresponse.getElementsByTagName("bookmark");
    for (i = 0; i < xmlEl.length; i++) {
        var div = document.createElement("div");
```

```
            // Create the row elements
            for (j = 0; j < xmlEl[i].childNodes.length; j++) {
                // Skip it if the type is not 1
                if (xmlEl[i].childNodes[j].nodeType != 1) {
                    continue;
                }
                var url = new RegExp("http");
                if (! xmlEl[i].childNodes[j].firstChild.nodeValue.match(url)) {
                    var pattern = "^" + text;
                    var title = xmlEl[i].childNodes[j].firstChild.nodeValue;
                    var nameRegexp = new RegExp(pattern, "i");
                    var existDiv = document.getElementById(title);
                    if (! existDiv) {
                        if (title.match(nameRegexp)) {
                            var anchor = document.createElement("a");
                            var xmlData =
                                document.createTextNode(xmlEl[i].childNodes[j].firstChild.
nodeValue);

                            var urls = AJAXresponse.getElementsByTagName("url");
                            anchor.setAttribute("href", urls[i].firstChild.nodeValue);
                            anchor.appendChild(xmlData);
                            div.appendChild(anchor);
                        }
                    }
                }
            }
            document.getElementById("data").appendChild(div);
        }
    }

    var requestObj = readyAJAX();
    var url = "http://www.braingia.org/books/javascriptsbs/bookmark.xml";
    requestObj.open("GET",url,true);
    requestObj.send();
    var AJAXresponse;
    requestObj.onreadystatechange = function() {
        if (requestObj.readyState == 4) {
            if (requestObj.status == 200) {
                AJAXresponse = requestObj.responseXML;
                listName("");
            } else {
                alert(requestObj.statusText);
            }
        }
    }

    if (window.attachEvent) {
        document.getElementById("textname").attachEvent("onkeyup",textsearch);
    } else {
        document.getElementById("textname").addEventListener("keyup",textsearch,false);
    }

</script>
</body>
</html>
```

The JavaScript portion of the code is broken into several functions, which will be discussed in due course. The HTML for the page consists mainly of only a few lines. Here's the Web form:

```
<form name="nameform" id="nameform" action="" method="post">
Bookmark Search: <input id="textname" type="text" name="textname">
</form>
```

And here's the *div* that will hold each of the bookmarks:

```
<div id="data"></div>
```

The JavaScript portion of the code declares several functions and executes the following code within the main block. This code is largely the same as you've seen throughout this chapter already, insofar as it uses the *readyAJAX()* function and sends an AJAX request for a bookmark XML file to the server. When the response is retrieved, the *listName()* function is called.

In addition to the AJAX code, an event handler is attached to the Web form's text box. The event to be handled is the *onkeyup* event, which detects when a key is released within the text box. The code is like this:

```
var requestObj = readyAJAX();
var url = "http://www.braingia.org/books/javascriptsbs/bookmark.xml";
requestObj.open("GET",url,true);
requestObj.send();
var AJAXresponse;
requestObj.onreadystatechange = function() {
    if (requestObj.readyState == 4) {
        if (requestObj.status == 200) {
            AJAXresponse = requestObj.responseXML;
            listName("");
        } else {
            alert(requestObj.statusText);
        }
    }
}

if (window.attachEvent) {
    document.getElementById("textname").attachEvent("onkeyup",textsearch);
} else {
    document.getElementById("textname").addEventListener("keyup",textsearch,false);
}
```

The event handler that handles key presses in the search form is contained in two functions, *textsearch* and *listName*. The *textsearch* function is responsible for removing bookmarks from the list, calling the *listName()* function.

```
function textsearch() {
    var textName = document.getElementById("textname");
    var dataNode = document.getElementById("data");
```

```
        while (dataNode.hasChildNodes()) {
            dataNode.removeChild(dataNode.firstChild);
        }
        listName(textName.value);
    }
```

Finally, the *listName()* function contains the code to display only those bookmarks that are related to the text that's been typed into the text box. If no text is in the text box, then all bookmarks are shown:

```
function listName(text) {
    var xmlEl = AJAXresponse.getElementsByTagName("bookmark");
    for (i = 0; i < xmlEl.length; i++) {
        var div = document.createElement("div");
        // Create the row elements
        for (j = 0; j < xmlEl[i].childNodes.length; j++) {
            // Skip it if the type is not 1
            if (xmlEl[i].childNodes[j].nodeType != 1) {
                continue;
            }
            var url = new RegExp("http");
            if (! xmlEl[i].childNodes[j].firstChild.nodeValue.match(url)) {
                var pattern = "^" + text;
                var title = xmlEl[i].childNodes[j].firstChild.nodeValue;
                var nameRegexp = new RegExp(pattern, "i");
                var existDiv = document.getElementById(title);
                if (! existDiv) {
                    if (title.match(nameRegexp)) {
                        var anchor = document.createElement("a");
                        var xmlData =
                            document.createTextNode(xmlEl[i].childNodes[j].firstChild.
nodeValue);

                        var urls = AJAXresponse.getElementsByTagName("url");
                        anchor.setAttribute("href", urls[i].firstChild.nodeValue);
                        anchor.appendChild(xmlData);
                        div.appendChild(anchor);
                    }
                }
            }
        }
        document.getElementById("data").appendChild(div);
    }
}
```

Exercises

1. Which of the HTTP request methods covered in this chapter is the most secure? Why?

2. Describe the differences between an *XMLHttpRequest* request/response using HTML, XML, and JSON.

3. Construct a server-side program to return the sum of two numbers that it receives as parameters. Call the program using an asynchronous *XMLHttpRequest* object.

Chapter 19
A Bit Deeper into AJAX

After reading this chapter you'll be able to

- Understand how Asynchronous JavaScript and XML (AJAX) and Cascading Style Sheets (CSS) can be used together.

- Understand more about the relationship between the Document Object Model (DOM), AJAX, and CSS.

- Use AJAX and CSS to create and style a Hypertext Markup Language (HTML) table with Extensible Markup Language (XML) data.

- Create an AJAX-based drop-down text box using CSS.

In the previous chapter, you saw how to use the *xmlHttpRequest* object to send, receive, and process requests and ultimately how to create an AJAX application. In this chapter, you'll see how to use CSS to display data retrieved with AJAX.

The relationship of JavaScript and CSS was covered in Chapter 15, "JavaScript and CSS." In that chapter, you learned that it's possible to change document styles programmatically using JavaScript. In Chapter 17, "JavaScript and XML," you saw how to display XML data as an HTML table. And in Chapter 18, "A Touch of AJAX," you saw how to create a live, searchable bookmarks Web page using some CSS and a lot of the DOM. This chapter shows how to use CSS to style the table from Chapter 17 and expand and retool the bookmark application from Chapter 18, again with the help of CSS and JavaScript.

Along the way, I hope to convey that AJAX is really pretty easy to use. Retrieving and parsing the information using *xmlHttpRequest* is the simple part; it's what you do with that data that matters. That's why CSS and the DOM matter! AJAX is where you put together all the JavaScript that you've learned throughout the book to create larger applications.

Creating an HTML Table with XML and CSS

Chapter 17 presented an example where XML was retrieved and its data was used as part of an HTML table, as depicted in Figure 19-1.

The code to create that table was developed within Chapter 17 and expanded to show not only the data, but also the column headings. The code ended up as shown at the end of Chapter 17.

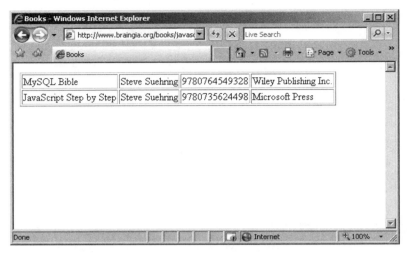

FIGURE 19-1 Displaying XML data in an HTML table

The code from Chapter 17 uses XML methods to obtain the data directly. The next exercise converts the code to retrieve the XML using *xmlHttpRequest*. Like the exercise in Chapter 18, this exercise requires that the XML file is stored on a Web server.

Using *xmlHttpRequest* to retrieve and display XML data

1. Use the books.xml file that you created in Chapter 17, or, if you didn't create one then or didn't save the file, create a file now called books.xml with the following data. Place this file on the same Web server as the HTML file that you create in the next step.

```
<books>
<book>
    <title>JavaScript Step by Step</title>
    <author>Steve Suehring</author>
    <isbn>9780735624498</isbn>
    <publisher>Microsoft Press</publisher>
</book>
<book>
    <title>MySQL Bible</title>
    <author>Steve Suehring</author>
    <isbn>9780764549328</isbn>
    <publisher>Wiley Publishing Inc.</publisher>
</book>
</books>
```

2. Using Microsoft Visual Studio, Eclipse, or another editor, edit the file ajaxbooks.htm in the Chapter19 sample files folder.

3. Within ajaxbooks.htm, add the code shown below in bold type. Be sure to replace the Uniform Resource Locator (URL) *YOUR SERVER HERE* with the correct URL for your Web server. Note that only the function definition and first line of the *displayData()* function are changed from the version in Chapter 17.

```
<!DOCTYPE HTML PUBLIC "-//W3C//DTD HTML 4.01//EN" "http://www.w3.org/TR/html4/strict.
dtd">
<html>
<head>
<title>Books</title>
</head>
<body>
<div id="xmldata"></div>
<script type="text/javascript">

function readyAJAX() {
    try {
        return new XMLHttpRequest();
    } catch(e) {
        try {
            return new ActiveXObject('Msxml2.XMLHTTP');
        } catch(e) {
            try {
                return new ActiveXObject('Microsoft.XMLHTTP');
            } catch(e) {
                return "A newer browser is needed.";
            }
        }
    }
}

var requestObj = readyAJAX();
var url = "http://YOUR SERVER HERE/books.xml";
requestObj.open("GET",url,true);
requestObj.send();
var AJAXresponse;
requestObj.onreadystatechange = function() {
    if (requestObj.readyState == 4) {
        if (requestObj.status == 200) {
            AJAXresponse = requestObj.responseXML;
            displayData(AJAXresponse);
        } else {
            alert(requestObj.statusText);
        }
    }
}

function displayData(response) {
    var xmlEl = response.getElementsByTagName("book");
    var table = document.createElement("table");
    table.border = "1";
    var tbody = document.createElement("tbody");

    // Append the body to the table
    table.appendChild(tbody);
    var row = document.createElement("tr");

    // Append the row to the body
    tbody.appendChild(row);

    for (colHead = 0; colHead < xmlEl[0].childNodes.length; colHead++) {
```

```
                if (xmlEl[0].childNodes[colHead].nodeType != 1) {
                    continue;
                }
                var tableHead = document.createElement("th");
                var colName = document.createTextNode(xmlEl[0].childNodes[colHead].nodeName);
                tableHead.appendChild(colName);
                row.appendChild(tableHead);
            }
            tbody.appendChild(row);

            // Create table row
            for (i = 0; i < xmlEl.length; i++) {
                var row = document.createElement("tr");
                // Create the row/td elements
                for (j = 0; j < xmlEl[i].childNodes.length; j++) {
                    // Skip it if the type is not 1
                    if (xmlEl[i].childNodes[j].nodeType != 1) {
                        continue;
                    }

                    // Insert the actual text/data from the XML document.
                    var td = document.createElement("td");
                    var xmlData =
                        document.createTextNode(xmlEl[i].childNodes[j].firstChild.nodeValue);
                    td.appendChild(xmlData);
                    row.appendChild(td);
                }
                tbody.appendChild(row);
            }
            document.getElementById("xmldata").appendChild(table);
        }

        </script>
        </body>
        </html>
```

4. View the page in a Web browser. You'll receive a page like this:

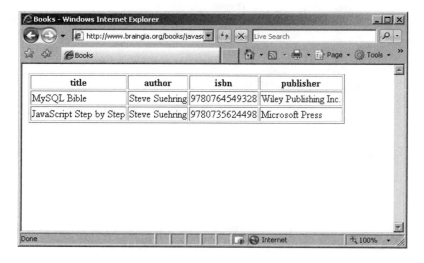

This exercise combined code from each of the last two chapters to show the retrieval and display of XML data using the *xmlHttpRequest* method associated with AJAX applications. Even though the original XML application shown in Chapter 17 is converted to use *xmlHttpRequest*, the table it displays is still rather ugly. This is where CSS styling comes into play.

Styling the Table with CSS

The main function to display the table within the previous exercise is the *displayData()* function. It's within this function where CSS styles can be applied to make the table look more like a table you'd see in a more modern Web application.

One of the first things to do is to remove the border by removing the following line from near the top of the *displayData()* function:

```
table.border = "1";
```

Within the *displayData()* function, there are two primary loops, one to display the column headings and one to display the data itself. The first loop to display the column headings looks like this:

```
for (colHead = 0; colHead < xmlEl[0].childNodes.length; colHead++) {
    if (xmlEl[0].childNodes[colHead].nodeType != 1) {
        continue;
    }
    var tableHead = document.createElement("th");
    var colName = document.createTextNode(xmlEl[0].childNodes[colHead].nodeName);
    tableHead.appendChild(colName);
    row.appendChild(tableHead);
}
tbody.appendChild(row);
```

And the second loop that displays the actual data looks like this:

```
for (i = 0; i < xmlEl.length; i++) {
    var row = document.createElement("tr");
    // Create the row/td elements
    for (j = 0; j < xmlEl[i].childNodes.length; j++) {
        // Skip it if the type is not 1
        if (xmlEl[i].childNodes[j].nodeType != 1) {
            continue;
        }
        // Insert the actual text/data from the XML document.
        var td = document.createElement("td");
        var xmlData = document.createTextNode(xmlEl[i].childNodes[j].firstChild.nodeValue);
        td.appendChild(xmlData);
        row.appendChild(td);
    }
    tbody.appendChild(row);
}
```

Most of the changes made to the table's display will be made within these loops, and I'll highlight the changes as they're made.

Another item to change is the font. (I've always been partial to the Arial font myself.) This is changed using the *fontFamily* style property in JavaScript. This change needs to be made within each of the loops if you'd like to make all the text in the table have an Arial font. The loops now look like this (note the two new lines in bold):

```
for (colHead = 0; colHead < xmlEl[0].childNodes.length; colHead++) {
    if (xmlEl[0].childNodes[colHead].nodeType != 1) {
        continue;
    }
    var tableHead = document.createElement("th");
    var colName = document.createTextNode(xmlEl[0].childNodes[colHead].nodeName);
    tableHead.style.fontFamily = "Arial";
    tableHead.appendChild(colName);
    row.appendChild(tableHead);
}
tbody.appendChild(row);

for (i = 0; i < xmlEl.length; i++) {
    var row = document.createElement("tr");
    // Create the row/td elements
    for (j = 0; j < xmlEl[i].childNodes.length; j++) {
        // Skip it if the type is not 1
        if (xmlEl[i].childNodes[j].nodeType != 1) {
            continue;
        }

        // Insert the actual text/data from the XML document.
        var td = document.createElement("td");
        var xmlData = document.createTextNode(xmlEl[i].childNodes[j].firstChild.nodeValue);
        td.style.fontFamily = "Arial";
        td.appendChild(xmlData);
        row.appendChild(td);
    }
    tbody.appendChild(row);
}
```

The results of these changes and the removal of the table border yields a table that looks like the one shown in Figure 19-2.

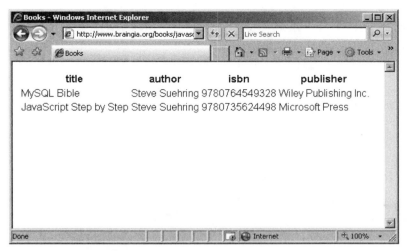

FIGURE 19-2 Beginning to style the table with CSS

Some color would certainly help make the table more readable, especially when there are several or even several hundred or more rows of data. Changing every other row to a slightly different shade and changing the table heading to a different color entirely might also be helpful. Here's what the loops look like with the addition of *backgroundColor* style properties. Again, the changes are in bold.

```
for (colHead = 0; colHead < xmlEl[0].childNodes.length; colHead++) {
    if (xmlEl[0].childNodes[colHead].nodeType != 1) {
        continue;
    }
    var tableHead = document.createElement("th");
    var colName = document.createTextNode(xmlEl[0].childNodes[colHead].nodeName);
    tableHead.style.fontFamily = "Arial";
    tableHead.style.backgroundColor = "#aaabba";
    tableHead.appendChild(colName);
    row.appendChild(tableHead);
}
tbody.appendChild(row);

for (i = 0; i < xmlEl.length; i++) {
    var row = document.createElement("tr");
    // Create the row/td elements
    for (j = 0; j < xmlEl[i].childNodes.length; j++) {
        // Skip it if the type is not 1
        if (xmlEl[i].childNodes[j].nodeType != 1) {
            continue;
        }

        // Insert the actual text/data from the XML document.
        var td = document.createElement("td");
        var xmlData = document.createTextNode(xmlEl[i].childNodes[j].firstChild.nodeValue);
```

```
        if (i % 2) {
            td.style.backgroundColor = "#aaabba";
        }
        td.style.fontFamily = "Arial";
        td.appendChild(xmlData);
        row.appendChild(td);
    }
    tbody.appendChild(row);
}
```

This code uses the modulo operator (%) to shade every other row of the table data with the light gray background. There are only two data rows in this table, so only the second row gets the gray shading. The results from the addition of color are shown in Figure 19-3.

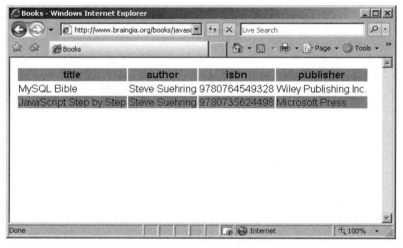

FIGURE 19-3 Adding color to the table using CSS

Creating a Dynamic Drop-down Box

A variation of the bookmark application shown in Chapter 18 can be used to create a live drop-down box. Sometimes this is known as a suggest-as-you-type drop-down box, because as you type, commonly entered values are shown within a drop-down box below the text box, thus making it easier to complete your entry. Google Suggest is one such application.

Another implementation of this same principle is a drop-down box whereby common items (such as U.S. states) are shown as the visitor types. The key to this variation is that there is a certain relatively manageable subset of data that can reasonably be retrieved to populate the live drop-down box quickly. For example, retrieving a subset from a list of the 50 U.S. states is a manageable amount of data to provide in real time as the visitor is typing a query into a text box. Retrieving 1,000,000 database records, on the other hand, is not. One use of this application in business might be to retrieve a list of employees for a company directory.

Here's a demonstration of this application. It retrieves, using *xmlHttpRequest*, a list of the 50 states. When the letter *w* is entered, all the states that begin with that letter are retrieved, as shown in Figure 19-4.

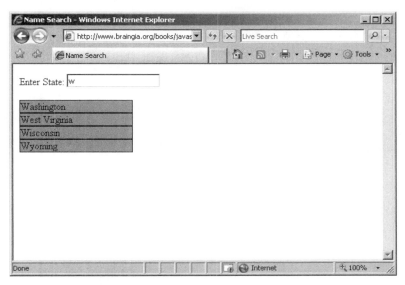

FIGURE 19-4 Retrieving a list of states that begin with the letter *w*

Moving the mouse over the various states changes their background color, as shown in Figure 19-5, where I moved the mouse over Wisconsin (the mouse pointer is not visible in this screenshot).

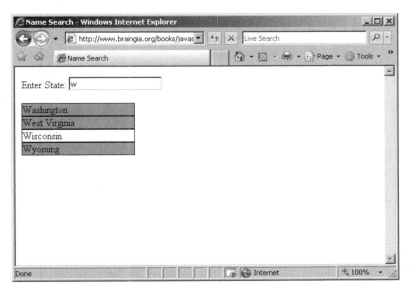

FIGURE 19-5 Moving the mouse over the states to change their background color

Finally, clicking one of the state names causes it to move up into the text box. The result of this action is shown in Figure 19-6. From here, the form might be submitted, taking whatever action is appropriate for the application based on that input.

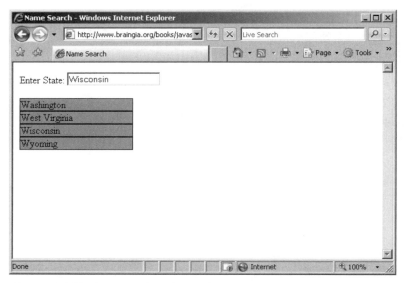

FIGURE 19-6 Moving a state into the text box

This code works the same as the bookmark application code from Chapter 18, insofar as the visitor can continue to type to narrow down or focus the search to their specific selection. Consider the case where the visitor typed the letter *n*. Doing so would reveal the 8 states that begin with the letter *n*. Further typing, say of the word *new*, would narrow that search down to 4 states, and typing more letters would narrow the results even more.

The code for this application is shown in Listing 19-1.

LISTING 19-1 A Search Application

```
<!DOCTYPE HTML PUBLIC "-//W3C//DTD HTML 4.01//EN" "http://www.w3.org/TR/html4/
strict.dtd">
<html>
<head>
<title>State Search</title>
</head>
<body>
<form name="nameform" id="nameform" action="" method="post">
Enter State: <input id="textname" type="text" name="textname">
</form>
<div id="data"></div>
<script type="text/javascript">

function textsearch() {
    var textName = document.getElementById("textname");
```

```
        var dataNode = document.getElementById("data");
    while (dataNode.hasChildNodes()) {
        dataNode.removeChild(dataNode.firstChild);
    }
    if (textName.value != "") {
        listName(textName.value);
    }
}

function readyAJAX() {
    try {
        return new XMLHttpRequest();
    } catch(e) {
        try {
            return new ActiveXObject('Msxml2.XMLHTTP');
        } catch(e) {
            try {
                return new ActiveXObject('Microsoft.XMLHTTP');
            } catch(e) {
                return "A newer browser is needed.";
            }
        }
    }
}

function listName(text) {
    var nameList = AJAXresponse.split(",");
    var pattern = "^" + text;
    var nameRegexp = new RegExp(pattern, "i");
    for (var i = 0; i < nameList.length; i++) {
        var existDiv = document.getElementById(nameList[i]);
        if (! existDiv) {
            if (nameList[i].match(nameRegexp)) {
                var displayDiv = document.getElementById("data");
                var newDiv = document.createElement("div");
                if (window.attachEvent) {
                    newDiv.attachEvent("onclick",function(e) {
                        document.forms["nameform"].textname.value =
                            e.srcElement.firstChild.nodeValue;});
                    newDiv.attachEvent("onmouseover",function(e) {
                        e.srcElement.style.background = "#FFFFFF"; });
                    newDiv.attachEvent("onmouseout",function(e) {
                        e.srcElement.style.background = "#aaabba"; });
                } else {
                    newDiv.addEventListener("click",function () {
                        document.forms["nameform"].textname.value =
                            this.firstChild.nodeValue; },false);
                    newDiv.addEventListener("mouseover",function() {
                        this.style.background = "#FFFFFF"; },false);
                    newDiv.addEventListener("mouseout",function() {
                        this.style.background = "#aaabba"; },false);
                }
                newDiv.setAttribute("id",nameList[i]);
                newDiv.style.background = "#aaabba";
```

```
                    newDiv.style.color = "#000000";
                    newDiv.style.border = "solid 1px";
                    newDiv.style.display = "block";
                    newDiv.style.width = "175px";
                    newDiv.appendChild(document.createTextNode(nameList[i]));
                    displayDiv.appendChild(newDiv);
                }
            }
        }
    }

    var requestObj = readyAJAX();
    var url = "http://YOUR SERVER HERE/statelist.php";
    requestObj.open("GET",url,true);
    requestObj.send();
    var AJAXresponse;
    requestObj.onreadystatechange = function() {
        if (requestObj.readyState == 4) {
            if (requestObj.status == 200) {
                AJAXresponse = requestObj.responseText;
            } else {
                alert(requestObj.statusText);
            }
        }
    }

    if (window.attachEvent) {
        document.getElementById("textname").attachEvent("onkeyup",textsearch);
    } else {
        document.getElementById("textname").addEventListener("keyup",textsearch,false);
    }
    </script>
    </body>
    </html>
```

Much of the code in Listing 19-1 has been seen throughout this book.

The list of states is retrieved through an external function, statelist.php. This file returns a simple comma-separated list of states, like this:

Alabama,Alaska,Arizona,California,Colorado,Delaware,Florida,Georgia, ...

These states are then split according to the comma delimiter and put into an array, like this:

```
var nameList = AJAXresponse.split(",");
```

Some additions to recent applications from the last two chapters include the code to create small CSS-styled drop-down boxes that can be clicked. This code went into the *listName()* function that had been seen in Chapter 18. Event listeners and CSS styles are applied to the HTML *DIV* elements in the *listName* function, shown here with the additional code in bold.

```
function listName(text) {
    var nameList = AJAXresponse.split(",");
    var pattern = "^" + text;
    var nameRegexp = new RegExp(pattern, "i");
    for (var i = 0; i < nameList.length; i++) {
        var existDiv = document.getElementById(nameList[i]);
        if (! existDiv) {
            if (nameList[i].match(nameRegexp)) {
                var displayDiv = document.getElementById("data");
                var newDiv = document.createElement("div");
                if (window.attachEvent) {
                    newDiv.attachEvent("onclick",function(e) {
                        document.forms["nameform"].textname.value =
                            e.srcElement.firstChild.nodeValue;});
                    newDiv.attachEvent("onmouseover",function(e) {
                        e.srcElement.style.background = "#FFFFFF"; });
                    newDiv.attachEvent("onmouseout",function(e) {
                        e.srcElement.style.background = "#aaabba"; });
                } else {
                    newDiv.addEventListener("click",function () {
                        document.forms["nameform"].textname.value =
                            this.firstChild.nodeValue; },false);
                    newDiv.addEventListener("mouseover",function() {
                        this.style.background = "#FFFFFF"; },false);
                    newDiv.addEventListener("mouseout",function() {
                        this.style.background = "#aaabba"; },false);
                }
                newDiv.setAttribute("id",nameList[i]);
                newDiv.style.background = "#aaabba";
                newDiv.style.color = "#000000";
                newDiv.style.border = "solid 1px";
                newDiv.style.display = "block";
                newDiv.style.width = "175px";
                newDiv.appendChild(document.createTextNode(nameList[i]));
                displayDiv.appendChild(newDiv);
            }
        }
    }
}
```

Accepting Input from the User and AJAX

The next logical step in developing AJAX applications is to accept input from the user and do something with that input. Building an AJAX application is all about providing a highly interactive application based on user actions. Unfortunately, to do justice to this subject, I would need to delve into the creation of server-side applications that would handle that input, and that is beyond the scope of this beginner-level book focusing just on JavaScript. With some luck, I'll write another book on intermediate JavaScript or building JavaScript applications that will show both the JavaScript and the server aspects of AJAX.

But I hope that even with this limited coverage, I've been able to convey that the building of AJAX applications is really nothing more than providing friendly, interactive ways for visitors to use applications, and that a large part of this task involves the design surrounding the JavaScript, not *xmlHttpRequest* alone. The *xmlHttpRequest* object is merely a carrier or delivery method for getting data into the program. The layer on which *xmlHttpRequest* operates is well below the presentation layer upon which the page is built. Therefore, the user will never see the *xmlHttpRequest* processing in the background, only the design that you put on the front end of the application.

Exercises

1. Create a *submit* event handler for the state example shown in this chapter such that the state submitted is displayed back to the user when she or he submits the form.

2. Create an application that uses *xmlHttpRequest* to return a list of names (such as an employee directory). You can use either plaintext or XML for the source data.

3. Congratulate yourself for completing the exercises in this book.

Appendix
Answer Key to Exercises

This appendix shows the answers and explanations for the exercises that have appeared throughout the book. In many cases, there is more than one way to solve a problem. Therefore, unless the question specified a particular way to solve the problem, any working implementation is acceptable. It's also expected that your function names will likely differ from the ones in this appendix.

Chapter 1

1. False. While JavaScript is indeed defined by a standards body, ECMA International, it is not supported on all Web browsers. And the support that does exist varies (sometimes widely) among browsers.

2. False. There are many reasons why a visitor to your Web site might have JavaScript disabled. The browser they're using might not support it; they might have special software installed that doesn't support it; or they simply might have JavaScript disabled as a personal preference. You should strive to make your site work without JavaScript, or at least have it fail gracefully for those visitors who don't have JavaScript enabled.

3. A typical JavaScript definition block looks like this:

```
<script type = "text/javascript" >
// JavaScript code goes here
</script>
```

4. False. The version of JavaScript isn't placed within the DOCTYPE definition. In fact, it's quite uncommon to declare the version of JavaScript being used at all.

5. True. JavaScript code can appear in both the head and the body of a Hypertext Markup Language (HTML) document.

Chapter 2

1. The code of mysecondpage.htm looks similar to this, though yours may differ slightly:

```
<!DOCTYPE HTML PUBLIC "-//W3C//DTD HTML 4.01//EN"
"http://www.w3.org/TR/html4/strict.dtd">
<html>
<head>
<title>My Second Page</title>
<script type="text/javascript">
```

```
    alert("Steve Suehring");
    </script>
    </head>
    <body>
    <p>My Second Page</p>
    </body>
    </html>
```

2. Here's the new code, with the changes shown in bold type:

```
<!DOCTYPE HTML PUBLIC "-//W3C//DTD HTML 4.01//EN"
"http://www.w3.org/TR/html4/strict.dtd">
<html>
<head>
<title>My Second Page</title>
<script type="text/javascript">
function callAlert() {
    alert("Steve Suehring");
}
</script>
</head>
<body>
<script type="text/javascript">
callAlert();
</script>
<p>My Second Page</p>
</body>
</html>
```

3. I created a file called 3.htm and a file called 3.js. Here they are (the reference in 3.htm to 3.js is shown in bold type):

3.js:

```
function callAlert() {
    alert("Steve Suehring");
}
```

3.htm:

```
<!DOCTYPE HTML PUBLIC "-//W3C//DTD HTML 4.01//EN"
"http://www.w3.org/TR/html4/strict.dtd">
<html>
<head>
<title>My Second Page</title>
<script type="text/javascript" src="3.js"> </script>
</head>
<body>
<script type="text/javascript">
callAlert();
</script>
<p>My Second Page</p>
</body>
</html>
```

Chapter 3

1. The valid statements are a, b, c, and d. The only invalid statement is e, because it uses a reserved word, *case,* as a variable name.

2. False. Not all JavaScript statements require a semicolon at the end. In fact, semicolons are usually optional.

3. The *orderTotal* variable is changed after the visitor is alerted to how many of an item are ordered, but before the value is returned from the function. The lesson here is that you must be careful not to alter the value or contents of variables unexpectedly. The visitor is expecting to order a certain quantity, but the code clearly changes that quantity after telling the visitor how many he or she ordered!

Chapter 4

1. Variable declarations:

   ```
   var first = 120;

   var second = "5150";

   var third = "Two Hundred Thirty";
   ```

2. Array:

   ```
   var newArray = new Array(10, 20, 30, "first string", "second string");
   ```

3. Escaped string:

   ```
   alert("Steve's response was \"Cool!\"");
   ```

4. Both the *first* and *second* variables should convert just fine. The *third* variable, "Two Hundred Thirty", is reported as *NaN* (not a number) when passed to the *Number()* function.

5. This exercise is for the reader to follow. There is no right or wrong answer.

Chapter 5

1. Alerts:

   ```
   var num1 = 1;
   var num2 = 1;
   var num3 = 19;
   var fourthvar = "84";
   var name1 = "Jakob";
   var name2 = "Edward";
   alert(num1 + num2);
   alert(num3 + fourthvar);
   alert(name1 + name2);
   ```

2. Postfix:

```
var theNum = 1;
alert(theNum);
alert(theNum++);
alert(theNum);
```

Prefix:

```
var theNum = 1;
alert(theNum);
alert(++theNum);
alert(theNum);
```

3. Code:

```
var num1 = 1;
var num2 = 1;
var num3 = 19;
var fourthvar = "84";
var name1 = "Jakob";
var name2 = "Edward";
alert(typeof num1);
alert(typeof num2);
alert(typeof num3);
alert(typeof fourthvar);
alert(typeof name1);
alert(typeof name2);
```

This should result in three alerts with the word *number* followed by three others with the word *string*.

4. False. Unary operators appear fairly often in JavaScript, especially within *for* loops that increment a variable using the ++ postfix operator.

5. False. While saving a few bytes is helpful, especially for Web applications, it's almost always preferable to spend those same few bytes making the code readable and maintainable.

Chapter 6

1. Replace *YOUR NAME* in the following code with the appropriate content:

```
var inputName = prompt("Please enter your name:");
switch(inputName) {
    case "YOUR NAME":
        alert("Welcome " + inputName);
        break;
    case "Steve":
        alert("Go Away");
        break;
    default:
        alert("Please Come Back Later " + inputName);
}
```

2. Here's the code:

```
var temp = prompt("Please enter the current temperature");
if (temp > 100) {
    alert("Please cool down");
} else if (temp < 20) {
    alert("Better warm up");
}
```

Note that it would also be a good idea to provide a default action in case the temperature is between 20 and 100!

3. This exercise is actually impossible to accomplish as specified. Because ternary operators expect a single test condition and Exercise 2 required two conditions, a ternary operator cannot be used to accomplish exactly the same task. The following code will create an alert that tells the visitor to cool down if the temperature is above 100 and tells her or him to warm up if the temp is less than or equal to 100:

```
var temp = prompt("Please enter the current temperature");
temp > 100 ? alert("Please cool down") : alert("Better warm up");
```

4. Here's the code:

```
for (var i = 1; i < 101; i++) {
    if (i == 99) {
        alert("The number is " + i);
    }
}
```

Note that because the variable *i* began counting at 1 (as was called for in the exercise), the counter needs to go to 101 to meet the requirement of counting from 1 to 100.

5. Here's the code:

```
var i = 1;
while (i < 101) {
    if (i == 99) {
        alert("The number is " + i);
    }
    i++;
}
```

Note the placement of the postfix increment of the *i* variable within the loop.

Chapter 7

1. Here's the code:

```
<head>
    <title>Chapter 7 Exercise 1</title>
<script type = "text/javascript" >
function incrementNum(theNumber) {
    if (isNaN(theNumber)) {
```

```
            alert("Sorry, " + theNumber + " isn't a number.");
            return;
        }
        return theNumber + 1;
    }
    </script>
    </head>
    <body>
    <script type = "text/javascript" >
    alert(incrementNum(3));
    </script>
    </body>
```

2. Here's the code:

```
function addNums(firstNum,secondNum) {
    if ((isNaN(firstNum)) || (isNaN(secondNum))) {
        alert("Sorry, both arguments must be numbers.");
        return;
    }
    else if (firstNum > secondNum) {
        alert(firstNum + " is greater than " + secondNum);
    }
    else {
        return firstNum + secondNum;
    }
}
```

3. This exercise is meant to show variable scoping problems. Note how the value of the *result* variable changes outside the function even though the change is made only within the function. The two locations for alerts are shown in bold within the following code:

```
function addNumbers() {
    firstNum = 4;
    secondNum = 8;
    result = firstNum + secondNum;
    return result;
}
result = 0;
alert(result);
sum = addNumbers();
alert(result);
```

4. Here's the code:

```
<head>
<title>Chapter 7 Exercise 4</title>
<script type="text/javascript">
var stars = ["Polaris","Aldebaran","Deneb","Vega","Altair","Dubhe","Regulus"];
var constells = ["Ursa Minor","Taurus","Cygnus","Lyra","Aquila","Ursa Major","Leo"];

function searchStars(star) {
    for (var i = 0; i < stars.length; i++) {
        if (stars[i] == star) {
            return constells[i];
```

```
            }
        }
        return star + " Not Found.";
    }
    </script>
    </head>
    <body>
    <script type = "text/javascript" >
    var inputStar = prompt("Enter star name: ");
    alert(searchStars(inputStar));
    </script>
    <p>Stars</p>
    </body>
```

Chapter 8

1. Here's the code:

```
var star = ["Polaris", "Deneb", "Vega", "Altair"];
for (var i = 0; i < star.length; i++) {
    alert(star[i]);
}
```

2. Here's one way:

```
function Song(artist,length,title) {
    this.artist = artist;
    this.length = length;
    this.title = title;
}

song1 = new Song("First Artist","3:30","First Song Title");
song2 = new Song("Second Artist","4:11","Second Song Title");
song3 = new Song("Third Artist","2:12","Third Song Title");
```

3. Assuming the code given in the exercise, this code in the body would concatenate all the names into one long string, as follows:

```
var names = new Array;
for (var propt in star) {
    names += propt;
}
alert(names);
```

To comma-delimit the names would look like this:

```
var names = new Array;
for (var propt in star) {
    if (names != "") {
        names += "," + propt;
    } else {
        names = propt;
    }
}
alert(names);
```

Chapter 9

1. Here's the code:

```
if (screen.availHeight < 768) {
    alert("Available Height: " + screen.availHeight);
}
if (screen.availWidth < 1024) {
    alert("Available Width: " + screen.availWidth);
}
```

2. The full code is shown here, including the code from the step-by-step exercise. The additional code for this exercise is shown in bold. Note the use of the *unescape()* function to remove the Uniform Resource Locator (URL)–encoded *%20* (space) character. This is necessary because the country name "Great Britain" specified in this exercise must be URL-escaped for HTTP GET requests.

```
<!DOCTYPE HTML PUBLIC "-//W3C//DTD HTML 4.01//EN"
"http://www.w3.org/TR/html4/strict.dtd">
<html>
<head>
    <title>Location, Location, Location</title>
    <script type = "text/javascript">
        function showProps() {
            var body = document.getElementsByTagName("body")[0];
            for (var prop in location) {
                var elem = document.createElement("p");
                var text = document.createTextNode(prop + ": " + location[prop]);
                elem.appendChild(text);
                body.appendChild(elem);
            }
            if (location.search) {
                var querystring = location.search.substring(1);
                var splits = querystring.split('&');
                for (var i = 0; i < splits.length; i++) {
                    var splitpair = splits[i].split('=');
                    var elem = document.createElement("p");
                    var text = document.createTextNode(splitpair[0] + ": " +
splitpair[1]);
                    if (splitpair[0] == "country") {
                        switch(unescape(splitpair[1])) {
                            case "Brazil":
                                alert("Obrigado");
                                break;
                            case "Great Britain":
                                alert("Thank You");
                                break;
                        }
                    }
                    elem.appendChild(text);
                    body.appendChild(elem);
                }
            }
        }
```

```
        </script>
</head>
<body onload="showProps()">
<p>Chapter 9</p>
</body>
</html>
```

3. This exercise doesn't have an answer in the answer key. The reader can install the User Agent Switcher to complete the exercise.

Chapter 10

1. Here's the code:

```
var newelement = document.createElement("p");
newelement.setAttribute("id","pelement");
document.body.appendChild(newelement);
newelement.appendChild(document.createTextNode("This is a paragraph, albeit a short
one."));
var anchorelem = document.createElement("a");
anchorelem.setAttribute("id","aelement");
anchorelem.setAttribute("href","http://www.braingia.org/");
document.body.appendChild(anchorelem);
anchorelem.appendChild(document.createTextNode("Go To Steve Suehring's Web Site."));
```

2. Here's the code:

```
var newelement = document.createElement("p");
newelement.setAttribute("id","pelement");
document.body.appendChild(newelement);
newelement.appendChild(document.createTextNode("This is a paragraph, albeit a short
one."));
var anchorelem = document.createElement("a");
anchorelem.setAttribute("id","aelement");
anchorelem.setAttribute("href","http://www.braingia.org/");
document.body.appendChild(anchorelem);
anchorelem.appendChild(document.createTextNode("Click Here"));

var existingp = document.getElementById("pelement");
existingp.firstChild.nodeValue="This is the new text.";
var newanchor = document.getElementById("aelement");
newanchor.setAttribute("href","http://www.microsoft.com/");
```

3. Here's the code:

```
<head>
<title>Chapter 10 Exercises</title>
</script>
</head>
<body>
<div id="thetable"></div>
<script type = "text/javascript" >
var table = document.createElement("table");
```

```
        table.border = "1";
        var tbody = document.createElement("tbody");

        // Append the body to the table
        table.appendChild(tbody);
        var row = document.createElement("tr");

        // Create table row
        for (i = 1; i < 3; i++) {
            var row = document.createElement("tr");
            // Create the row/td elements
            for (j = 1; j < 3; j++) {
                // Insert the actual text/data from the XML document.
                var td = document.createElement("td");
                var data = document.createTextNode("Hello - I'm Row " + i + ", Column " + j);
                td.appendChild(data);
                row.appendChild(td);
            }
            tbody.appendChild(row);
        }
        document.getElementById("thetable").appendChild(table);
    </script>
</body>
```

Chapter 11

1. See the section titled "Working with Select Boxes" in Chapter 11 for an example solution for this exercise.

2. Based on the pizza.htm example, the *<head>* portion of code now looks like this, with the additions shown in bold:

```
<head>
    <title>Pizza</title>
    <script type = "text/javascript">

    function prepza() {
        var checkboxes = document.forms["pizzaform"].toppingcheck.length;
        var crusttype = document.forms["pizzaform"].crust;
        var size = document.forms["pizzaform"].size;
        var crustlength = crusttype.length;
        var sizelength = crusttype.length;
        var newelement = document.createElement("p");
        newelement.setAttribute("id","orderheading");
        document.body.appendChild(newelement);
        newelement.appendChild(document.createTextNode("This pizza will have:"));

        for (var c = 0; c < crustlength; c++) {
            if (crusttype[c].checked) {
                var newelement = document.createElement("p");
                newelement.setAttribute("id","crustelement" + i);
                document.body.appendChild(newelement);
                newelement.appendChild(document.createTextNode(
```

```
                                crusttype[c].value + " Crust"));
                }
        }

        for (var s = 0; s < sizelength; s++) {
            if (size[s].checked) {
                    var newelement = document.createElement("p");
                    newelement.setAttribute("id","sizeelement" + i);
                    document.body.appendChild(newelement);
                    newelement.appendChild(document.createTextNode(size[s].value + "
Size"));
            }
        }

        for (var i = 0; i < checkboxes; i++) {
            if (document.forms["pizzaform"].toppingcheck[i].checked) {
                    var newelement = document.createElement("p");
                    newelement.setAttribute("id","newelement" + i);
                    document.body.appendChild(newelement);
                    newelement.appendChild(document.createTextNode(
                        document.forms["pizzaform"].toppingcheck[i].value));
            }
        }
    }
    </script>
</head>
```

The HTML looks like this, with the additions again shown in bold:

```
<form id="pizzaform" action="#" onsubmit="return false;">
<table>
<tr><td>Toppings</td><td>Crust</td><td>Size</td></tr>
<tr>
<td><input type="checkbox" id="topping1" value="Sausage" name="toppingcheck"
/>Sausage</td>
<td><input type="radio" name="crust" value="Regular" checked="checked" id="radio1"
/>Regular</td>
<td><input type="radio" name="size" value="Small" checked="checked" id="radiosize1"
/>Small</td>
</tr>
<tr>
<td><input type="checkbox" id="topping2" value="Pepperoni" name="toppingcheck"
/>Pepperoni</td>
<td><input type="radio" name="crust" value="Deep Dish" id="radio2" />Deep Dish</td>
<td><input type="radio" name="size" value="Medium" id="radiosize2" />Medium</td>
</tr>
<tr>
<td><input type="checkbox" id="topping3" value="Ham" name="toppingcheck" />Ham</td>
<td><input type="radio" name="crust" value="Thin" id="radio3" />Thin</td>
<td><input type="radio" name="size" value="Large" id="radiosize3" />Large</td>
</tr>
<tr>
<td><input type="checkbox" id="topping4" value="Green Peppers" name="toppingcheck"
/>Green Peppers</td>
<td></td>
</tr>
```

```
<tr>
<td><input type="checkbox" id="topping5" value="Mushrooms" name="toppingcheck"
/>Mushrooms</td>
<td></td>
</tr>
<tr>
<td><input type="checkbox" id="topping6" value="Onions" name="toppingcheck" />Onions
</td>
<td></td>
</tr>
<tr>
<td><input type="checkbox" id="topping7" value="Pineapple" name="toppingcheck"
/>Pineapple</td>
<td></td>
</tr>
</table>
<p><input type="submit" id="formsubmit" name="formsubmit" value="Prep Pizza"
onclick="prepza();" /></p>
</form>
```

3. Add the following code to the *<head>* portion of the pizza application from the previous exercise:

```
function flip(pizzatype) {
    if (pizzatype.value == "Veggie Special") {
        document.getElementById("peppers").checked = "true";
        document.getElementById("onions").checked = "true";
        document.getElementById("mushrooms").checked = "true";
    } else if (pizzatype.value == "Meat Special") {
        document.getElementById("sausage").checked = "true";
        document.getElementById("pepperoni").checked = "true";
        document.getElementById("ham").checked = "true";
    } else if (pizzatype.value == "Hawaiian") {
        document.getElementById("ham").checked = "true";
        document.getElementById("pineapple").checked = "true";
    }
}
```

Use the following HTML form. (Note the addition of three buttons and the change to each ingredient's *id* attribute.)

```
<form id="pizzaform" action="#" onsubmit="return false;">
<p>
<input type="button" onclick="flip(veggiespecial)" name="veggiespecial" value="Veggie
Special" />
<input type="button" onclick="flip(meatspecial)" name="meatspecial" value="Meat
Special" />
<input type="button" onclick="flip(hawaiian)" name="hawaiian" value="Hawaiian" />
</p>
<table>
<tr><td>Toppings</td><td>Crust</td><td>Size</td></tr>
<tr>
<td><input type="checkbox" id="sausage" value="Sausage" name="toppingcheck"
/>Sausage</td>
<td><input type="radio" name="crust" value="Regular" checked="checked" id="radio1"
/>Regular</td>
```

```
<td><input type="radio" name="size" value="Small" checked="checked" id="radiosize1"
/>Small</td>
</tr>
<tr>
<td><input type="checkbox" id="pepperoni" value="Pepperoni" name="toppingcheck"
/>Pepperoni</td>
<td><input type="radio" name="crust" value="Deep Dish" id="radio2" />Deep Dish</td>
<td><input type="radio" name="size" value="Medium" id="radiosize2" />Medium</td>
</tr>
<tr>
<td><input type="checkbox" id="ham" value="Ham" name="toppingcheck" />Ham</td>
<td><input type="radio" name="crust" value="Thin" id="radio3" />Thin</td>
<td><input type="radio" name="size" value="Large" id="radiosize3" />Large</td>
</tr>
<tr>
<td><input type="checkbox" id="peppers" value="Green Peppers" name="toppingcheck"
/>Green Peppers</td>
<td></td>
</tr>
<tr>
<td><input type="checkbox" id="mushrooms" value="Mushrooms" name="toppingcheck"
/>Mushrooms</td>
<td></td>
</tr>
<tr>
<td><input type="checkbox" id="onions" value="Onions" name="toppingcheck" />Onions</
td>
<td></td>
</tr>
<tr>
<td><input type="checkbox" id="pineapple" value="Pineapple" name="toppingcheck"
/>Pineapple</td>
<td></td>
</tr>
</table>
<p><input type="submit" id="formsubmit" name="formsubmit" value="Prep Pizza"
onclick="prepza();" /></p>
</form>
```

Chapter 12

1. A variation on an example in the chapter:

```
<!DOCTYPE HTML PUBLIC "-//W3C//DTD HTML 4.01//EN"
"http://www.w3.org/TR/html4/strict.dtd">
<html>
<head>
<title>Hello Cookie</title>
<script type = "text/javascript">
var cookName = "cookie1";
var cookVal = "testvalue";
var date = new Date();
date.setTime(date.getTime()+86400000);
var expireDate = date.toGMTString();
```

```
       var myCookie = cookName + "=" + cookVal + ";expires=" + expireDate;
       document.cookie = myCookie;
       </script>
       </head>
       <body>
       <p>Hello</p>
       </body>
       </html>
```

2. Basically the same as Exercise 1, with the changed lines shown in bold:

```
       <!DOCTYPE HTML PUBLIC "-//W3C//DTD HTML 4.01//EN"
       "http://www.w3.org/TR/html4/strict.dtd">
       <html>
       <head>
       <title>Hello Cookie</title>
       <script type = "text/javascript">
       var cookName = "cookie2";
       var cookVal = "testvalue";
       var date = new Date();
       date.setTime(date.getTime()+86400000);
       var expireDate = date.toGMTString();
       var myCookie = cookName + "=" + cookVal + ";expires=" + expireDate + ";secure";
       document.cookie = myCookie;
       </script>
       </head>
       <body>
       <p>Hello</p>
       </body>
       </html>
```

3. Unless you're using a Secure Sockets Layer (SSL) connection, you won't be able to read a cookie with the *secure* flag set.

4. In Exercise 1, I set a cookie named *cookie1*; therefore, that's the only one I want to display for this exercise. The code is as follows:

```
       <!DOCTYPE HTML PUBLIC "-//W3C//DTD HTML 4.01//EN"
       "http://www.w3.org/TR/html4/strict.dtd">
       <html>
       <head>
       <title>Reading Cookie</title>
       <script type = "text/javascript">
       var incCookies = document.cookie.split(";");
       for (var c = 0; c < incCookies.length; c++) {
           var splitCookies = incCookies[c].split("=");
           if (splitCookies[0] == "cookie1") {
               alert(incCookies[c]);
           }
       }
       </script>
       </head>
       <body>
       <p>Hello</p>
       </body>
       </html>
```

Chapter 13

1. See Listing 13-2 in Chapter 13 for an example of this exercise.

2. Within the slideshow example, there is a function called *nextimage()*. That's where the changes should be made for this exercise. The changes are shown in bold here.

```
function nextimage() {
    var img = document.getElementById("slideimage");
    var imgname = img.name.split("_");
    var index = imgname[1];
    if (index == images.length - 1) {
        var startover = confirm(
            "You've reached the last image. Start over from the beginning?");
        if (startover)  {
            index = 0;
        } else {
            return;
        }
    } else {
        index++;
    }
    img.src = images[index];
    img.name = "image_" + index;
}
```

3. See Listing 13-2 in this chapter for an example of preloading images. That same code logic would be applied to the image map that you make for this exercise.

Chapter 14

1. Here's the code:

```
<!DOCTYPE HTML PUBLIC "-//W3C//DTD HTML 4.01//EN"
"http://www.w3.org/TR/html4/strict.dtd">
<html>
<head>
<title>Onclick</title>
<script type="text/javascript">
function handleclick() {
    alert("You Clicked Here");
    return false;
}

</script>
</head>
<body>
<p><a href="#" onclick="return handleclick();">Click Here</a></p>
</body>
</html>
```

2. Here's the code:

```
<!DOCTYPE HTML PUBLIC "-//W3C//DTD HTML 4.01//EN"
"http://www.w3.org/TR/html4/strict.dtd">
<html>
<head>

<title>Onclick</title>
<script type="text/javascript">
function handleclick() {
    alert("You Clicked Here");
    return false;
}

</script>
</head>
<body>
<p><a id="link1" href="#">Click Here</a></p>
<script type = "text/javascript" >
var link1 = document.getElementById("link1");
if (typeof window.addEventListener != "undefined") {
    link1.addEventListener("click",handleclick,false);
} else {
    link1.attachEvent("onclick",handleclick);
}
</script>

</body>
</html>
```

3. No JavaScript is necessary for this. The code looks as follows:

```
<!DOCTYPE HTML PUBLIC "-//W3C//DTD HTML 4.01//EN"
"http://www.w3.org/TR/html4/strict.dtd">
<html>
<head>
<title>New Tab</title>
</head>
<body>
<p><a target="Microsoft" href="http://www.microsoft.com" id="mslink">Go To Microsoft
</a></p>
</body>
</html>
```

4. Here's the code:

```
<!DOCTYPE HTML PUBLIC "-//W3C//DTD HTML 4.01//EN"
"http://www.w3.org/TR/html4/strict.dtd">
<html>
<head>
<title>window open</title>
<script type="text/javascript">
function openwin(event) {
    if (typeof window.open != "undefined") {
        var opened =window.open(
            "http://www.braingia.org","",
```

```
"height=300,width=250,menubar=yes,location=yes,resizable=yes,scrollbars=yes,status=
yes");
        event.preventDefault();
        return false;
    } else {
        return true;
    }
}
</script>
</head>
<body>
<p><a target="Microsoft" href="http://www.microsoft.com" id="mslink">Go To Microsoft
</a></p>
<p id="braingia"><a href="DYNAMIC URL GOES HERE" id="braingialink">
Go To Steve Suehring's Page</a></p>
<script type = "text/javascript">
var braingialink = document.getElementById("braingialink");
if (window.addEventListener) {
    braingialink.addEventListener("click",openwin,false);
} else {
    braingialink.attachEvent("onclick",openwin);
}
</script>
</body>
</html>
```

Chapter 15

1. Here's an example page:

```
<!DOCTYPE HTML PUBLIC "-//W3C//DTD HTML 4.01//EN"
"http://www.w3.org/TR/html4/strict.dtd">
<html>
<head>
<title>CSS</title>
</head>
<body>
<h1 id="h1element">The Title</h1>
<p id="firstelement">The first element.</p>
<p id="secondelement">The second element.</p>
</body>
</html>
```

2. This code will change the element named *firstelement* so that its font color is blue:

```
<script type = "text/javascript" >
var element1 = document.getElementById("firstelement");
element1.style.color = "#0000FF";
</script>
```

3. This code hides all the *<p>* elements using the Cascading Style Sheets (CSS) visibility property:

```
<script type = "text/javascript" >
var pelements = document.getElementsByTagName("p");
```

```
    for (var i = 0; i < pelements.length; i++) {
        pelements[i].style.visibility = "hidden";
    }
    </script>
```

4. This code shows the visibility setting both before and after it has been set within the script. When you run the code, notice that the alert is empty prior to the property being set.

```
<script type = "text/javascript" >
var pelements = document.getElementsByTagName("p");
for (var i = 0; i < pelements.length; i++) {
    alert(pelements[i].style.visibility);
    pelements[i].style.visibility = "hidden";
    alert(pelements[i].style.visibility);
}
</script>
```

5. This solution uses the form.htm file found in Chapter 15:

```
<!DOCTYPE HTML PUBLIC "-//W3C//DTD HTML 4.01//EN"
"http://www.w3.org/TR/html4/strict.dtd">
<html>
<head>
<title>Form Validation</title>
<script type="text/javascript" src="form.js"></script>
</head>
<body>
<form name="formexample" id="formexample" action="#">
<div id="citydiv">City: <input id="city" name="city"></div>
<div><input id="submit" type="submit"></div>
</form>
<script type="text/javascript">
    function init() {
        document.forms[0].onsubmit = function() { return checkValid() };
    }
    window.onload = init;
</script>
</body>
</html>
```

The form.js file is where the new element with the error text is created and appended. Here it is, with the additional lines shown in bold type:

```
function checkValid() {
    var cityField = document.forms[0]["city"];
    if (cityField.value != "Stevens Point") {
        cityField.style.background = "#FF0000";
        var citydiv = document.getElementById("citydiv");
        var feedbackdiv = document.createElement("div");
        feedbackdiv.setAttribute("id","feedback");
        citydiv.appendChild(feedbackdiv);
        feedbackdiv.appendChild(document.createTextNode("Incorrect City."));
        return false;
    } else {
```

```
        return true;
    }
}
```

Chapter 16

1. Listing 16-1 in Chapter 16 provides a solution for this exercise.

2. An alert provides visual feedback, so that works as a solution to this problem. Better visual feedback can be found in the solution to Exercise 5 in Chapter 15, shown previously, where a new element was used. Here's the basic solution to this problem:

```
<!DOCTYPE HTML PUBLIC "-//W3C//DTD HTML 4.01//EN"
"http://www.w3.org/TR/html4/strict.dtd">
<html>
<head>
<title>Try/Catch</title>
<script type="text/javascript">
</script>
</head>
<body>
<form name="formexample" id="formexample" action="#">
<div id="citydiv">Enter a City: <input id="city" name="city"></div>
<div><input id="submit" type="submit"></div>
</form>
<script type="text/javascript">
function checkValid() {
    try {
        var cityField = document.forms[0]["city"];
        if (cityField.value != "Stockholm") {
            throw "It's not Stockholm";
        }
    }
    catch(errorObject) {
        alert(errorObject);
    }
}
function init() {
    document.forms[0].onsubmit = function() { return checkValid() };
}
window.onload = init;
</script>
</body>
</html>
```

3. Here's the code:

```
<!DOCTYPE HTML PUBLIC "-//W3C//DTD HTML 4.01//EN"
"http://www.w3.org/TR/html4/strict.dtd">
<html>
<head>
<title>Try/Catch</title>
<script type="text/javascript">
</script>
```

```
        </head>
        <body>
        <form name="formexample" id="formexample" action="#">
        <div id="citydiv">Enter a Number Between 1 and 100: <input id="num" name="num"></div>
        <div><input id="submit" type="submit"></div>
        </form>
        <script type="text/javascript">
        function checkValid() {
            try {
                var numField = document.forms[0]["num"];
                if (isNaN(numField.value)) {
                    throw "it's not a number";
                }
                if ((numField.value > 100) || (numField.value < 1)) {
                    numField.style.background = "#FF0000";
                    return false;
                }
                else {
                    numField.style.background = "#FFFFFF";
                    return true;
                }
            }
            catch(errorObject) {
                alert(errorObject);
            }
            finally {
                alert("Thank you for playing.");
            }
        }
        function init() {
            document.forms[0].onsubmit = function() { return checkValid() };
        }
        window.onload = init;
        </script>
        </body>
        </html>
```

Chapter 17

1. This solution requires the books.htm and books.xml files that are used within Chapter 17. Only books.htm is changed for the solution. The few changes to this file are highlighted in bold.

```
<!DOCTYPE HTML PUBLIC "-//W3C//DTD HTML 4.01//EN"
"http://www.w3.org/TR/html4/strict.dtd">
<html>
<head>
<title>Books</title>
</head>
<body>
<div id="xmldata"></div>
<p><a href="#" id="displaytable">Display Table</a></p>
<script type="text/javascript">
```

```
var tablelink = document.getElementById("displaytable");
if (typeof window.addEventListener != "undefined") {
    tablelink.addEventListener("click",getXML,false);
} else {
    tablelink.attachEvent("onclick",getXML);
}


function displayData() {
    var xmlEl = docObj.getElementsByTagName("book");
    var table = document.createElement("table");
    table.border = "1";
    var tbody = document.createElement("tbody");

    // Append the body to the table
    table.appendChild(tbody);
    var row = document.createElement("tr");

    for (colHead = 0; colHead < xmlEl[0].childNodes.length; colHead++) {
        if (xmlEl[0].childNodes[colHead].nodeType != 1) {
            continue;
        }
        var tableHead = document.createElement("th");
        var colName = document.createTextNode(xmlEl[0].childNodes[colHead].nodeName);
        tableHead.appendChild(colName);
        row.appendChild(tableHead);
    }
    tbody.appendChild(row);


    // Create table row
    for (i = 0; i < xmlEl.length; i++) {
        var row = document.createElement("tr");
        // Create the row/td elements
        for (j = 0; j < xmlEl[i].childNodes.length; j++) {
            // Skip it if the type is not 1
            if (xmlEl[i].childNodes[j].nodeType != 1) {
                continue;
            }

            // Insert the actual text/data from the XML document.
            var td = document.createElement("td");
            var xmlData = document.createTextNode(xmlEl[i].childNodes[j].firstChild.
nodeValue);
            td.appendChild(xmlData);
            row.appendChild(td);
        }
        tbody.appendChild(row);
    }
    document.getElementById("xmldata").appendChild(table);
}

function getXML()
{
    tablelink.style.visibility = "hidden";
    if (typeof document.implementation.createDocument != "undefined")
```

```
    {
        docObj = document.implementation.createDocument("", "", null);
        docObj.onload = displayData;
    }
    else if (window.ActiveXObject)
    {
        docObj = new ActiveXObject("Microsoft.XMLDOM");
        docObj.onreadystatechange = function () {
            if (docObj.readyState == 4) displayData()
        };
    }
    docObj.load("books.xml");
}

</script>
</body>
</html>
```

Bonus: The following code adds a "Display Table" link, and then, when the table is displayed, it adds a "Hide Table" link. This wasn't part of the exercise.

```
<!DOCTYPE HTML PUBLIC "-//W3C//DTD HTML 4.01//EN"
"http://www.w3.org/TR/html4/strict.dtd">
<html>
<head>
<title>Books</title>
</head>
<body>
<div id="xmldata"></div>
<p><a href="#" id="displaytable">Display Table</a></p>
<script type="text/javascript">

var tablelink = document.getElementById("displaytable");
if (typeof window.addEventListener != "undefined") {
    tablelink.addEventListener("click",getXML,false);
} else {
    tablelink.attachEvent("onclick",getXML);
}


function displayData() {
    var xmlEl = docObj.getElementsByTagName("book");
    var table = document.createElement("table");
    table.setAttribute("id","bookstable");
    table.border = "1";
    var tbody = document.createElement("tbody");

    // Append the body to the table
    table.appendChild(tbody);
    var row = document.createElement("tr");

    for (colHead = 0; colHead < xmlEl[0].childNodes.length; colHead++) {
        if (xmlEl[0].childNodes[colHead].nodeType != 1) {
            continue;
        }
        var tableHead = document.createElement("th");
```

```
                var colName = document.createTextNode(xmlEl[0].childNodes[colHead].nodeName);
                tableHead.appendChild(colName);
                row.appendChild(tableHead);
        }
        tbody.appendChild(row);


        // Create table row
        for (i = 0; i < xmlEl.length; i++) {
                var row = document.createElement("tr");
                // Create the row/td elements
                for (j = 0; j < xmlEl[i].childNodes.length; j++) {
                        // Skip it if the type is not 1
                        if (xmlEl[i].childNodes[j].nodeType != 1) {
                                continue;
                        }

                        // Insert the actual text/data from the XML document.
                        var td = document.createElement("td");
                        var xmlData = document.createTextNode(xmlEl[i].childNodes[j].firstChild.
nodeValue);
                        td.appendChild(xmlData);
                        row.appendChild(td);
                }
                tbody.appendChild(row);
        }
        var tableanchor = document.createElement("a");
        var tableanchortext = document.createTextNode("Hide Table");
        tableanchor.setAttribute("id","hidetable");
        tableanchor.setAttribute("href","#");
        tableanchor.appendChild(tableanchortext);
        if (typeof window.addEventListener != "undefined") {
                tableanchor.addEventListener("click",hideTable,false);
        } else {
                tableanchor.attachEvent("onclick",hideTable);
        }
        document.getElementById("xmldata").appendChild(tableanchor);
        document.getElementById("xmldata").appendChild(table);
}

function hideTable() {
        var bookstable = document.getElementById("bookstable");
        bookstable.style.display = "none";
        tablelink.style.display = "";
        var tableanchor = document.getElementById("hidetable");
        tableanchor.style.display = "none";
}

function getXML()
{
        tablelink.style.display = "none";
        if (typeof document.implementation.createDocument != "undefined")
        {
                docObj = document.implementation.createDocument("", "", null);
                docObj.onload = displayData;
        }
```

```
        else if (window.ActiveXObject)
        {
            docObj = new ActiveXObject("Microsoft.XMLDOM");
            docObj.onreadystatechange = function () {
                if (docObj.readyState == 4) displayData()
            };
        }
        docObj.load("books.xml");
    }

</script>
</body>
</html>
```

2. This solution requires the books.xml file as well. Most of the code is the same as the
   final books.htm code in Chapter 17, with the differences shown in bold:

```
<!DOCTYPE HTML PUBLIC "-//W3C//DTD HTML 4.01//EN"
"http://www.w3.org/TR/html4/strict.dtd">
<html>
<head>
<title>Books</title>
</head>
<body>
<div id="xmldata"></div>
<script type="text/javascript">

window.onload = getXML;

function displayData() {
    var xmlEl = docObj.getElementsByTagName("book");
    var table = document.createElement("table");
    table.border = "1";
    var tbody = document.createElement("tbody");

    // Append the body to the table
    table.appendChild(tbody);
    var row = document.createElement("tr");

    for (colHead = 0; colHead < xmlEl[0].childNodes.length; colHead++) {
        if (xmlEl[0].childNodes[colHead].nodeType != 1) {
            continue;
        }
        var tableHead = document.createElement("th");
        var colName = document.createTextNode(xmlEl[0].childNodes[colHead].nodeName);
        tableHead.appendChild(colName);
        row.appendChild(tableHead);
    }
    tbody.appendChild(row);


    // Create table row
    for (i = 0; i < xmlEl.length; i++) {
        var row = document.createElement("tr");
        // Create the row/td elements
```

```
        for (j = 0; j < xmlEl[i].childNodes.length; j++) {
            // Skip it if the type is not 1
            if (xmlEl[i].childNodes[j].nodeType != 1) {
                continue;
            }

            // Insert the actual text/data from the XML document.
            var td = document.createElement("td");
            if (i % 2) {
                td.style.background = "#aaabba";
            }
            var xmlData = document.createTextNode(xmlEl[i].childNodes[j].firstChild.
nodeValue);
            td.appendChild(xmlData);
            row.appendChild(td);
        }
        tbody.appendChild(row);
    }
    document.getElementById("xmldata").appendChild(table);
}

function getXML()
{
    if (typeof document.implementation.createDocument != "undefined")
    {
        docObj = document.implementation.createDocument("", "", null);
        docObj.onload = displayData;
    }
    else if (window.ActiveXObject)
    {
        docObj = new ActiveXObject("Microsoft.XMLDOM");
        docObj.onreadystatechange = function () {
            if (docObj.readyState == 4) displayData()
        };
    }
    docObj.load("books.xml");
}

</script>
</body>
</html>
```

3. False. Browsers that are compliant with the World Wide Web Consortium (W3C) requirements use different methods than Microsoft Windows Internet Explorer does.

4. False. Before you can work with XML data, you must wait for *readyState* to be equal to 4.

Chapter 18

1. None of the Hypertext Transfer Protocol (HTTP) methods discussed in the chapter offer more security than any of the others. Only the addition of Secure Sockets Layer (SSL) adds a layer of security on top of the HTTP methods. It should be noted that using the *POST* method does not hide the input data, and only the *POST* method should be used with SSL because the *GET* method would place the parameters right on the URL where they could be seen regardless of SSL.

2. Responses using standard HTML are retrieved with the *responseText* method and can contain just about anything that could be obtained through HTTP. Extensible Markup Language (XML) responses must be obtained with the *responseXML* method and must be served as an XML content type by the server. JavaScript Object Notation (JSON) responses are JavaScript responses; therefore, they offer some performance advantages over the other methods.

3. This solution was discussed in the chapter itself, but here is the asynchronous call (replace *YOUR SERVER* appropriately for your environment):

```
<!DOCTYPE HTML PUBLIC "-//W3C//DTD HTML 4.01//EN"
"http://www.w3.org/TR/html4/strict.dtd">
<html>
<head>
<title>Async</title>
</head>
<body>
<div id="xmldata"></div>
<script type="text/javascript">
function readyAJAX() {
try {
    return new XMLHttpRequest();
} catch(e) {
    try {
        return new ActiveXObject('Msxml2.XMLHTTP');
    } catch(e) {
        try {
            return new ActiveXObject('Microsoft.XMLHTTP');
        } catch(e) {
            return "A newer browser is needed.";
        }
    }
}
}
var requestObj = readyAJAX();
var url ="http://YOUR SERVER/sum.php?num1=2&num2=2";
requestObj.open("GET",url,true);
requestObj.send();
requestObj.onreadystatechange = function() {
    if (requestObj.readyState == 4) {
        if (requestObj.status == 200) {
            alert(requestObj.responseText);
        } else {
            alert(requestObj.statusText);
        }
    }
}
</script>
</body>
</html>
```

The file sum.php is a woefully small and inadequately secured server-side program in PHP that looks like this:

```php
<?php
print $_GET['num1'] + $_GET['num2'];
?>
```

Chapter 19

1. This solution uses Listing 19-1 and requires the addition of a submit button to the form. The form now looks like this:

```html
<form name="nameform" id="nameform" action="" method="GET">
Enter State: <input id="textname" type="text" name="textname">
<input type="submit" name="submit" id="statesubmit">
</form>
```

An event handler and new function are all that's required for this solution. These are added within the existing JavaScript.

```javascript
var submitbtn = document.getElementById("nameform");
if (window.addEventListener) {
    submitbtn.addEventListener("submit",showstate,false);
} else {
    submitbtn.attachEvent("onsubmit",showstate);
}

function showstate() {
    alert(document.forms[0].textname.value);
}
```

2. This solution is a variation of the previous solution and others shown in Chapter 19. The server-side program will need to return the comma-delimited list of people for the company directory, much as the state example returned a list of U.S. states.

3. Congratulations!

Index

About the Author

Steve Suehring is a technology consultant with a diverse business and computing background. Steve's extensive experience enables him to work cross-functionally within organizations to help create computing architectures that fit the business need. Steve has written several books and magazine articles and contributed to many others. Steve has spoken internationally at user groups and conventions. When he has the chance, Steve plays just about any sport or any musical instrument, some with better success than others.

What do you think of this book?

We want to hear from you!

Do you have a few minutes to participate in a brief online survey?

Microsoft is interested in hearing your feedback so we can continually improve our books and learning resources for you.

To participate in our survey, please visit:

www.microsoft.com/learning/booksurvey/

...and enter this book's ISBN-10 or ISBN-13 number (located above barcode on back cover*). As a thank-you to survey participants in the United States and Canada, each month we'll randomly select five respondents to win one of five $100 gift certificates from a leading online merchant. At the conclusion of the survey, you can enter the drawing by providing your e-mail address, which will be used for prize notification only.

Thanks in advance for your input. Your opinion counts!

**Where to find the ISBN on back cover*

ISBN-13: 000-0-0000-0000-0
ISBN-10: 0-0000-0000-0

00000

0 000000 000000

Example only. Each book has unique ISBN.

Microsoft®
Press